Schools and Kindergartens – A Design Manual

For Ben (The Royal College of Art), Matthew (University of Liverpool), Amy and Grace (St Michael's Primary School, London)

Layout and cover design: Oliver Kleinschmidt, Berlin

Editor: Ria Stein, Berlin

Translation from German (texts by Hofmann, Baumann and Niederstätter, Hübner): Margot Stringer, Nieuil

Cover: Zürich International School, Galli & Rudolf
Photographer: Hannes Henz, Zürich

Lithography: Licht & Tiefe, Berlin

Printing: Kösel, Altusried

Library of Congress Cataloging-in-Publication data
A CIP catalog record for this book has been applied for at the Library of Congress.

Bibliographic information published by the German National Library
The German National Library lists this publication in the Deutsche Nationalbibliografie;
detailed bibliographic data are available on the Internet at http://dnb.dnb.de.

This publication is also available as an e-book pdf (ISBN 978-3-03821-481-6),
an EPUB (ISBN 978-3-03821-670-4) and in a German language edition (ISBN 978-3-03821-637-7).

First edition 2007 (hardcover) and 2008 (softcover)
Second and revised edition 2015

© 2015 Birkhäuser Verlag GmbH, Basel
P.O. Box 44, 4009 Basel, Switzerland
Part of Walter de Gruyter GmbH, Berlin/Munich/Boston
Printed on acid-free paper produced from chlorine-free pulp. TCF ∞

Printed in Germany
ISBN 978-3-03821-636-0

www.birkhauser.com
9 8 7 6 5 4 3 2

A DESIGN MANUAL

Schools and Kindergartens

Mark Dudek

Second and Revised Edition

CONTRIBUTIONS BY

Dorothea Baumann
Mohamed Boubekri
Susan Herrington
Susanne Hofmann
Peter Hübner
Pamela Loeffelman
Heather Marsden
Christina Niederstätter

Birkhäuser
Basel

Principles of Schools and Kindergartens

9
Preface

Building for Education

10
Historical Paradigms

16
Educational Systems

18
Schools in the Community

19
School Typologies

Requirements of School Design

22
Spatial Configurations
Pamela Loeffelman

28
Acoustic Design
Dorothea Baumann and Christina Niederstätter

34
Lighting Design
Mohamed Boubekri

40
Sustainability
Heather Marsden

42
Outdoor Spaces
Susan Herrington

46
Designing Learning Landscapes
Peter Hübner

50
Schools and Kindergartens under Reconstruction
Susanne Hofmann

Selection of Projects

NURSERIES AND KINDERGARTENS (0-6 years)

56
Kita Sinneswandel
Berlin, Germany
Baukind

60
Cherry Lane Children's Centre
Hillingdon, London, UK
Mark Dudek Associates

62
San Antonio de Prado Kindergarten
Medellin, Colombia
Ctrl G Estudio de Architectura and
Plan B (Federico Mesa)

66
Lavender Children's Centre
Mitcham, Surrey, UK
John McAslan + Partners

68
Sondika Kindergarten
Sondika, Bilbao, Spain
Eduardo Arroyo, No.mad arquitectos

70
San Felice Nursery and Preschool
San Felice, Reggio Emilia, Italy
ZPZ Partners

74
Hoyle Early Years Centre
Bury, Northwest England, UK
DSDHA

76
National Day Nurseries Association
Grantham, United Kingdom
Mark Dudek with
Michael Stiff and Andy Trevillion

78
Kindergarten Jerusalemer Straße
Berlin, Germany
Staab Architekten

80
Sheerness Children's and
Family Centre
Isle of Sheppey, Kent, UK
Architype

82
École Maternelle ZAC Moskowa
Paris, France
Frédéric Borel Architectes

84
Shenyang Xiaohajin
International Kindergarten
Shenyang, China
Shenyang Huaxin Designers

86
Bubbletecture Maihara Kindergarten
Maihara, Japan
Shuhei Endo Architect Institute

PRIMARY SCHOOLS (4-12 years)

112
Kingston International School
Hong Kong, China
Kwong & Associates

114
Montessori Primary School
De Eilanden, Amsterdam,
The Netherlands
Herman Hertzberger

116
Druk White Lotus School
Ladakh, India
Arup Associates

120
Little Village Academy
Chicago, Illinois, USA
Ross Barney Architects

122
Ranelagh
Multi-denominational School
Dublin, Ireland
O'Donnell + Tuomey Architects

124
Mary Poppins Primary School
Berlin, Germany
Carola Schäfers Architekten

126
North Kildare
Educate Together School
Celbridge, County Kildare, Ireland
Grafton Architects

128
Burr Elementary School
Fairfield, Connecticut, USA
SOM 'Education Lab'

130
Hachoresh School
Zichron Yaacov, Israel
Shimon and Gideon Powsner

132
Westcliff Primary School
and After School Club
Westcliff on Sea, UK
Cottrell and Vermeulen

134
Joint Denominational School
Sheffield, UK
DSDHA

136
Heinz Galinski School
Berlin, Germany
Zvi Hecker

138
Mossbrook Primary School
Norton, Sheffield, UK
Sarah Wigglesworth Architects

140
Taxham School Extension
Taxham, Salzburg, Austria
Maria Flöckner and Hermann Schnöll

142
Kingsmead Primary School
Northwich, Cheshire, UK
White Design Associates

144
Energy-plus Primary School
Hohen Neuendorf, Germany
IBUS Architects and Engineers

148
Jubilee School
Brixton, London, UK
Allford Hall Monaghan Morris

152
Jockey Club Primary School
Hong Kong, China
Aedas + Design Consultants

154
Zürich International School
Wadenswil, Switzerland
Galli & Rudolf

156
South Bronx Charter School
for The Arts
Hunts Point, New York, USA
Weisz + Yoes Studio

158
Recycled Brick School
Tongjiang, Jianxi, China
Joshua Bolchover and John Lin,
Rural Urban Framework

SPECIAL SCHOOLS (6-18 years)

90
BSBO De Bloesem School
St. Truiden, Belgium
VBM Architecten

92
Swiss Cottage SEN School
Camden, London, UK
Penoyre & Prasad

96
Pistorius School
for Disabled Children
Herbrechtingen, Germany
Behnisch, Behnisch & Partner

100
Special School Sursee
Sursee, Switzerland
Scheitlin-Syfrig+Partner

102
Osborne School
Winchester, UK
Hampshire County Council Architects

104
Feather River Academy
Yuba City, California, USA
Architecture for Education – A4E

108
Special Pedagogic Centre
Eichstätt, Germany
Diezinger & Kramer Architekten

SECONDARY SCHOOLS (10-18 years)

162
Collège Nicolas Robert
Vernouillet, Eure-et-Loir, France
Berthelier Fichet Tribouillet

166
Ale Upper Secondary School
Nödinge, Sweden
Wingårdh Arkitektkontor

168
Lycée Camille Corot
Morestel, France
Hérault Arnod Architectes

170
Gunma Kokusai Academy
Ohta City, Gunma, Japan
Kojima, Uno, Akamatsu

172
Montessori School
Ingolstadt, Germany
Behnisch & Partner

174
Kuoppanummi School Centre
Nummela, Finland
Perko Architects
Meskanen & Pursiainen

176
Instituto Rafael Arozarena
La Orotava, Tenerife, Spain
AMP arquitectos

180
Kvernhuset Junior High School
Fredrikstad, Norway
PIR II Arkitektkontor, Duncan Lewis

182
Public School Jardim Ataliba Leonel
São Paolo, Brazil
Angelo Bucci, Alvaro Puntoni

184
Exemplar School
Lambeth, London, UK
Alsop Architects

186
Lycée François Magendie
Bordeaux, France
Brojet Lajus Pueyo

188
Greenwich Academy
Greenwich, Connecticut, USA
SOM 'Education Lab'

190
St. Andrew's College
Aurora, Ontario, Canada
Kuwabara Payne McKenna Blumberg

192
Nærum Amtsgymnasium
Nærum, Copenhagen, Denmark
Arkitekter Dall & Lindhardtsen

194
Albert Einstein Oberschule
Berlin, Germany
Stefan Scholz Architekten

196
Sankt Benno Gymnasium
Dresden, Germany
Behnisch, Behnisch & Partner

198
Lachenzelg School Extension
Zürich, Switzerland
ADP, Beat Jordi, Caspar Angst

200
Perspectives Charter School
Chicago, Illinois, USA
Perkins+Will

202
Bishops Park College
Clacton, Essex, UK
Architects Co-Partnership (ACP)

204
Gymnasium Markt Indersdorf
Markt Indersdorf, Germany
Allmann Sattler Wappner Architekten

206
Instituto Villanueva del Rio y Minas
Sevilla, Spain
J. Terrados Cepeda +
F. Suarez Corchete

208
Collège des Tuillières
Gland, Switzerland
Graeme Mann & Patricia Capua Mann

212
Colegio Secundaria Industrial
Santiago de Cali, Colombia
Luis Fernando Zùñiga Gàez

214
Oskar Maria Graf Gymnasium
Neufahrn, Germany
Hein Goldstein Architekten

216
Instituto La Serra
Mollerussa, Lleida, Spain
Carme Pinós Desplat

218
Protestant Comprehensive School
Gelsenkirchen, Germany
Plus+ Bauplanung

222
Jo Richardson Community School
Dagenham, London, UK
Architecture PLB

ACADEMIES AND VOCATIONAL SCHOOLS (6-18 years)

226
Flims Comprehensive School
Flims, Switzerland
Werknetz Architektur

228
Education Centre 'Tor zur Welt'
Hamburg, Germany
BOF Architekten

234
Bexley Business Academy
Bexley, London, UK
Foster and Partners

236
Montessori College Oost
Amsterdam, The Netherlands
Herman Hertzberger

238
Aurinkolahti Comprehensive School
Vuosaari, Helsinki, Finland
Jeskanen-Repo-Teränne
and Leena Yli-Lonttinen

240
Marie Curie Gymnasium
Dallgow-Döberitz, Berlin, Germany
Grüntuch Ernst Architekten

242
Diamond Ranch High School
Pomona, California, USA
Morphosis, Thomas Blurock

244
Ivanhoe Grammar School
Mernda, Victoria, Australia
Bates Smart

246
**Secondary Intermediate
Vocational School**
Hoorn, The Netherlands
Herman Hertzberger

248
Packer Collegiate Institute
Brooklyn, New York, USA
H³ Hardy Collaboration Architecture

APPENDIX

252
Authors

253
Selected Bibliography

254
Index of Places

255
Index of Names

255
Illustration Credits

Preface

What is the relationship between pedagogical visions and space for children? I ask this question because it is in my view a key to understanding good school or pre-school architecture, and is a primary idea which lies at the heart of this publication. Whilst we want and need buildings which respond to the immediate requirements of contemporary society, the schools we build now are also for a future which is hard to predict. Designers of school buildings need 'the vision thing'. And one might ask the question, what should dictate the vision, education or architecture?

Eight years ago when this book was first published the talk then was all about how we could raise the quality of our learning environments. Architectural quality was at the focus of the agenda which promoted the power of good design to boost the educational and social attainment of students using the new schools, particularly those in deprived areas. Now it seems the world has changed. In this new age of austerity, the prevailing attitude appears to play down the role of architecture, it is simply too expensive. Much of the emphasis is now on simple solutions which are cheap and practical.

In England the so-called new Free Schools usually operate from converted premises at minimal refurbishment costs. In the secondary schools sector the approach often calls for one standard solution prepared by a contractor which will be rolled out across the country with no regard to consultation with the users or the site-specific issues that make every new building particular to its context. However we reiterate here, the original values presented in the book's first edition remain fundamental to the well-being of future generations. Good quality architecture is essential in raising educational standards. It is timely that a second edition coincides with the reactionary and regressive views currently dominating the public discussion. We also include a number of austerity case studies which illustrate the more positive aspects of the contemporary debate where sustainability and the green agenda are rightly coming to the fore.

The best new school builders recognise that education should lead architecture to the extent that many of the case studies featured here are explicit renditions of the latest educational theories, almost like a three-dimensional curriculum plan. Rightly so in my view; the pedagogical vision is of fundamental importance when designing a new school. If it is to have a direct bearing on the contemporary needs of teachers, pupils and future generations of school users, it must reflect the parallel needs of children's education and their social development in its design. The relationship between pedagogical visions and space is never linear, where the pedagogical vision dictates the architecture. Rather, education and architecture enter into a relationship where, if everything goes according to plan, the two dimensions mesh together in a symbiotic formula to create a complex child-orientated environment which enables children to learn and the community to prosper. I trust this book will inspire and help design teams to order priorities and create the best possible school environments for all of our futures.

I would like to thank the many people who have contributed to the creation of this book, all of the case study contributors and numerous teachers and educationalists who have provided observations and support during its development. In particular I would like to acknowledge Ria Stein and the team at Birkhäuser who have stuck with the project over more years than I care to remember. In her determination to get the book published, Ria has shown a degree of tolerance and understanding towards me beyond the call of duty. It is to her that I offer my greatest thanks for the final version of this publication.

I also wish to thank Penny Terndrup for her pastoral care and wisdom during the book's difficult gestation and birth, and Ken Macdonald who got me started with all of this more than 20 years ago. Finally, recognition goes to the School of Architecture, University of Sheffield, where I am engaged as a part-time Research Fellow. Without their support this publication would not have been possible.

Mark Dudek
London, September 2014

Historical Paradigms

The first Margaret McMillian nursery school, Deptford,
South London, 1923. School yard during recess

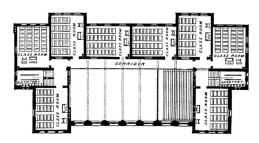

Margaret McMillan nursery school,
Deptford, South London, 1923

Nurseries and kindergartens

Architecture for the education of young children aged 5 or 6 to 11 years has been a distinct building type
for over a century. Early years architecture for preschool children aged 0 to 5 or 6 years has been less distinct. Nevertheless early years and elementary school design can be discussed generally within the framework of a number of themes and building typologies. Three approaches have distinctive pedagogical concepts built into the architectural approach and are discussed here.

Firstly, there are new buildings where design priorities focus upon a strictly codified room schedule.
This alone will dictate the architectural approach. Here is a case in point: 'There is a soft corner with a comfortable adult sized sofa, a large rug and some cushions and a child sized bookcase, and an additional accessible storage shelf. Each group room has its own bathroom and a side room exclusively used for naps and
sleeping, and equipped with small mattresses.'[1]

Because the schedule is expressed primarily as a series of quasi-functional zones underpinned by a pre-
determined floor area relating to child numbers, the architectural narrative tends to be two-dimensional and
very limited. There is an emphasis on a prescriptive approach where rules and regulations guide the architectural strategy. Everything is very much pre-determined by the zones or territories which are strictly imposed upon children. The main determinant of the architecture are age-related groupings such as 0-1 year
olds, 1-2 year olds, 2-3 years olds etc. Although they are usually described as 'homebase' areas, many are
similar in character to school classrooms. Each homebase area may be further designated into functional
zones such as the cloakroom, the wet zone (with sinks for art and craft activities) and the quiet zone. This is
a range of activities which is so tightly prescribed that the architecture tends to reduce and limit the scope
for learning rather than extending and opening it up. The focus is on adult needs, such as safety and security, rather than on child needs, such as the promotion of exploration and discovery.

Clearly this approach can obscure the potential for creativity and imagination. The free spirit of young
children is somehow narrowed down to a set of activities which are deemed to have educational value. Ultimately, the quality of the architecture is very much down to the skills of the architect selected, and his or
her ability to interpret the brief in a truly child-orientated way. This is in my view a highly dysfunctional relationship between pedagogy and space, yet it is the basis of much contemporary practice.

The second design typology applies to those institutions which have adapted premises to suit new
forms of pedagogy. This is space which emerges organically as a result of enlightened forms of education
around which an existing school or nursery building adapts itself. Here the architecture follows the pedagogy. E. F. O'Neill's work at Prestolee School, Kearsley, set the tone for this approach.

Prestolee School was an unremarkable county elementary school in Lancashire, northwest England,
which was transformed between the years 1918 and 1953. Its head teacher throughout this time was Edward Francis O'Neill (1850-1975). He pioneered an active learning approach which flew in the face of convention with its emphasis on structured discipline dictating school design formulaically as, for example, a
number of classrooms grouped around an assembly hall with an outside playground.

O'Neill objected to the concept that the child's day must be divided up between work and play and
neatly segmented across the week into hour long subject lessons delivered by a specialist teacher with
the aid of a blackboard. His thesis was that children learnt by doing, and he developed a school environment which enabled the children to work at their own pace following their own course of development. He
viewed children as constructors and researchers of their own worlds, utilising their time best in a way which
developed their own interests. O'Neill fashioned the school interior and exterior as a single seamless environment, which was a deliberate response to what he considered to be the artificial and damaging division
between 'work' (indoors) and 'play' (outdoors).

Children at Prestolee could carry out their tasks indoors or outdoors as they wished. He gradually developed the hard tarmac play yard introducing flower beds, a vegetable garden, water fountains, bathing
pools and opportunities for construction; a windmill, 4 metres high standing on a 1.8 metre wall was constructed by the oldest junior boys.

Inside, one of the important transformations was the conversion of the assembly hall into an open plan
classroom, accessible to pupils of all ages. Screens and other furniture were moved in, with long tables

Typical Robson school plan, Hackney, East London, 1911

The windmill, built by senior pupils, at Prestolee School, Kearsley, Lancashire, 1946

Nine year old playing with Froebel blocks

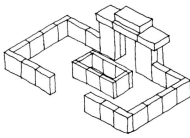

Froebel blocks

placed back to back forming large flat areas for specialised learning activities such as music, reading, art and construction. The idea was that learning materials could be used informally when individuals or small groups of children required them. The emphasis was on self-generated research rather than forced learning, and the flexibility of the environment became a key component. The school was open for 12 hours per day with children returning voluntarily for evening sessions. O'Neill's school became known as the 'learn by doing school'. Broadly speaking this was not high architecture in the tightly pre-planned form. Rather it emerges and develops, as educational needs are defined. Radical pedagogy goes hand in hand with spatial adaptations, which are constantly changing to match the needs of the evolving curriculum.[2]

There are many other examples of such developments during the 20th century from Margaret McMillan's ideal nursery school in London's east end in 1923 to Loris Malaguzzi, the renowned Italian educator who developed the Reggio Emilia system from 1963 on. What they have in common is the leadership of a visionary individual educator from which all else follows, including architecture and space.

The third distinct category is where an architect, strongly influenced by his or her personal experiences of childhood, develops a particularly child-orientated approach to design. Because the architect is in tune with his or her own early experiences and is aware of their architectural potency, this category has usually created the most advanced form of pedagogical building design.

Perhaps the prime example is the master architect Frank Lloyd Wright. Due to his fame in designing and building all types of architecture and inspiring subsequent architectural movements in the 20th century the story of his childhood inspiration is well known.

The youthful Wright explained how he and his mother worked together with the Froebel 'gifts', which became the source of profound pleasure and his subconscious awakening to the primacy of shape, texture and form. He describes his engagement with the Froebel block system as follows: 'The smoothly shaped maple blocks with which to build, the sense of which never afterwards leaves the fingers: form becoming feeling.'[3] To understand the roots of this theory we have to go back further.

Friedrich Froebel (1782-1852), the important early years educator, had initially worked in the field of crystallographic science. In the first German edition of *The Education of Man* (1826), he makes the observation that whether organic or inorganic, crystalline or non-crystalline, developmental processes seemed to be the same; in essence they tend to develop outward from within, striving to maintain balance between inner and outer forces.[4] His study of the natural sciences gave him a clear conception of the importance of geometric numbering systems and their underlying relationship to natural phenomena such as plant forms and crystals. Much of Froebel's slightly mystical theorising can now be dismissed (although it is important to recognise how seriously the Froebel idea is taken particularly in Japan and North America). Froebel's speculations brought him to the view that the random nature of child like play could be directed into an organised learning system, by somehow connecting this innate knowledge within the child to an appropriate systematic process. He called the system 'The Gifts and Occupations.'

In purely architectural terms, what was important about Froebel's system were the building blocks or 'building boxes.' Each set became progressively more complex as the child's understanding developed. Although they contained different shapes, rectangular, square and triangular spheres, they were all based on the same modular system. The child is unaware of the mathematical significance of his or her playthings, but the child's eye becomes accustomed to a correct sense of form; as a result, notions of proportion and harmony are lodged deep within the child's psyche.

On an intuitive level, it is clear how many of Wright's designs incorporated this precocious knowledge. The external view of his Avery Coonley Playhouse (1912), a kindergarten in the suburbs of Chicago for a private client, is formed by pure horizontal and vertical plains of materiality which can be precisely constructed in miniature.

Taking the logic of this towards more detailed features in the same building, we can see in the triptych stained glass windows of the main façade the use of coloured circles and squares in an abstract composition which Wright himself ascribed to the 'Seventh Froebel Gift.' (I have described the window designs as abstract but they are open to imaginative interpretation. At the time of their creation, discussion about their meaning between Wright and his client centred on balloons, American flags and confetti.) Wright claimed

Avery Coonley Playhouse with triptych stained glass windows.
Chicago, Frank Lloyd Wright, 1912

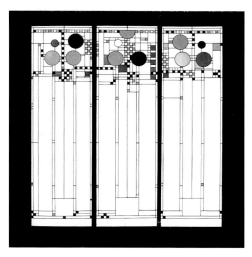

The piazza of Reggio Emilia preschool in Northern Italy.
Nursery and Preschool San Felice, ZPZ Partners, 2000

that these circles and squares of brilliant primaries 'interfere less with the function of the window and add a higher architectural note to the effect of light itself.'[5] They form what Wright called a 'kinder-symphony,' once again evoking Froebel's kindergarten education.

So what was the pedagogical vision in the work of Wright and other architects who followed him? The buildings which promote these principles develop an empathy with their users, by way of a sort of colour and form language. Rather than relying on a schedule of accommodation to dictate space, there is an altogether richer, more spatially coherent frame of reference. What Wright did in the Avery Coonley Playhouse was to develop a way in which children could quite literally read their environment as they moved around. For pre-literate children in particular, this means that the building becomes an integral part of the learning process, yet in a smooth natural process of seeing, touching and smelling the environment. In other words, perception comes through all of the senses rather than just sight.

Of course, it is difficult to place a quantifiable pedagogic value on what ultimately may simply be described as good design which promotes a particular type of learning for children (which some people call environmental awareness). A child's conception of space is such a cerebral concept; developers and government funding bodies in charge of developing early years environments today usually seek more pragmatic values. In the UK at present this educational orthodoxy, which relates children's activities to educational values in an overly simplistic way, is threatening to diminish the richness of a children's culture which has in the past been closely linked to pedagogical visions and architectural space.

It cannot be conclusively proven that all children depend or indeed need good architectural space to thrive and learn during the early years. However, there is a growing body of evidence to suggest that a child's perception of space is critical, particularly where children come from deprived or abusive homes. Good perceptive design really makes a difference for children at every age, but in particular for those growing towards the end of primary school and the advent of secondary school, it is fundamental.

When discussing early years architecture, its culture and historical development, one must mention the municipal infant-toddler centres and pre schools of Reggio Emilia in Northern Italy. The system has evolved over the past 40 years, largely as a result of the inspirational childcare specialist and visionary, Loris Malaguzzi and his early work on how children learn. 'Reggio,' as it is known, is widely recognised as the best system in the world, where an advanced pedagogy connects with some of the most pleasing early years buildings anywhere. Reggio recognises that spaces for children are a fundamental part of the complex development support system which enables young children to gain knowledge.

The system is one which speaks about the exciting process of cognitive and cultural development for young children. This is a highly developed science where a language has evolved which goes beyond the negative discourse which characterises much of the debate currently taking place in the UK and the USA. As mentioned previously, there appears to be a complete separation between the articulation of architectural and educational ideas; early years is often seen as a subject relating mainly to safety and social control rather than a great opportunity for young children. By contrast at Reggio, architecture and pedagogy is fully integrated and the level of discourse is deep and philosophical. Children's rights are the priority.

Reggio recognises that the development of knowledge does not take place in a simplistic linear way, but rather as a complex network of rich interconnecting influences which the world has to offer; therefore, the more complex and rich the learning environment is, the better the pace of knowledge and understanding will become. The school environment becomes a sort of workshop for research and experimentation where perception of things, and in particular, the relationships between children, become fundamental strategies for building individual cognition and knowledge. Reggio buildings are often beautiful by any subjective opinion, but the extent to which they encourage interaction with the users really defines their success.

'Reflections on the tools of design, with indications on spatial distribution and on the 'soft qualities': light, colour, materials, sound, smell and microclimate. The aim is to provide instruments of analysis and practical indications for designing the interiors and exteriors of infant-toddler centres and pre-schools.'[6]

The Reggio research group have developed a series of guidelines which are framed in a strong pedagogical language. For example 'recognisability' means creating an architectural language and an environmental atmosphere which has a precise identity. It speaks of non-hierarchical space, where every area of

the childcare building is potentially open to children and adults alike because there should be a democracy of function; every space is a potential area for learning and development. Another important feature which appears in every centre is a large central square called the piazza. The piazza is a place of meeting, a public place of the school which plays the same role as the piazza does in the town. It fosters encounters, group interactions, stories, social relations and the children's assumption of a public identity.

Many other influences and inspirations are cited as being important within this list of ingredients for the successful early years centre, including light, colour, the use of materials, smell, sound, the quality of environmental conditions and changeability, i.e. the extent to which the environment can be transformed over the year by its users. This is a philosophy which rides through the mediocrity and subjective basis of much contemporary design for early years.

Schools

One of the earliest examples of school buildings with a converging educational and architectural agenda was the work of E. R. Robson, surveyor, architect and educational theorist, who was the main driving force in the development of the London Board Schools at the end of the 19th and into the early 20th century. Indeed the group of school buildings which comprise the Phoenix School campus includes a Robson influenced elementary school which is still in use today, 100 years after it first saw the light of day. In this section we will provide a brief over-view of the key historical movements which influenced architecture for mass education from its inception to the present time.

England was the first country to experience industrialisation and sought educational provision for the so-called industrial classes from the beginning of the 19th century. From the implementation of the 1833 Factory Act, which enforced two hours of instruction daily for factory children, reform developed as an all too evident response to the plight of the exploited masses. However, the level of government grants allocated to erect schoolhouses in Great Britain was slow to get off the mark when compared with similar developments in other European countries at that time. For example the Irish Government provided a 2.5 million GBP subsidy to assist education in Ireland between 1821 and 1828. In Germany at that time, vast resources were being allocated, as the nation geared up to a period of sustained economic growth. In the United States, spending on school buildings in one year, 1851, in one town, Philadelphia, was 184,842 USD, as the population increased at a rate of 20,000 per annum.

It was not until the implementation of the UK Elementary Education Act in 1870, that made education compulsory for all children between the ages of 6 and 11, that the need to construct large elementary schools within the urban areas became an overriding necessity and similar sums were allocated from general taxation. At this time, the London School Board advertised for an architect and surveyor to direct the massive expansion anticipated throughout the mainly working class areas of the capital. The then architect surveyor to the Liverpool Corporation, E. R. Robson, was appointed.

Whilst school systems in some shape or form had been developing throughout the world from the earliest part of the enlightenment, there was no coherent idea as to how an architectural and educational theory should be integrated to create a new form of school building appropriate to its special function. Treatises on the subject were either written from a purely architectural perspective (with an emphasis on the external style rather the internal functioning) or from an essentially pragmatic viewpoint emphasising the health and safety needs of the children during their time in school.

Robson had travelled widely following his appointment in 1872. His view of overseas systems, particularly those he viewed in the USA, Switzerland and Germany, led him to the conclusion that although there was a tradition of secondary school education in those countries upon which England could draw, there was no such tradition in elementary schooling. Nevertheless observing the best systems of education the world had to offer proved to be a valuable experience in balancing his professional background in architecture with his broader remit as a promoter of good educational practice.

Robson's emerging theories were set out in a book published in 1874, *School Architecture: Practical Remarks on the Planning Designing, Building and Furnishing of School Houses*. This landmark publication covered key areas of the agenda in some detail such as the layout of schools, the interior environment,

David Stow's ideal plan for a classroom where all ages are educated simultaneously (1834-1836). According to Robson, the British and the Americans were still practicing the simultaneous method when Germans were developing age-related classrooms.

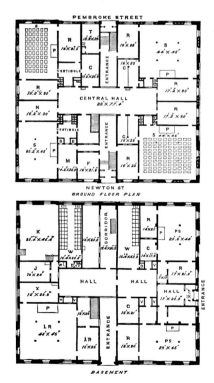

The High and Normal School for Girls in Boston, 1870

school furniture and architectural style. The publication was rich in advice on natural ventilation, orientation and heating. For example, on lighting Robson concluded that the coolest and steadiest light was from the north and recommended that there should be a minimum of 30 square inches of glass to every square foot of floor space (0.22 m² per 1 m²). This he asserted was sound guidance based on previously unpublished German research. In fact, the most interesting dimension of this landmark publication was the extensive reference he made to the projects he had seen during his study trips abroad.[7]

Based on his first hand observations, Robson introduced the Prussian system of separate classrooms organised around a communal hall into his new school buildings in London. Previously lessons had taken place 'simultaneously' in vast communal halls. For the first time in English state schools, strict age-related class sizes were proscribed along with advice on their use, for example the need for circulation spaces around desks and at the front of the room for presentations was defined in precise feet and inches. No detail seemed unimportant to Robson. His great skill was to integrate both sides of the agenda by making himself proficient in both the architectural and educational aspects of school buildings.

Robson's work both in the theory and the practice of school design had far reaching consequences. Having developed many of his original ideas following his study visits to Europe and the USA, his buildings then became a source of great influence for others during the first 20 years of their usage. Visitors from abroad took what they needed, often re-importing the ideas Robson had originally taken from their own country; Robson was particularly influential to the developing school system in North America at the turn of the century.

Robson's comments on his American sojourn are interesting. He notes how school houses in America, and in particular those of New England, were ingenious, using new approaches to construction and in particular mentioning how important the school edifice was, perhaps for the first time recognising that school architecture communicated to children on a number of levels. One project example he cites as of particular merit is The High and Normal School for Girls in Boston. Erected in 1870, it had five storeys and a various range of accommodation including classrooms with single desks for 50 children, large classrooms for 100 students and rooms for the withdrawal of smaller study groups. The total number of pupils was 1,225. It was a model of robust, high quality space making which set a new standard in terms of advanced environmental design.

Robson is critical of the lack of convergence between educational and architectural theories stating that: "As in England, there is much critical investigation and discussion of education itself, but no trace that some of the vital points affecting buildings (and, therefore, indirectly the education) [...] have as yet been sufficiently tackled at close quarters or in the careful manner common to Germany."[8] There is a genuinely held esteem for the German system of building for education, which he recognises as highly influential to most of what he had seen in America. Robson even asserts that it is their superior system of education to which the Prussians owe their success over the French in war, referring to the compulsory primary schooling which had been in place for over a century; it was not surprising to him that the Germans were so far ahead of the UK in many aspects of the developing urban culture. In 1870, Robson eulogised about the German system of mass education, especially that of Saxony and Prussia, describing it as the best system in the world. From the age of six, he observed, a German boy attends an elementary school. "Theoretically he goes under compulsion, practically of his own pleasure, for the German parents no more think of depriving their child of tuition than of breakfast."[9]

Building for education developed in juddering movements over long periods of time with phases of relative inactivity, followed by periods of frenetic investment and usually very speedy re-development. This happens in roughly 30-year cycles. So for example in the UK, there were major developments from the end of the 1950s through the 1960s, where architects experimented with system build solutions and high modernism, a reflection of 1960s Premier Harold Wilson's 'white hot heat of technological advancement'. An important forerunner was the Hunstanton School in Norfolk designed by Alison and Peter Smithson (1953). However, much of its technology was underdeveloped and has not stood the test of time. Currently there is a massive wave of renewal, with virtually every school in the country having at least a make-over, if not a total re-build by 2010, a case perhaps of political expediency finally recognising what a good social and economic investment education is.

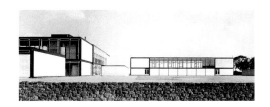

Secondary Modern School, Hunstanton, Norfolk,
Alison and Peter Smithson, 1953

Volksschule Düsseldorf
Paul Schneider-Esleben, 1959-1961

Cantonal School in Freudenberg
Zürich, Jacques Schader, 1960

In Germany, there was a significant investment during the 1980s, although it has to be stated that the German economic model has facilitated a much more steady investment. In the years following the Second World War, for understandable reasons, education in Germany took on a new significance; Nazi indoctrination which had infected the body politic during the years leading up to hostilities, was viewed by the allies as an anti-education mentality which helped Hitler to power with little widespread resistance from the people. The new education would stress a more progressive attitude developing thinking individuals with a democratic spirit and a responsibility to the liberal federal constitution rather than to the state.

Many of the new school buildings would help to express this mentality by adopting a modernistic, almost Bauhaus aesthetic (the design school founded by Walter Gropius which had been condemned and closed by the Nazis as being degenerate). A key idea was the open-air school, which was interpreted as a symbol of liberation from authoritarian rules and regulations – a concept which looked back to late 19th century Prussian ideas.

However, the new post war buildings did not mimic the open-air concept literally, instead extensive single-storey pavilion-like structures were created during the 1950s with dual aspect windows so they could be passively ventilated and naturally lit. Towards the end of the decade there was a tendency towards sober functionalism. For example, architect Paul Schneider-Esleben created a clearly articulated three-storey structure in exposed concrete, which became a much-imitated model of good practice.[10] In Switzerland, with its clear functional school design, there was a different reaction to political developments. Jacques Schader's cantonal school in Freudenberg near Zürich (1960) is more of a reference to the Modern Movement in architecture than to historical concepts and ideologies.[11]

The work of Hans Scharoun with his unbuilt proposal for an elementary school in Darmstadt (1951), followed by Günter Behnisch from the 1970s, for example his Secondary School at Lorch (1973), illustrate how some German States were interested in new architectural concepts for an educational system which had for too long been obsessed with control and regimentation at the expense of creativity and imagination. Whilst Robson, 100 years previously, had invested in his own research, looking at the best 'foreign' examples of school design, sadly little of this visionary ethos was explored within UK and USA settings during the 1950s and 1960s, and architects and architecture perhaps from the 1970s on took a back seat in the evolution of school design until quite recently.

References

1 Helen Penn, *Comparing Nurseries*,
London: Paul Chapman Publishing, 1997, p. 58.

2 Catherine Burke, 'The school without tears: E. F. O'Neill of Prestolee,'
in: *History of Education*, vol. 34, no. 3, May 2005, p. 263-275.

3 Frank Lloyd Wright, *Frank Lloyd Wright – An Autobiography*,
New York: Duel, Sloan and Pearce, 1943, p. 13-14.

4 Friedrich Froebel, *The Education of Man* (trans. W. N. Hailmann),
New York and London: Appleton and Co., 1887
(originally published as *Die Menschenerziehung* in 1826)

5 Frank Lloyd Wright, 'In the Cause of Architecture: VI. The Meaning of
Materials – Glass,' *Architectural Record*, April 1928.

6 Giulio Ceppi and Michele Zini (eds.), *Children, Spaces, Relations –
Metaproject for an Environment for Young Children*, Milan: Reggio
Children/Domus Academy, 1998, p. 35.

7 E. R. Robson, *School Architecture* (with an introduction by Malcolm
Seaborne), Leicester, Leicester University Press,1972 (first published
1874), p. 167.

8 Ibid, p. 25

9 Ibid, p. 30

10 *Detail*, special issue,'Konzept Schulbau,' no. 3, 2003, p. 175.

11 Ibid, p. 168

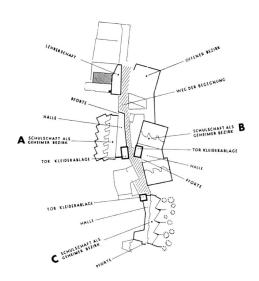

Hans Scharoun's project for a primary school in Darmstadt, 1951
Floor plan

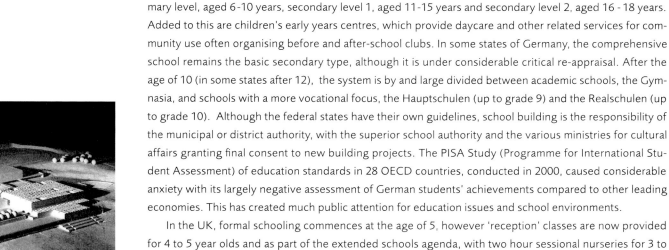

Educational Systems

In Germany as in most European systems, the structure of education is divided into a number of tiers: primary level, aged 6-10 years, secondary level 1, aged 11-15 years and secondary level 2, aged 16 - 18 years. Added to this are children's early years centres, which provide daycare and other related services for community use often organising before and after-school clubs. In some states of Germany, the comprehensive school remains the basic secondary type, although it is under considerable critical re-appraisal. After the age of 10 (in some states after 12), the system is by and large divided between academic schools, the Gymnasia, and schools with a more vocational focus, the Hauptschulen (up to grade 9) and the Realschulen (up to grade 10). Although the federal states have their own guidelines, school building is the responsibility of the municipal or district authority, with the superior school authority and the various ministries for cultural affairs granting final consent to new building projects. The PISA Study (Programme for International Student Assessment) of education standards in 28 OECD countries, conducted in 2000, caused considerable anxiety with its largely negative assessment of German students' achievements compared to other leading economies. This has created much public attention for education issues and school environments.

All-day secondary school, Osterburken, Germany, Bassenge, Puhan-Schultz and Schreck, 1967

In the UK, formal schooling commences at the age of 5, however 'reception' classes are now provided for 4 to 5 year olds and as part of the extended schools agenda, with two hour sessional nurseries for 3 to 4 year olds in some schools, which are being developed as a coherent 'foundation stage' whenever funding permits. Outside of this school based provision there is also the children's centre programme, with subsidised daycare for children in deprived areas, along with a range of community facilities for other local children and their families. The money for this comes from a new government funding regime called 'Sure Start', which is distinct from education funding for schools. The commitment is to open 3,500 children's centres in the UK by 2010, providing a centre in every community.

Infant schools which are often organised into two separate schools (yet usually within the same site) provide education for children aged between 4 and 7. Junior schools cater for the educational needs of children aged between 7 and 11 years. Secondary school commences at age 11 and runs through to age 18, although often the sixth form, aged 16 to 18, will be in a separate part of the school or on a different site operating as an institution in its own right, the so-called sixth form college. There are a range of different school types, such as the academically orientated grammar school, and the more vocationally orientated comprehensive school; these are both leftovers from an earlier regime which run along-side new initiatives such as the academy programme. The UK system has traditionally been de-centralised and run by local education authorities, under the guidance of the government department for education (DfES). Funding was allocated on the basis of required school places within each authority, with a certain level of capital allocated to provide maintainance on an annual cycle. However, the system has been subject to radical change to cope with huge investment currently underway; this is explained in more detail below.

Tulse Hill Comprehensive School
London, London County Council, 1953-1966

In the early 1960s, the vertical, hierarchical organisation of the secondary school system in Germany was questioned. A more horizontal structure was proposed, similar to so-called comprehensive models first introduced to the UK and the USA during the 1950s. This was based on a more socially egalitarian approach, where all students of whatever academic ability attended the same institution. The new educational structure would require a new school building type, which reflected this evening-out of opportunities. In the UK many examples of this new school type were introduced during the 1950s, with mixed results architecturally and educationally; for example Tulse Hill Comprehensive School (1956) was a perversely inhumane nine-storey slab block catering for 2,210 boys located on a single inner city site. Designed by the London County Council Architect's Department, it was an example of all that was wrong with arrogant local authority architects of the period. Middle class people, many of whom had attended private schools themselves, showed little care or respect for the well-being of their working class clients. Memories are still vivid, and it is understandable that for the current wave of school building public architecture has been placed in the hands of private practices with a proven track record in big public buildings.

The comprehensive school in Germany usually took the form of a similarly large complex albeit low-rise and horizontal in plan. However, because the designers had to use deep plan structures, the result were dingy, artificially lit, air-conditioned groups of rooms. One of the first projects of this type was the all-day secondary school in Osterburken (1967) by Bassenge, Puhan-Schultz and Schreck. The system over-loaded the programme with rooms, mixing large and socially complex groups together, which brought inevitable

conflicts. Added to this, the new pre-fabricated form of construction was technically poor and aesthetically disastrous virtually wherever it was used. Buildings made of exposed concrete with little colour or textural variety were to a certain extent forced upon architects and developers, as a result of tight budgets and limited time frames. For 'comprehensive', read 'bog-standard' as one politician was heard to describe the secondary school system during the early stages of the new Labour government in 1997. This referred as much to the sad, run-down architecture of these places as it did to the grim social and educational experience many students received.

As part of the Labour government's social inclusions policies, since 2000 it has been investing heavily in the nation's school building stock. Tony Blair's strategy for power was exemplified by the watchwords he repeatedly used throughout his first term in office, 'education, education, education'. Secondary schools have been at the forefront of this huge capital investment, a process that will be ongoing for the next 20 years. The sheer lack of investment over a sustained period of 40 years previously, exacerbated mainly during the tax restrictive Thatcher governments (1979-1997), meant the pent-up need to invest in school buildings quickly and efficiently was clear. Quite simply when Labour came to power in 1997 the condition of many if not most schools was appalling. Something had to be done.

The results of this investment so far has been mixed in terms of the quality of many new secondary schools built since 2000. Whilst central government has attempted to micro-manage all aspects of the educational curriculum, its control over the quality of the new buildings it has commissioned has been less successful. A complex system of private finance combined with public funding, where the schools effectively lease their new school premises from private developers who build and maintain them over a duration of 25 years, has been operating. It is fair to say that many of the private developers involved in this sector have been cavalier in the delivery of quality; of equal concern has been the lack of a coherent framework in which quality can be defined and evaluated. If good design is concerned with complex, often subjective criteria, how can you leave design quality to the marketplace?

Another contentious area of policy is a semi-privatised approach to what was considered the most pressing problem, the replacement of large comprehensive schools located in deprived urban areas. The strategy promoted had been successfully implemented in a number of locations across the USA in the form of the Charter Schools. These are semi-autonomous public schools, founded by educators, community groups or private organisations that operate under a written contract with the state. This contract, or charter, details how the school will be organised and what students will be taught. Many charter schools enjoy freedom from rules and regulations affecting other public schools, as long as they continue to meet the terms of their charters. In the UK, this model gives a degree of autonomy to a private group or individual willing to invest a figure of GBP 2 million towards the capital cost of a new secondary school. As the cost of building the new school will be in excess of GBP 20 million, this is a relatively small amount in return for a degree of power not previously known. Although the school is subject to inspection by the government's office for education standards, the fear remains that a private backer may have influence in areas of the curriculum such as its religious ethos, which would undermine the parents' role.

Recent investment in educational initiatives, such as numeracy and literacy hours, has done much to improve primary school pupil performance within the UK. Educational reform has sought to increase central control of both processes and outcomes, with close monitoring and evaluation of curriculum, inspection and assessment. There has been some objection to this change, on the basis of an overly proscriptive system imposed across the board; however, the effects of reform since the introduction of a national curriculum in 1998 have mostly had great educational benefits.

The refurbishment and replacement of the majority of primary schools is still at its inception. The UK case studies illustrated here are the best and most innovative examples, however, many if not most of the new secondary schools built within the UK since 2000 are at best adequate and at worst dull and uninspiring. There is a long way to go in the provision of high quality school buildings, equipped with modern facilities, which run hand in hand with ongoing educational reforms.

A limited budget spent on small-scale improvement raises the quality of the environment immeasurably. Nursery in Loup, Northern Ireland, 2005. Mark Dudek Associates, before and after refurbishment.

Schools in the Community

Schools whose classrooms are filled with the most challenging students need a modern day Marshall Plan. This plan should be centred on the needs of the children and, where possible, their local community. Key to the plan are a number of interrelated elements: smaller class sizes; full-time, permanent teachers judged to be good or better, continuous professional development, extensive range of extra-curricular activities, involvement of professionals other than teachers, such as social workers, counsellors and educational psychologists, plus parental engagement and family learning. A good physical environment [is required], good resource level, strong links with the wider community including business and community leaders.
William Atkinson, headteacher of the Phoenix High School, London

Phoenix High School, White City, London, 1970 -1996

William Atkinson is on many levels an exemplar. In charge of a 'challenging' inner city secondary school in west London with students from some of the most socially deprived sections of the community including a potentially explosive mix of recent refugees and long standing white and black working class poor, he has nevertheless revived the school's reputation over the past decade. No longer does it tolerate bad behaviour and bullying, it is more outward looking with significantly improved examination results. Atkinson's achievements have been widely recognised to the point where he advises the UK government on strategies for improving similar 'problem' schools. He is a modern celebrity teacher.

His diagnosis for what represents a good school is one which focuses on the needs of the children and the community. It is important to answer the question, where and how did Atkinson succeed? The answer lies in the community message.

William Atkinson was often seen striding around the area, visiting shops, talking to local people, often accosting them on the street. For him the learning environment was not limited to the confines of the school grounds, it was the surrounding streets, the public places which children frequented and the adults, not just parents, who came into contact with the students; in short, his remit was to the community as a whole, and not just to the academic welfare of the pupils under his wing.

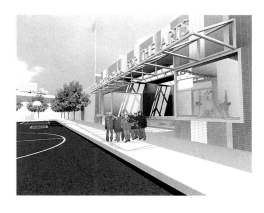

This school is a converted factory building. South Bronx Charter School for the Arts, Hunts Point, New York, Weisz + Yoes Studio, 2004

This aspiration is widely held, and there are many examples of good community schools cited within this publication which are taking a particularly inclusive line with their new buildings. For example, the South Bronx School for the Arts (pages 158-159) is a building located in the heart of a downtown area so that it is readily available to people who wish to use its facilities outside school hours. Its very presence within the community is a manifesto of how schools can contribute towards a renaissance of public life and public space.

An ambitious project at the Archbishop Ramsey Technology College in Southwark, South London, will offer local people multiple opportunities to enrich the life of their community and their own lives. The so-called Communiversity project has revolutionary ambitions which reach out well beyond the traditional school agenda. Like many inner city school communities up and down the country, the Communiversity project is located in an area which currently has a socially and economically deprived populace; one in five students are refugees or are in public care, almost three out of four are entitled to free school meals (a recognised poverty index). Sporadic acts of violence in the neighbourhood might depress attendance or lower motivation, yet academic results have improved substantially during the past three years.

The key to its success is the development of partnerships with external agencies such as the church, the police, local government and leading businesses such as Motorola and Ernst and Young. Students are encouraged to be outward looking; they are constantly made aware of their relationship to the community which serves them. Their education is as much social as it is academic. The success of their education will help in the development of good community relations through the social spirit of the school's alumni.

There is also an interesting dual-purpose entrepreneurial aspect to the Communiversity, an earning and learning capability for the school. It is planned that the new complex will include a business/workshop village, leased office and shop space, an Internet café, a fitness and leisure centre. These activities will provide role models and mentors for students as well as jobs for local people.

Schools are for the people who effectively own and run them, and one of the key priorities for the future must be to make their resources available to the wider community, to optimise the huge investment in school buildings currently underway. The future is in making these facilities open to the public, yet at the same time safe, secure and effective for those attending as full-time students.

School Typologies

In England, the Department for Education and Skills takes a strategic role in advising and, to a considerable extent, determining the size, layout and organisation of new schools. For example it produces what are called Building Bulletins, which proscribe many critical areas of the design agenda. Similar guidance is promoted by other national systems in Europe and the USA, most of which is developed in an effort to maintain critical standards and in order to control costs. For example, a floor area of 1.8 to 2.2 metres square per pupil is a commonly held standard for schools, whereas, 2.5 to 3.5 metres square is common for early years facilities. Because standards such as this relate directly to the budget provided, even if the designer feels more space is required, they would not be able to afford to do it without going over budget.

The thinking here is that since the school has a pre-determined technical specification and is paid for out of public taxation, the government has a responsibility to exert commonly held standards. It will be acting as a distant client to the local development group, comprising architect, school users and sometimes the building contractor. Whilst almost every national system promotes de-centralisation where each new school project is controlled and developed at local level, key strategic decisions will be set out and pre-determined by central government. The user clients who will be consulted during design development may have unique aspirations; in reality they will be working within the framework of tight planning and technical constraints.

Often this guidance is conflicting, for example the need for schools to be open to the community, yet at the same time secure and safe for the children using them. Many new early years facilities currently being developed within the UK and Germany include adult training rooms, adjacent to children's activity areas. Schools will need to be fully accessible to wheelchair users, however, a single-storey building, the most practical in that respect, will be less economical than a multi-storey building, particularly when the size of the site is restricted. This kind of tension runs through much of the guidance produced by central government.

As with any generic directive, it is impossible to take account of local site and community-related variables when designing a building as inherently complex as a new school. So whilst it is helpful to discuss plan types, it can become mischievous and in certain situations confusing. Nevertheless it is useful to be aware of key spatial design criteria and to discuss the main design opportunities which will contribute towards a successful and distinctive learning environment.

Modern school buildings cover a broad spectrum of layouts, some with free and open-plan forms, similar to the modern office, with a predominantly open-plan arrangement. However, the majority have traditional closed cellular structures, with the basic teaching space a classroom, providing lessons for groupings between 14 and 30 pupils. The classroom will either be a standard room for general teaching, acting as a secure homebase for a single age group of children, as is the case with most elementary schools for children up to the age of 11. Alternatively, the classroom may be subject-related, with distinct areas of the building for dedicated subject areas such as humanities, arts and design, science and technology, sports and drama.

Subject specific classrooms will be the most common arrangement for secondary schools, since most subjects studied at this level will require specialist facilities to a greater or lesser extent, such as language laboratories, acoustically insulated music rooms and indoor sports halls. Today all of these subject specific classrooms will have integrated ICT (information and communications technology) and sometimes a range of smaller seminar rooms for group or individual tuition. Lots of storage will be required, not just for student and staff belongings, but also for teaching resources. The school will need to have staff facilities, for study and relaxation; these rooms will usually be grouped together and out of bounds to students, to promote a collegiate spirit and perhaps to give teachers some respite from the 'chalk face.' In addition there will be whole school dining/cafe and refreshment areas, which will provide a full catering service. The school will comprise a main entrance or reception area, a main hall for assemblies (although it may double as a sports, drama or dining room), a library and safe, hygienic toilet and washroom areas for the use of students and staff, strategically positioned throughout the building.

These rooms will be the basic schedule of accommodation, and the architects will bring their planning skills to bear and organise the schedule in the most efficient and aesthetically pleasing form. Often the planning will be extremely complicated, with room and area relationships set out within a 300-room brief. It should not be allowed to dominate the design development as the sheer joy of architecture is of fundamen-

Images of classrooms: Geography lesson at Alma School, London, 1908, and art lesson at King Alfred School, London, 2002

The central atrium at this Waldorf School acts as a multi-functional space for school assemblies and community events. Waldorf School, Chorweiler near Köln, Peter Hübner, 1996

tal importance too. However, whilst the location of storage in relation to teaching areas may seem like a secondary issue when discussing exciting architectural concepts, if it is in the wrong position, the subsequent generation of teachers who have to use the building will not thank you.

Circulation

Beyond this functionally specific area schedule, there will be the internal circulation areas which link individual rooms or subject departments. Circulation is not merely a function of teaching; it is the space between, where students will spend much of their time outside the classroom as they move around the campus between lessons. These circulation areas will often be described as 'break-out spaces,' or 'covered streets' in order to invest them with a positive aura. Poorly designed circulation can make movement around the building difficult and even facilitate bullying. Generous well-designed circulation will promote a positive ethos and make sense of the building as a coherent public institution. Circulation should never be merely conceived of as a corridor. It is a critical dimension where good design can make a real difference to spatial quality. The cynical observer might note that since the tight constraints of the normal school brief allow architects little scope for fantasy and imagination, spatial quality usually manifests itself in the concept and design of the intermediate zones.

Plan types

In the UK government's Building Bulletin 95, generic plan types are proposed for secondary and primary schools (Schools for the Future – Designs for Learning Communities, Building Bulletin 95, Department for Education and Skills, 2002, p. 54, www.teachernet.gov.uk/schoolbuildings). In reality these have little to say about the rich language of architecture, rather they treat school design as a slightly simplistic two-dimensional diagram. Nevertheless, they help to rationalise the various strategic approaches in a systematic way, which is easy to communicate at an early stage of the design. In this respect they have value within the framework of a broader conceptual discussion with end users, parents and school governors, when consulting during the design development stages.

Early years buildings are different from schools or at least they should be. They must relate to the smaller scales of young children with the emphasis on learning through play as the essential aspect of the curriculum, which inevitably makes them distinct and very special environments in their own right. Whilst age-related groupings might be the basic organising principles for many daycare facilities, the ethos that children at this age are not there for formal education must shine through.

In terms of secondary schools, three plan types can be distinguished. Firstly, the street plan, secondly, the campus plan and thirdly, linked pavilions. The 'street plan' is based on a main linear volume, which might be two or three storeys high and covered over with a translucent roof. The main street may have subsidiary streets, or in order to extend the metaphor, what might be described as 'lanes' which run at right angles off the main street. The street provides a focus for the school community as a whole and acts as an internal recreation area, with cafés and shops running inside. Whilst reminiscent of the shopping mall, this concept can be used to develop an economical three- or four-storey building which will be easy to adapt and extend at a later date. An example is the Jo Richardson Community School (pages 222-223).

The so-called campus plan adopts the language of the suburban university, with individual buildings set within a green landscape, with circulation predominantly outside in the fresh air. The school is seen as a semi-autonomous series of buildings, which may be dedicated to particular subject areas. In theory each block can be different so that a degree of variety becomes part of the architectural language. Each building can operate as an individual year or house base, and one or more can be opened outside of school hours, such as a sports building for community use. The downside is that different areas can be far apart. It may take time to get around, a problem when students change lessons. Also it may be more suitable to sunny climates, for obvious reasons. An example is the Feather River Academy (pages 104-105), which is a special school that benefits from the idea of individual smaller scale units for special groups of students, which are deliberately detached from each other.

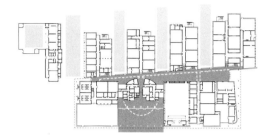

Street plan: the 'main street' provides a focus for the school. Jo Richardson Community School, Dagenham, London, Architecture PLB, 2005

View of circulation area in street plan school. Central Tree Middle School Rutland MA, USA, HMFH Architects, 1998

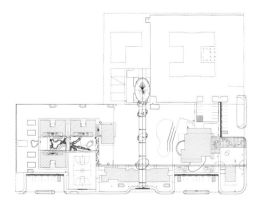

A campus plan school has individual buildings set within a landscape; most circulation is outside. Feather River Academy, Yuba City, California, Architecture for Education – A4E, 2005

Classroom blocks surrounding a central space.
Nærum Amtsgymnasium, Copenhagen,
Dall & Lindhardtsen, 2004

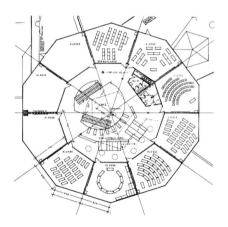

Polygonal plan centred around a shared hall. Secondary school
Auf dem Schäfersfeld, Lorch, Germany, Günter Behnisch, 1973

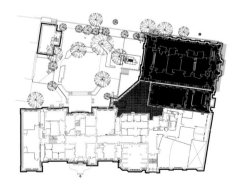

Incorporation of existing buildings at Packer Collegiate Institute,
Brooklyn, New York, H³ Hardy Collaboration Architecture, 2003

The third plan type cited, which is clearly a hybrid of the first and second, comprises of classroom blocks surrounding a double-height central space which is covered over by a semi-translucent roof. Larger spaces are formed as separate blocks, linked but not necessarily attached to the main central space. An example of this would be Nærum Amtsgymnasium near Copenhagen in Denmark (pages 192-193). The advantages of this are that each block can reflect a faculty or school within a school idea, so for example a different colour of cladding panel provides a subtle but very legible organising devise avoiding too much fragmentation. In addition, the central space can form a shared resource area, easily accessed by surrounding spaces. This may result in a slightly corporate image relying on transparency and open planning to get light into the inherently deep-plan arrangements.

As far as the primary school typologies are concerned, Building Bulletin 95 firstly identifies a deep-plan form with classrooms and resource areas on each side of a circulation route, with the main hall positioned centrally. The linear plan has classrooms on one side of a circulation route with support spaces on the other side. The hall and entrance are usually at one end of the classroom run. With classrooms all orientated in one direction, it is a fluid and environmentally effective arrangement. However, it is going to be less economical than an arrangement with classrooms at both sides of the central space. This is the final primary school type and is described as the 'deep linear plan.' Here classroom bases are on two sides of a circulation/resource area. Main hall and entrance are located at one or both ends.

The need for rationalisation of this type disguises the complexity of designing for education in the 21st century. Even trying to categorise a school in this way may reduce its richness as an organisation, which is responding to a unique set of local influences. A good example is the work of Günter Behnisch, particularly in his secondary school Auf dem Schäfersfeld in Lorch (1973) which is characterised by dynamic free forms and essential quality of openness, whilst retaining the basic classroom form. It is a creative novelty, defeating typologies, yet it has influenced a subsequent generation of school builders with its theme of expressive individualism.

Perhaps the most important factor to bear in mind is that the diagnosis for most school sites will incorporate existing buildings, for example the Burr Elementary School (pages 128-129) or the Packer Collegiate Institute (pages 248-251), which is an amalgamation of five loosely connected historical buildings dating back to 1854. In a situation like this, the correct diagnosis will spring from the most creative yet cost effective response to a given situation for which generic advise will be largely irrelevant. It is clear that spatial quality emerges as a direct reaction to the site problems to which the architect is responding. As with any great architecture, it is as much the juxtaposition of beautiful materials, nice to the touch and good to look at, which are as fundamental as the correct technical specification for light, space and acoustics.

PAMELA LOEFFELMAN

Spatial Configurations

Atelier art room addition in the Cyert Center
for Early Education, Carnegie Mellon University,
Pittsburgh, Pennsylvania, Perkins Eastman Architects

Today kids are different, even 5 year olds have opinions. Both little kids and big kids are looking for meaningful changes that allow them to better utilise their facilities in a way that connects learning with the world as it is. As designers, we have a chance to connect architecture with learning. Today's school design should reflect a powerful commitment to the potential for education reform, a kind of reform that allows for the appropriate connection between learner and teacher, between the individual and society. We need to provide facilities that link curriculum development with the community and balance comprehensive learning with personalised outcomes.

It is no longer acceptable to allow lowrisk, status quo designs for schools which result in standard facilities that are average in their appearance and average in their students' academic achievements. New benchmarks based on innovative design approaches for primary schools are converging, supporting an impetus for change. While there is a lack of substantive research that links the actual cause and effects of changing designs on student outcomes, anecdotal evidence, by way of these benchmarks, is starting to demonstrate through examples how certain schools have successfully reshaped a specific learning community through design, thereby reducing the risks inherent in innovation and encouraging change.

At least four emerging trends can be recognised as contributing to the innovative school designs of tomorrow. Individually, these trends can act as incremental catalysts in the design of specific programme components that make up traditional elementary schools design; together they can also be viewed as components of a larger transformation.

The separate trends themselves, however, are worth individual consideration before we take a closer look at how they have jointly influenced the spatial relationships that are becoming more pervasive in 21st century schools:

- Ubiquitous technology
- Integrated break-out spaces and project rooms
- Specialised learning environments
- Multi-functional spaces that support schools as centres of community

Ubiquitous technology

Technology has changed the world. I believe it will continue to do so at an ever-increasing rate. Today's 5- to 7 year olds are the fastest-growing segment of computer users. If you look only a few years ahead, their teenage siblings typically have five to six applications running at once on their computers, with either e-mail or instant messaging as their preferred methods of communication with friends, with blogs as their method for discerning truth, and Web sites around the world providing them with the "facts" they seek. While technology alone is not the answer to 21st century learning, an understanding of how it can appeal to a child's frame of reference and capture their attention needs to be incorporated into the development of the building programme. As students become increasingly computer savvy, more schools are responding to the challenge of engagement by becoming media-rich.

As a result of this infusion of evolving technology, school designs must develop from plans and infrastructures that are flexible and adaptable to new models of instruction that can support students' needs for access to maximum resources. It is sometimes difficult to remember that widespread use of computers and the availability of the World Wide Web are fairly recent occurrences. Initially, computers were added to established classrooms, taking up valuable real estate. As the cost of wireless laptops and PDAs have decreased, and as software programmes that are student and teacher friendly have been developed, the integration of technology into the elementary school classroom has fostered a change in the pedagogy of early education. Today's elementary school student can be involved in everything from word processing to concept mapping, drawing and animation to scientific research. Learning is hands-on and project-based. In response to this change in pedagogy, a much wider variety of spaces and configurations are emerging as the norm. Schools today need to be more flexible than the traditional double-loaded corridors of uniform classrooms of the past.

'Pod' break-out space adjacent to four classroom clusters for students and faculty, Helen S. Faison Academy, Pittsburgh, Pennsylvania, Perkins Eastman Architects

Integrated break-out spaces and project rooms

First and foremost among the changes in 21st century learning environments are spaces that enhance and embrace an individual student's ability to learn both on- and offline. Elementary school should be a time when children are nurtured and encouraged to explore. They should be allowed to proceed at their own paces, consistent with their own 'intelligence.' Technology has given instructors the tools to allow this to happen. Physical learning environments need to be adapted to further enable and encourage this shift.

Dedicated spaces within classrooms and dedicated computer labs are being replaced with the opportunities to change the entire classroom or parts of it into 'labs' through wireless technology and PDAs. Online or computer-based learning tools for small group instruction can also be provided in break-out spaces to meet these needs. The ability to instruct a few children or individuals on similar topics, at different paces and in different ways, allows for the customisation of each student's personal profile.

Break-out spaces can also be places that support project-based learning, where informal interaction focuses on group interactions versus just the individual. More and more, break-out spaces are developing into scalable environments that nurture both individual students and small-group work with an emphasis on collaborative work and the recognition of the need to accommodate multiple learning styles.

Interior windows and openings can further allow for effective break-out spaces in the nooks and crannies of circulation that were previously perceived as unusable spaces. These spaces have become secondary instructional areas by allowing an instructor to maintain supervision over more than one area at a time.

Break-out space at classroom clusters
West Haven Elementary School, West Haven, Utah.
VCBO Architecture

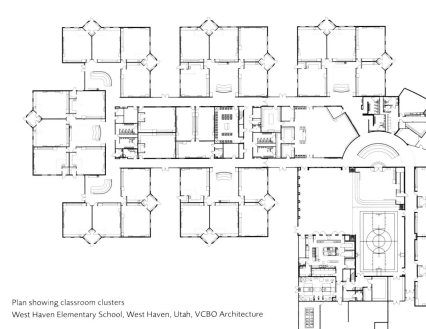

Plan showing classroom clusters
West Haven Elementary School, West Haven, Utah, VCBO Architecture

Specialised learning environments

Most elementary schools' specialised learning environments consist of media centres, gymnasiums, art and music classrooms. Sometimes included are science centres and outdoor learning places. With an ever increasing need for facilities and a finite pool of resources, there is a tendency to make as many of the public spaces as multi-functional as possible; however, specialized learning environments all have specific programme functions that must be met in order to be successful. It is important to remember that it is often hard to excel if the list of priorities is too broad.

These are the spaces that should be thought of as the 'jewels in the crown', serving as places of wonder for kids. Let it be said that kids today are wired differently. It is not enough to say, 'If it was good enough for me,' thus implying that change is not required. There are too many children that are still not graduating from secondary schools. How can design make a difference?

Specialised learning places are opportunities to provide the places and the mechanisms that engage every student. Each student may enter school from a different starting place than their respective peers.

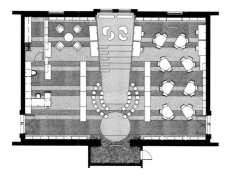

Plan diagram showing central storytelling area at P.S. 106 Edward Everett Hale School Library, Brooklyn, New York, Rockwell Architecture

Storytelling area. P.S. 106 Edward Everett Hale School Library, Brooklyn, New York, Rockwell Architecture

Treehouse designed to support environmental curriculum. Island Wood, Bainbridge Island, Washington. Mithun Architects

These are the kinds of places that can equalise, that should allow for every student to find their specific area of interest. These are the places for invention, places for reflection, also places to just blow off steam.

Rather than locating them in one central area, these spaces should be considered transitional zones that can serve as semi-public places. Locating these transitional zones throughout a school provides equal accessibility to all, while also connecting both the more public areas of a school and the front doors to the classroom environment.

Multi-functional spaces

In addition to specialised learning environments, there is a need for group gathering spaces that are flexible and allow for many different types of configurations. Both the size and the proportions of multi-functional rooms need to accommodate furnishings that can be easily adjusted on a day-to-day, if not a function-by-function basis. This does not mean that the spaces should be lacking in character; rather, these kinds of spaces need 'signals' as to how the rooms should and can be configured. Careful consideration of furniture, acoustics, sound systems and lighting are also very important in designing these kinds of rooms.

Having reviewed these four emerging trends, let us now study how these individual trends have started to affect the spatial relationships of the components that make up a traditional elementary school's space programme. This will allow us to synthesise and suggest new design paradigms for classrooms, specialised learning environments and places for public gathering. As in any building design, there needs to be a balance between perceiving the whole and breaking the whole down into precincts that are easily understood and negotiated. One has to look at designing from both the inside out and from the outside in, all for a variety of users:

- First and foremost, the students. Even this group of users comprises multiple sub-groups in elementary school. The difference between pre-Kindergarten and Kindergarten (4-5 year olds), second and third graders (7-8 year olds), and the 'big guys' in fourth and fifth grades (9-10 year olds) all need to be considered.
- The administration and the faculty
- The parents
- The community at large. After all, in most communities, this is the constituency that ultimately votes to fund the construction of schools.

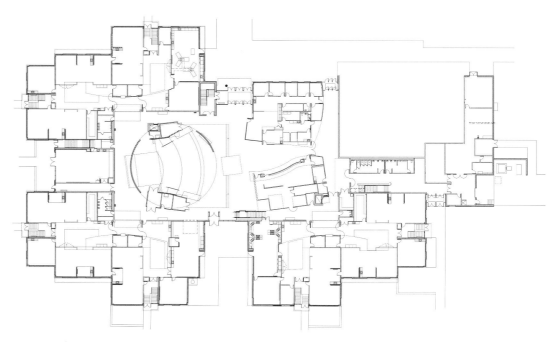

Plan showing single-loaded corridor leading to indoor public spaces.
Crosswinds Arts and Science Middle School, Woodbury, Minnesota, Cuningham Group

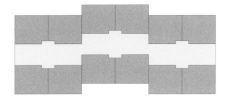

Diagram of break-out spaces in oversized double-loaded corridor

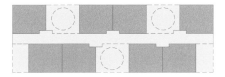

Diagram of integrated break-out spaces

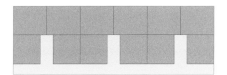

Diagram of break-out spaces in oversized single-loaded corridor

View of indoor public spaces with commons, cafeteria and performance spaces. Crosswinds Arts and Science Middle School, Woodbury, Minnesota, Cuningham Group

Multi functional gathering space. West Metro Education Programme (WMEP) Interdistrict Downtown School, Minneapolis, Minnesota, Cuningham Group

Inside out

Designing from the inside out, one must first consider the student. The domain of the student is, of course, the classroom. The classroom should feel different than the more public areas of the school. It should be a student space. This does not mean that it should feel childish, but rather scaled to their developmental needs. The evolution of instructional spaces continues to change, particularly in terms of how these spaces are configured. While many elementary schools still feature the traditional double-loaded corridor, there are variations on this theme. The most common approach allows for either enlarged corridors with media-rich breakout spaces that can be shared by a cluster of classrooms, or an E or H shaped configuration that allows for secondary circulation to classroom clusters and shared facilities. This results in neighbourhoods that are grade specific and scaled to an environment that is very child-friendly.

The alternative basic configuration is the single-loaded corridor which provides a direct relation between the classrooms, in the centre to both the outdoors on one side and to the indoor public spaces on the other side. This type of configuration allows for the public and students to progress from the community as represented by the context outside to a classroom focus which is more on the individual. It also incorporates circulation areas into interior public spaces resulting in an open, commodious feel.

Another consideration to be taken into account in classroom design is the dramatic range in ages. Pre-K students live in a much different world than fifth-graders. The elementary school should act as a learning tool that allows younger students to grow and transition as they move from grade to grade. Pre-Kindergarten and Kindergarten classrooms are often located in their own precincts with dedicated bus/parent drop-off and pick-up areas. Travel distances to other activities such as the gym or the library should be kept to a minimum.

As students matriculate, their use of the school should expand, always allowing them to see more and more of the school and the activities that are offered at various grade levels. This allows students to be proud of where they have been and look forward to where they are going.

Diagram illustrating a typical elementary school programme

Prevalent programme spaces

- Classrooms
- Shared facilities
- Administration
- Circulation

Outside in

When looking at the design from the outside in, one must consider the sequence from public to semi-public to private. Within the various areas of the school, there should be differentiation so that wayfinding can easily be achieved. Public zones should clearly feel like public zones. Student zones should clearly feel like student zones.

Starting at the front door, there is typically one point of access for the public during school hours with the administration located nearby. This provides both security and central access for students, faculty and parents alike. From this point, the community needs clear and direct access to the specific areas within the building that they are using. With more and more schools becoming true centres of community, the relationship of these spaces to the overall plan has changed to accommodate typical requirements for zoneable, secure 24-hour access.

Just as there are designs to accommodate the core curricula, there are two basic variations on how to arrange the public spaces. The public spaces typically consist of the gymnasium, the auditorium and the cafeteria. These spaces can be collocated into one multi-functional group, either at the perimeter of the school or as a central gathering space. If all of the public functions are central to the school with classroom spaces ringing the perimeter, issues such as service to the public spaces and off-hour use have to be carefully considered. However, this model can be particularly persuasive when the public 'commons' combines dining and group assembly in such a way to provide a true heart for the school.

In contrast, public functions can be located at key points around the perimeter. This can allow for separate off-hour use, such as access to a gymnasium/auditorium for local community use or the use of cafeterias or media centres for public town meetings.

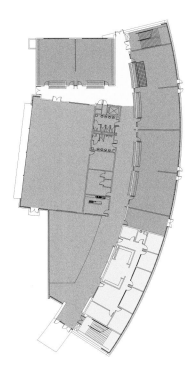

Plan illustrating public spaces located at the perimeter. Concordia International School, Shanghai, China, Perkins Eastman Architects

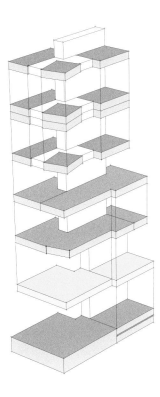

Diagram of vertically stacked public spaces in the center of the school. Lucile S. Bulger Center for Community Life, New York, Perkins Eastman Architects

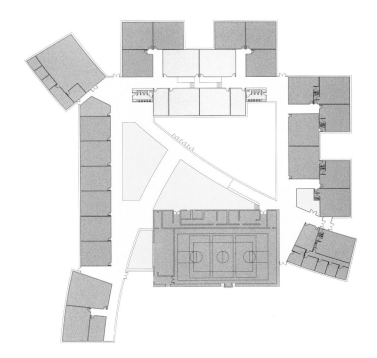

Plan showing public spaces at the key locations on the perimeter. Glenville Elementary School, Greenwich, Connecticut, Perkins Eastman Architects

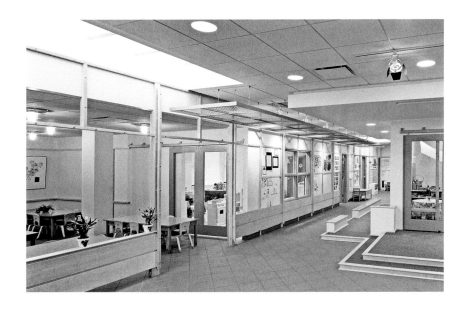

Learning pathway and central piazza at Cyert Center for Early Education, Carnegie Mellon University, Pittsburgh, Pennsylvania, Perkins Eastman Architects

Whether one designs from the inside out or the outside in, the biggest factors affecting spatial relationships in the design of any school can be the requirements related to the ratio of net to gross. Net represents the area of all spaces that are designed for specific functions. Gross is the area required to connect and service these functional spaces. Often this relationship is integrally linked to funding, where the perception is the lower the number, the more efficient the building, and therefore, the better. Most public schools in the United States will allow, on average, state funding for school construction typically in a range of 1.35 to 1.4 net to gross.

Contrary to this requirement is the potential inherent if lobbies, corridors and other circulation spaces become enlarged to support a variety of activities. This is particularly true in elementary schools where the changes from class to class are more limited in nature. Recent developments support new design approaches that make connecting spaces functional space. Rather than laying out the corridors, architects are designing connections as "learning pathways," resulting in more usable spaces and a more efficient building. Whether one creatively labels space to be fundable, or whether one successfully argues that "learning pathways" provide for increased learning opportunities, the outcome will be the same.

Just as there are common characteristics among learning environments and how they are spatially configured, there must also be differences. Every institution should have distinguishing traits that are a direct reflection of the curriculum, context, student body and the community. As citizens of the 21st century, we must also recognise that the world at large is also changing. As globalisation continues, the discussion of what makes world-class facilities is an increasingly important topic.

• How can one learn from the projects that take risks, thereby creating outcomes that are better than average?
• How can one benefit from a more global dialogue?
• What are the common traits that lead to success?
• What are the regional differences that create context?
• How can we be sure that personalisation of learning environments is focused on students?

First and foremost, be sure you know your client, listen well, anticipate change and understand that no two students are alike. Allow a „loose fit" so that a certain amount of adaptability over time is possible as curriculum requirements, programme and politics change occurs. This is crucial to the development of a value-based design appropriate for today's schools and adaptable to the needs of tomorrow.

Building systems (structural, mechanical, electrical) should also incorporate a sustainable approach to design. If the initial cost of a building represents less than 20% of the lifelong cost of the building, a "loose fit" should anticipate and allow for cost-effective renovations and adaptations over time. The interiors must balance traditional approaches to layout and materials that focus on durability, with design ideas and finishes that are adaptable to that they can accommodate changing students and communities long into the 21st century. To sum it up, one size, shape or spatial organisation no longer fits all.

Acoustic Design

The architectural acoustics of school buildings and schoolrooms are often not taken into account until late in the design phase. The following considerations should help to explain why it makes sense to include them at the earliest possible stage, and why careful acoustic design is both aesthetically and financially worthwhile.

One reason for assuming that room acoustics are a secondary design function lies in the traditional belief that they are primarily dependent upon the absorption characteristics of the internal finishing materials. The factors which govern room acoustics are more complex, however, and will already have been predetermined by the choice of construction and spatial form. Also, a condition fundamental to the psychology of perception is that the quality of an acoustic will be judged according to the personal experiences of the listener. This judgement and the auditory reception itself will ultimately be influenced by the individual's perceptual expectations. Recent neurological investigations have confirmed that perception is an active process and extends to the regulation of the sensitivity of the ear for amplitude and frequency. This can be intensified or reduced via nerve fibres which send feedback from the brain to the ear, which explains why the judgements formed of acoustic or room acoustic impressions are sometimes very different. The definition of an acoustic sound as opposed to unpleasant noise is subjective. Nevertheless, quality factors may be defined to which value ranges can be assigned that apply for certain listener groups and types of use.

Sensory perception and acoustics

Sound experiences trigger emotions and activate numerous areas of the brain. They are strongly linked to the autonomic nerve system and may effect a variety of changes, including fluctuations in blood pressure and respiratory rate. Acoustic impressions may mask other nerve signals (like Tinnitus, but also discomfort and even pain); they may have a calming effect, but may also cause fear (e.g. a sudden noise). It is known that rooms with excessive sound insulation may induce breathlessness, unease and fatigue because perceptible spatial dimensions have been lost. But it is also true that a good acoustic may have a liberating, invigorating effect and may promote concentration and communication. Seldom do we consciously perceive acoustics unless they are unpleasant. The perception of sound is a way of detecting meaningful structures in our environment, guided by our expectations. Acoustic signals assist social communication. In this sense, acoustics are an integral part of the whole design process.

Temporal resolution of the senses

Of all the sensory organs, the ear transmits the most finely attuned temporal orientation. Binaural perception from the side towards the front enables us to experience differences in direction of only 1 cm or 3°, corresponding to the unbelievably minute time differential of 0,03 ms (milliseconds). Only 3 ms are needed to perceive middle frequency pitches with a soft attack. Our sense of touch is able to detect vibrations through the fingertips with the same temporal resolution. The ear requires up to 28 ms to perceive tone colours and pitches produced with a hard attack, and up to 50 ms (1/20 secs.) to perceive low pitches. It is known that a continuous film sequence needs at least 20 images per sec., and that at least 50 ms are required for the visual perception of each individual image. Much longer, namely 160 ms, is needed to feel an object. The conscious recognition of a smell or taste takes seconds if not minutes. An important consequence of this is that the slower sensory perceptions benefit from faster auditory perception. This is a reason for the strong coordination between eye and ear, but also for the importance of room acoustics in architectural design.

Sensory experiences in preschool and school-age children

These physiological data clearly show how important the opportunity for acoustic experiences is during early childhood and school years. Investigations show that small children are very active and sensitive in exploring their acoustic environment. In teenagers, however, the emotional perspective already predominates over acoustic impressions. Nevertheless, an analytical approach to listening can be stimulated in every individual through independent acoustic events. The attention can be tuned in both to the sound source and to the quality of the sound. Generally, adults can only sustain this approach to listening for a few moments before making a comparison with the spectrum of standard sounds stored in the memory. Just as we say that snow is white even though it is a shimmering blue in evening light, so do we store stereotyped images of sound for

certain situations and sound sources. We have a preconception that a gymnasium should be reverberant, a bedroom muted and a busy street noisy. These 'preconceived opinions,' which help us to orientate ourselves quickly, are essentially formed during childhood. Subsequently, they can only be corrected if we are constantly subjected to different experiences. We know that threatening or happy moments leave behind deep impressions which also stamp our acoustic perception of the world, so from the number of hours a child spends in school, we can make a direct conclusion as to the importance of the sensory experiences gained there.

Noise and silence

Noise is an invasive nuisance which masks important acoustic signals. Insulation against outside noise is therefore regarded as a great relief. Also, it is only in periods of continuous silence that our aural perception achieves its highest level of sensitivity. Building technology has made enormous progress by sealing windows and doors against penetrating airborne sound and by decoupling mechanical connections with elastic elements (footstep damping, floating floors, softening rigid wall and conduit junctions). Building standards provide clear guidelines in this respect. In the USA and the UK high levels of acoustic performance has been made a statutory requirement in all new school buildings. For example, the 2006 UK publication, Acoustic Design of Schools – Building Bulletin 93 recognises that teaching and learning are acoustically demanding activities. In particular, there is a consensus that low ambient noise levels are required particularly to integrate pupils with special needs into mainstream schools. The most serious acoustic problems are due to noise transfer between rooms and excessive reverberation in rooms. This is often the case in old Victorian buildings or in more recent open plan school design, which is particularly problematic at primary school level.

The quality of room acoustics

It is much more difficult to define the quality criteria by which the architectural acoustics of internal rooms should be designed. This is where the standards are less helpful. Often, the correction of reverberation may lead to excessive damping, even if the calculated absorption measures are exceeded only slightly. This in turn produces unpleasant acoustic discolouration in the high frequency range when conventional absorbing materials are used. A room acoustic must never be dead but should preserve a quality of spaciousness.

clockwise

Music school in Auer
South Tyrol, Italy,
Christina Niederstätter, 2005
Room for flute lessons

Music school in Auer
South Tyrol
Room for piano lessons and chamber music

Gustav Mahler Hall,
Arts Centre and School of Music
Toblach, South Tyrol,
Wachter & Partner, 1999/2006

Sports hall, Gasteiner Upper School
Bolzano, South Tyrol, O. Zoeggeler, 2001

Zoned areas offering different acoustic experiences

Of particular benefit to children, who receive essential acoustic experiences in schoolrooms, would be the conscious creation of different zones offering a variety of acoustic characteristics: places of silence and concentrated tranquillity (library); places for eating; places for speaking (classroom, lecture hall), singing and making music in small groups (music rooms); and rooms for a larger number of listeners (music hall). Children are among the first to recognise the use of acoustic signals such as the gentle splashing of a fountain to denote relative peace in the refectory, and to discover that a corridor channels sound and carries it over long distances, or that their voices and other sounds reverberate longer in the cellar. It is not always the case that children will be less aggressive in a dampened acoustic and will shout more in a reverberant one. However, as with adults, children experience a feeling of well-being if the acoustic design suits the function of the room.

Refectory, Manzoni Elementary School
Bolzano, South Tyrol, Christina Niederstätter, 2004

Direct sound

One of the first acoustic experiences we perceive is that we hear better when we can see the sound source, but good visual contact with the sound source alone is not enough for a good acoustic. Nevertheless, direct sound improves speech intelligibility because it is ideal for transmitting high frequencies. This can be achieved by banking rows of seats, or, if the room has an adequately high ceiling, raising the sound source may be sufficient.

Indirect sound, reflection and diffraction

Sound is reflected off the room boundaries like light off a mirror. An effective reflector must be substantially bigger than the length of the sound waves. (Wavelengths within audible range are approximately between 17 m at 20 Hz and 17 mm at 20.000 Hz). As with light, when a sound wave encounters a barrier or surface undulation within its wavelength, it will be diffracted. By texturing the surface with raised and recessed areas, harsh reverberations are prevented, flutter echoes between parallel walls avoided, and the required amount of absorption achieved in the higher frequency range (diffuse reflection). Architecturally, these rules relating to reflector dimensions and surface texture touch upon an aesthetically sensitive design realm, which should be taken into account when designing a space. In the temporally staggered field of reflections, we talk about useful early reflections which amplify and clarify the sound, and late reflections which are heard as reverberation. They add spaciousness and fullness.

x = time (in milliseconds)
y = volume (in decibel)
D = direct sound
R_1, R_2, R_3 = reflections from walls,
ceiling, rear wall and other surfaces

The reverberation formula of Wallace C. Sabine

Around 1900 Boston physicist Wallace C. Sabine successfully demonstrated that there was a relationship between room volume V, absorption A and reverberation time T (time taken for the sound pressure level to

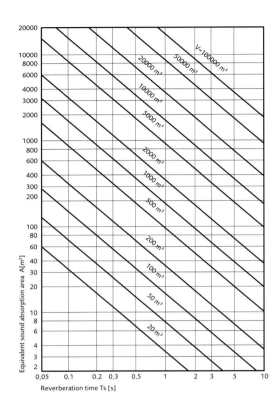

Realtion between sound absorption and reverberation time

fall by 60 dB): T (sec.) = 0.163 V/A, whereby A = $\alpha_1 S_1 + \alpha_2 S_2 + \alpha_3 S_3$... This equation can be used in the design phase to calculate reverberation time if the precise absorption factors α_x and joint faces S_x of the materials used are known. The coefficients of A for a planned reverberation time can thus be determined for the given room volumes. In the absence of laboratory measurements, calculations can be made using the α-values given in the technical specifications (e.g. the α-database of the PTB, Physical-Technical State Institute, Brunswick), but a reserve margin should always be planned for essential fine-tuning of the room acoustic. Measuring the reverberation of the shell of the building has proved useful for clarifying the acoustic properties of the construction. A measurement taken after essential internal elements have been completed allows the planning of final adjustments.

Absorption

The application of absorption materials reduces not only the intensity of sound reflections but may also prevent the formation of energy accumulation, which may in turn cause unpleasant late spatial responses. Modern construction now rarely uses surface textures. Vibrating floors and wall claddings are absent and mostly hard and heavy materials are preferred which absorb little acoustic energy, particularly within the 100 - 200 Hz range (this applies to concrete but also glass).

It is technically easier to dampen high and mid range frequencies. This is achieved by using porous surfaces such as mineral and organic fibre materials, but they are also absorbed by people in the room and textured surfaces. The sound absorbing effect of curtains increases from the high to the middle frequency range with increasing weight per unit area and distance from the wall covered. However, curtains may also impair the lateral acoustic so important to the perception of direction and sound amplification. Depending on the surface, carpets are effective in the mid to high frequency range. Carefully chosen upholstered seating may also compensate acoustically in a lecture room when few people are present.

Invasive low frequencies require more extensive corrective measures. Perforated and slotted absorbers are used (absorbed frequency range depends on the thickness of the panel, the size of perforation, the proportion of slotted surface, width of slot, the distance between perforations, the surface distance and the sound-absorbing infill). Panel absorbers may also be used (soft, pliable panels with an enclosed air cavity, positioned in front of acoustically hard, heavy structural components), as well as cavities lined with absorbing materials, which can be very precisely adjusted to the frequency range to be dampened. Especially suitable for schoolrooms are non-fibrous absorbers in micro-perforated plastic, metal sheeting or plywood

Details of elastic suspension of walls and ceiling in Aula Magna at Gasteiner Upper School
Bolzano, South Tyrol, V. Andrialo, 2001

(diameter of perforation: 0.5-0.7mm) which, depending on construction, can be effective in a broad frequency range. A regular distribution of sound-absorbing areas alternating with reflecting areas is acoustically advantageous.

Acoustic standards and guidelines relevant to school buildings

For the design of room acoustics, standards specify reverberation times for the best reception of speech and music within a minimal frequency range of 60 - 4,000Hz. (The narrower frequency range of 500 - 1,000 Hz given in the German norm DIN 18041 for speech does not include the frequency band between 2,000 - 3,000 Hz, which is important for the carrying capacity of the voice and the masking effect of low frequency reverberation). The ideal average reverberation time, T, for speech is 0.7 secs., but for music lessons it is 0.4 to 1.2 secs., depending on the volume of the room and the musical instrument. In a smaller public hall the average reverberation time for music should not lie below 0.9 secs. to guarantee a pleasant sound. This time should be proportionally longer for larger room volumes.

Experiences in the construction of acoustically sensitive rooms (music schools, auditoria and concert halls, children's schoolrooms etc.) have shown that the linearisation of upper reverberation, i.e. the most even reverberation time possible within the 50 to 5,000 Hz frequency range, permits longer reverberation times because of less masking. This satisfies the requirements of multi-purpose use of rooms for speech and music. Flexible use can also be facilitated by moveable absorbers (reflecting or absorbing partition walls, moveable reflectors with different textures, upholstered seating, curtain with the correct wall coverage, etc.).

It is particularly important to consider children with impaired hearing, who require special measures, to create good hearing conditions. According to standards, to be intelligible without strain, speech in a classroom should be twice as loud as the sum of all interfering background noises (the level differential to the ambient noise should therefore be about 10 dB). For those with impaired hearing, however, the ideal level differential is 15 to 20 dB. Difficulties in perceiving sound and speech can be overcome by the position in the room of the listener with impaired hearing (proximity to, and good visibility of, the speaker). Experts will need to be consulted on this point.

Geometric room acoustic

The shape of the room determines the geometric diffusion of the sound. Concave surfaces concentrate the sound while convex surfaces diffuse it. Narrow angles, niches and rooms linked by openings cause so-called sound accumulations, which may produce unpleasant delayed reverberations. Asymmetrical shapes produce an uneven sound distribution, especially when reflections bounced off two or three surfaces before reaching the listener. Because the ear is more sensitive to lateral sounds, it is important that the height of the room is adequate to allow lateral reflection from above.

It is known that shoe-box shaped, rectangular rooms give the most even sound distribution. Nevertheless, parallel walls may produce standing waves and flutter echoes, which must be carefully attenuated by texturing/structuring the surfaces, or at least by absorbing specific frequencies. Even in the absence of right angles, standing waves may occur over several surfaces. In smaller rooms absorbing measures are often sufficient on only one of the interacting surfaces.

Masking and summation

An acoustic event comprises a constant temporal overlaying of direct sound and reverberation. It therefore moves within the range of masking – too loud, delayed or discoloured reflections – and the summation of useful reflections. Depending on what is being perceived, reflections of 15 ms to 150 ms blend to form a complete impression. From this quality factors are derived such as the extent of syllabic recognition, clarity, transparency, spatial impression, level of lateral sound, sound colour of the early reflections, amplitude etc. If there are numerous reflections, temporally well-layered and converging from all directions, the sound is more transparent and the listener can tolerate a higher sound level and longer reverberation times.

Classroom at Middle school
Schlanders, South Tyrol, T. Simma, 2002

Multi-purpose hall at school Vella
Graubünden, Switzerland, V. Bearth & A. Deplazes, 1997

Seminar room, University of Zürich Musicology Institute
Beate Schnitter, 1997

Music school in Auer
South Tyrol, Christina Niederstätter, 2005

Teaching room for flute: length 5.5 m, width 3.5 m, average height 3.4 m, volume approx. 65 m³. Teaching room for piano: length 6.5 m, width 6.0 m, height 3.0 m, volume approx. 115 m³. Linear reverberation times 0.5 - 0.9 secs., depending on the instrument taught.

Absorbing resonators in the walls and in some rooms in the ceiling, covered and concealed by perforated metal sheeting. The ceilings are clad with sheets of perforated plasterboard. Tube-traps were installed in the corners of the rooms as excellent low-frequency absorbers. Flexible lining shells of plasterboard are installed in some rooms to act as low-frequency absorbers. Fine tuning for high frequencies was accomplished by applying colourful highly absorbent foam structures as necessary, particularly in sharp angles. The floor structures were produced throughout in floating Keene's cement; the doors were checked for sound transmissions and sound-insulated wherever necessary using double-sealed door panels of sufficient weight, soundproof door frames and flush rubber seals. The partition walls achieved sound insulating coefficients of Rw'= 57dB. To reduce resonance in the windows, melamine resin foam elements were installed between the panes. Some of the timber cladding in the rooms was designed as undulating panelling for low-pitch absorption. By applying precise measures and step-by-step optimisation, each room has an acoustic matched exactly to its purpose. The goal was to sound-insulate the rooms and to achieve the best possible acoustic transparency and appropriate sound volume to ensure undisturbed teaching.

Gustav Mahler Hall, Arts Centre and School of Music
Toblach, South Tyrol
Wachter & Partner, 1999/2006

Length 32 m, width 16 m, height 10 m, volume approx. 5.200 m³. Linear reverberation time 1.8 secs. with 430 persons in the hall.

Shoe-box hall room with carefully textured wall and ceiling cladding in wood. Acoustic installations: following measurement taken in the shell, 1,000 exactly calculated absorbing cavity resonators were installed behind the wall and ceiling cladding. Seating in light-weight upholstery enables use of the hall with a small audience and for recording when the hall is empty. Outstanding acoustic for orchestral concerts, chamber music and recordings.

Sports hall, Gasteiner Upper School
Bolzano, South Tyrol, O. Zoeggeler, 2001

Length 46 m, width 34,6 m (ceiling), 28 m (floor), average width 31 m, height 8 m, volume approx. 11.400 m³. Average reverberation time 2.3 secs. (reverberation times before non-linear correction 4 - 6.5 secs).

A fully equipped sports hall used as a venue for handball tournaments. Acoustic renovation: installation of approx. 340 m² absorbing cavities (approx. 162 m² in the ceiling, approx. 108 m² in the side walls, approx. 70 m² in the front and rear walls). The coefficients achieved conform to the standard. The absorbing resonators in the walls were deliberately designed as 'windows' in this architecturally distinctive 'urban' inner space.

Refectory, Manzoni Elementary School
Bozen, South Tyrol, Christina Niederstätter, 2004

Average length 20.5 m, width 11 m, height 2.60 m, total volume approx. 590 m³. Linear reverberation time 0.8 secs. (before correction non-linear 2-2.5 secs. with a noise level of 86 dB(A)).

Absorbing resonators in the ceiling, additional high pitch absorption using insulating panels in mineral wool covered with fibreglass; additional absorbing wall panels as notice boards and sound-absorbing partitions. The sound absorbers are deliberately designed as playful or technical elements. The acoustics, and therefore the sense of well-being of the children, were also optimised by organisational and design measures: this long, low room was subdivided into areas for small groups of pupils; passage ways were rationalised; mealtimes in three shifts were introduced so that the room did not become overcrowded; meal waiting times were reduced; and a pleasant acoustic ambience is created by the sound of flowing water.

Aula Magna, Gasteiner Upper School
Bolzano, South Tyrol, V. Andriolo, 2001

Length 22.5 m, width 19.2 m, maximum height 9 m, average height 6.5 m, volume approx. 2.600 m³. Linear reverberation time 1.1 secs. when the room is full (reverberation times before correction non-linear 3-6 secs.).

Acoustic renovation: installation of approx. 90 m² absorbing cavities (approx. 54 m² in the ceiling, mainly to the back and side, and approx. 32 m² evenly distributed on both sides of the stage). The Aula Magna had been unused for many years because of acoustic pollution from the sports hall located immediately above it. The whole acoustic ceiling (reflectors in the ceiling with resonators) and all the timber cladding with absorbing resonators on the side walls were suspended to provide elastic decoupling. Noise transmission from the sports hall above was thus prevented. Today it is possible to use both the Aula and the gym at the same time without any problem. Light-weight upholstered seats were installed to improve the acoustic when the hall is not full. Linearisation of reverberation ensures good acoustics for speech. The clear, pleasant acoustics also make the Aula ideal for theatrical and musical events.

Middle school in Schlanders
South Tyrol, T. Simma, 2002

Room height 2.83 m; rooms of differing dimensions. Linear reverberation time of 0.7 secs. (reverberation times before renovation: 1.4 to 2.5 secs.).

Acoustic optimisation of three existing classrooms used for music lessons. The absorbing resonators were installed in the ceiling between the rows of lights. Additional high-pitch absorption was achieved by the installation of wall panels (Acoustichoc – glass wool covered with a fibreglass fabric), designed as notice boards. Two types of resonators were combined which absorb at 315 Hz and 125 Hz respectively. The timber of the resonators was stylised painted in a metallic silver-grey to give the visual effect of technical elements. The acoustics achieved are pleasant and transparent in all rooms.

Multi-purpose hall and classrooms at school Vella
Graubünden, V. Bearth & A. Deplazes, 1997

Length of hall 27 m, length of stage 7 m, width 15 m, maximum height 12.40 m, height of side walls 7 m, total volume approx. 4.350 m³. Reverberation time in hall (stage open) with 200 persons present: from 125 to 4000 Hz, virtually linear 1.8 secs., dropping to 1.2 secs. above and below this frequency range. The reverberation time in the empty sports hall when the stage is closed off by a folding door: 3 secs. between 315 Hz and 5000 Hz, reducing to 1.5 secs. above and below this frequency range (reverberation time in shell 3.5 to 1.4 secs.).

The room is used, without changes, as a sports hall, assembly hall, theatre and concert hall. Thanks to early planning and measurements taken in the shell, an aesthetically attractive solution with good linearisation of the reverberation was achieved by optimising the ceiling (slightly convex, vaulted gable areas) and installing absorbing cavities behind the timber walls and in the stage door.

Seminar room, University of Zürich, Musicology Institute
Beate Schnitter, 1997

Length 9.85-11.50 m, width 7.40-7.90 m, height of side walls 4,80 m, total volume approx. 290 m³ (room slightly asymmetrical without right angles). Linear reverberation time when the room is full 0.9 secs.

Teaching room with 50 seats maximum, in which music is also made. Owing to the water-tight outer walls of this room, which is barely above the ground water level, no wall mountings were possible. The convex ceiling, which curves downwards, houses the ventilation and lighting systems. The acoustics could only be corrected by using free-standing cubic hollow bodies in the room, fixed to the floor. To linearise reverberation, they absorb standing waves which form at 250 Hz and 125 Hz diagonally across the walls, although the surfaces are not parallel. Absorption with this newly developed type of resonator does not occur through the braking effect of an opening with a neck (Helmholtz principle), but by lining the cavity with absorbing rock wool (Kirchhoff principle). They are positioned at points where maximum disturbing soundwaves accummulate. Thanks to the corrective measures taken, are pleasant acoustics are now ensured for speech intelligibility and music whether the room is empty or full.

Literature

α-database: PTB Braunschweig. www.ptb.de/de/org/1/17/173/datenbank.htm

Acoustic Design of Schools – Building Bulletin 93, Department for Education and Skills, 2006, www.teachernet.gov.ok/schoolbuildings

Dorothea Baumann, 'Können wir unseren Ohren trauen?', in: *Schweizer Musikzeitung* 1,1998, p. 1-9

Jens Blauert (ed.): *Communication Acoustics* Berlin/Heidelberg: Springer, 2005.

Classroom Acoustics, A resource for creating learning environments with desirable listening conditions, Acoustical Society of America ASA 2000. http://asa.aip.org (15. Sep. 2006)

DIN 18041: 2004-05, Audibility in small to medium-sized rooms.

Wolfgang Fasold and Eva Veres, *Schallschutz und Raumakustik in der Praxis* Berlin: Verlag für Bauwesen, 2003.

Guidelines of the Swiss Acoustical Society (Schweizerische Gesellschaft für Akustik SGA) for the acoustics of school rooms and other speech rooms, SGA, 2004.

Stephen Handel, *Listening. An Introduction to the Perception of Auditory Events,* Cambridge, MA: MIT Press, 1989.

Ludowika Huber, Joachim Kahlert, Maria Klatte (eds.), *Die akustisch gestaltete Schule. Auf der Suche nach dem guten Ton.* Göttingen: Vandenhoeck & Ruprecht, 2002.

Christina Niederstätter *Studie über den Zusammenhang zwischen akustischer Qualität und Wohlbefinden der Kinder in den Grundschulmensen der Stadt Bozen / Studio sulla relazione tra qualità acustica e benessere dei bambini nelle mense delle scuole elementari del Comune di Bolzano*, unpublished manuscript, Unterinn, 2002.

Rudolf Schricker, *Kreative Raum-Akustik für Architekten und Designer,* Stuttgart: DVA, 2001.

www.uni-oldenburg.de/psychologie/mub/meis.htm#pub (Sep.15, 2006)

Lighting Design

Background and significance of daylighting

The presence of daylight in educational buildings plays a significant role in the process of learning. Performance of students is measured by a number of yardsticks, among them are students' performance on tests and level of absenteeism. In the five years between 2000 and 2007, more than 1,000 schools will be built each year in order to meet the demand of students in kindergarten and elementary schools in the United States. With calls for energy conservation, improving the health of children and the quality of the educational settings of kindergartens and schools, some major studies using rigorous scientific methods were undertaken to assess the impact of daylight on the well-being and the scholastic achievements of pupils at all levels. One of such major studies[1] analysed test scores of more than 21,000 students in three school districts in three different US states, namely California, Colorado and Washington. The following results were obtained:

- Students in classrooms with the most daylight progressed 20% faster on math tests and 26% faster in reading tests
- Classrooms with the most window area were associated with a 15-23% faster rate of improvement
- Classrooms with skylights were associated with a 19-20% faster rate of improvement
- Classrooms with operable windows were associated with a 7-8% faster improvement in three out of four cases that have been investigated when compared to classrooms with non-operable windows

Students who attend daylight schools seem to perform up to 14% better than those who do not according to another major survey of 1,200 elementary students in North Carolina. The authors of the study did not provide daylight illuminance levels but they characterised the conditions of the daylight schools as 'average illumination levels in the skylit classrooms are two or three times higher than in classrooms with electric lighting in peak conditions.'

There seems to be a direct correlation between the presence or lack of daylight and the way pupils perform. But why do students perform better with daylight?

Daylight and circadian rhythm

One of the most obvious relationships between humans and daylight is that of the circadian rhythm, i.e. the cycle of day and night and the complex chemical and physiological variations that control our bodies 24 hours a day. The timing and functions related to these processes depend on our biological clock. Arguably the most influential factor in this timing is the presence of daylight.[2] This rhythm directs the body to release hormones and trigger functions that control our days. Researchers found that from ten o'clock until noon our immediate memory is at its best, and is therefore a positive factor in schoolwork, concentration and debate; whereas the hours from six in the evening to midnight are favourable for studying since then our long term memory is at its best. This circadian rhythm is especially important in children since their systems seem to be more sensitive to change and variation. The presence of daylight in classrooms is crucial to the preservation of this rhythm and the body's natural clock.

Seasonal Affective Disorder and depression

One possible effect of lack of daylight or lack of the presence of daylight is Seasonal Affective Disorder. Depression, fatigue, irritability and lack of concentration are just a few of the many symptoms that SAD sufferers usually confront. Similar symptoms were found in children confined to windowless classrooms for entire school days. Children exhibited restlessness and much more irritability in these classrooms. Concordantly, children in classrooms with sufficient daylight were able to develop concentration skills with more ease. A by-product of SAD and its symptoms are frequent absences and a lack of resistance towards diseases. Although many of the studies related to SAD have been performed on hospital patients and people in northern latitudes, the results are still relevant to the long term impact on school children.

It has been hypothesised by many studies that melatonin, a hormone which is produced by the pineal gland located in the centre of the brain and is inhibited by light and permitted by darkness. Melatonin may help our bodies know when it's time to go to sleep and when it's time to wake up. At night melatonin is produced to help our bodies regulate our sleep-wake cycles. Research indicates that it may ameliorate SAD and circadian misalignment. It is believed that it is the key chemical messenger in SAD. It is also widely believed that higher levels of melatonin caused by fewer hours of daylight contribute to SAD. The rate of release of melatonin, like so many other body functions, is controlled by environmental illumination. Melatonin levels in children seem to fluctuate more rapidly than those in adults, and daylight illumination is proven to be of great significance to the health of children.

Daylight and stress

Cortisol, a stress hormone, is also associated with daylight presence indicated by high levels during the day and low levels at night. The release of cortisol is directly related to the body's circadian rhythm and is often used as a chronobiological indicator in studies. Cortisol levels are higher in summer and lower in winter.

High levels of cortisol are associated with an inclination towards sociability; medium levels seem to promote concentration and increased focus, according to a Swedish investigation of 90 elementary school students. Both too much and too little cortisol is negative for concentration. A hormone imbalance influences children's ability to focus and concentrate, it affects their growth and fosters absenteeism.[3]

Full spectrum lighting which mimics certain spectral characteristics of daylight makes a positive contribution to the learning process in school children according to a Canadian study.[4] Students studying with full spectrum lighting were a lot less absent than those with conventional fluorescent lighting.

It is evident that daylight has a dramatic effect on health both in adults and children. In fact, most of the effects are interrelated and dependant on each other on multiple levels. Melatonin has an inverse relationship to cortisol. SAD is commonly said to be caused by a melatonin deficiency which disturbs the natural sleep-and-wake cycle in humans. Vitamin D deficiency can drastically alter the production of vital nutrients. Meanwhile, our body's circadian rhythm has control over almost all of these factors and has the ability to drastically affect our system. Most functions overlap and create chain reactions all controlled by daylight. Growth and development are particularly important in children; the amount of time spent in school directly points to the need for these facilities to be designed for their health and well-being. A facility properly designed will have fewer absences and more productive days than one that is ill-fitted for education.

Daylighting strategies for schools and kindergartens

An appropriate daylighting strategy in schools and kindergarten would be one that provides an adequate amount of light where needed while ensuring no visual discomfort and good visual performance. Typologies of school architecture tend to favour single-storey buildings. These are often appropriate for simple yet effective daylighting strategies that include both side-lighting as well as top-lighting principles.

All daylighting systems harvest the daylight available outside and distribute it in a way that optimises the area inside the room. Daylight is comprised of a non-directional diffuse component and a direct component which is directional and dynamic. Fenestrations systems must be sized and placed to account for the dynamic characteristic of daylight. Sunlight, the direct component of daylight, is the most dynamic. It can be harsh, and it can create shadows as well as extreme disparities in illuminance levels inside a room. It can also produce visual discomfort and glare if not controlled properly.

Daylighting systems are of two general categories: 1. top-lighting systems where daylight is distributed inside the room from the ceiling or the roof; 2. side-lighting systems where daylight is distributed from the sides of the room.

Studies have shown that successful daylighting principles are:
- The building should be elongated along an east-west axis. Daylight apertures can be placed on the north side where diffuse daylight is available and the south side where it is relatively easy to control the sunlight in winter and summer.
- Apertures placed high in the wall such as clearstoreys or tall side windows optimise daylight distribution and bring light deeper into the space.
- Bringing daylight from two different directions reduces the chances of discomfort glare and evens out thedaylight distribution.
- Use indirect daylighting to control sunlight inside the classroom. Direct sunlight inside a room can cause glare and discomfort.

Side windows

Light levels are much more intense near the window and decrease rapidly as one moves away from the window. The height of the window dictates to a great extent the effective depth of illumination with daylight. Low ceiling and deep classroom could experience a gloomy feeling due to the disparity in light levels between the back of the room and the peripheral area near the window. Effective illumination can be obtained for room depth as much as 2 ½ times the height of the window above the workplane. For example, a classroom with a ceiling height of 3.5 metres and desk height of 0.75 metre, if the top of the window is 2 metres above desk height, the area that is adequately daylit is approximately up to (2 x 2.5 metres) 5 metres deep from the window wall.

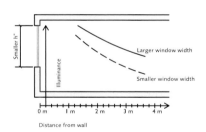

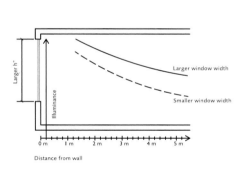

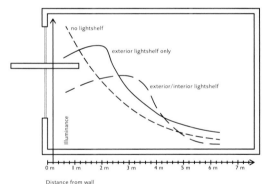

from left to right:

Narrow window allows narrow daylight distribution with the effective daylit area depending on the height of the window above the window sill.

Large window allows wider daylight distribution but the effective daylit area remains a function of the window height.

Daylight distribution with and without a light shelf

Light shelves

When designing with side windows, attention must be given not to create very brightly lit areas near the window and dark ones in the back. Light shelves can provide a good remedy to this problem. They are designed such that the clearstory portion above the light shelf catches sunlight or diffuses daylight and reflects it toward the back of the room away from the window. The protruding portion of the light shelf, in the case of a combined or exterior light shelf, acts as a shading device and prevents sunlight from falling on the work area immediately adjacent to the window. It also cuts on glare and minimises brightness near the window. As a result, more uniform light levels are achieved throughout the room. The clearstory portion of the window may be made of clear glass for maximum daylight harvesting. The lower portion below the shelf is referred to as the view window. The glass in it may be tinted to reduce glare.

Skylights

Skylights are another top-lighting strategy used for single-storey schools to bring daylight from the top rather than the side. The drawing indicates the recommended spacing between skylights as function of the mounting height of the skylight, or the distance between the bottom of the skylight and the workplane. The depth of the skylight well, the size of the opening of the skylight dictates largely the efficiency of the skylight system. A very large portion (up to 75% or even more) of the luminous energy incident on the outside of the skylight may be lost within the skylight if the skylight well is too deep or too dark.

A single skylight could create large disparity in light levels between the area underneath the skylight and the rest of the room. The size of the skylight opening also dictates the daylight distribution. More than one skylight will help balance daylight inside the space.

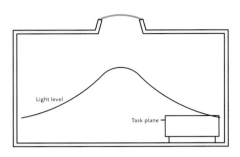
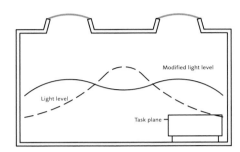

left: Top-lighting using a single skylight

right: Difference in the daylight distribution between one and two skylights

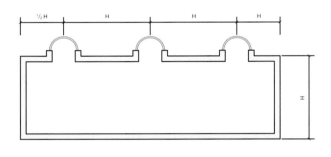
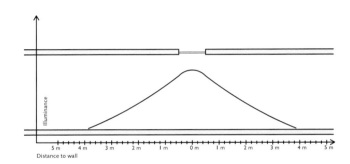

left: Recommended spacing between skylights for uniform daylight distribution in the classroom

right: Single skylight may create large disparities in daylight levels underneath the skylight and areas away from it

below from left to right:

Clearstories allow the daylight to reach wall opposite the clearstory wall

Large clearstories allow deep penetration and larger amounts of daylight. Adding a clearstory to a side window provides a more even daylight distribution

The combination of a side window and a clearstory result in deep and uniform daylight penetration

Clearstory windows

Clearstory windows admit light deep towards the back of the room and henceforth create a more uniform daylight distribution throughout if there is another side window. The relationship between illumination from side window and clearstory depends on size, height and position. With typical narrow window arrangements for clearstories, the recommended depth from the plane of the clearstory to the opposite wall is about equal to the distance from the mounting height of the clearstory above the workplane level. For wider clearstories the depth could be one and half the mounting height. To obtain adequate and more uniform daylight distribution, the height of the clearstory window should be about one half the side wall window height. Not only the height of the clearstory affects the depth of the daylight penetration but also the width of the clearstory window.

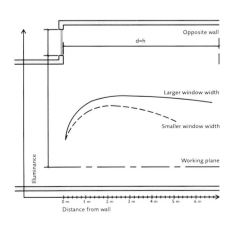
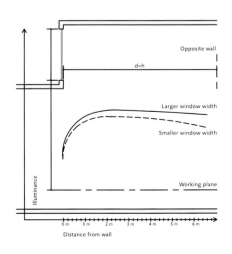
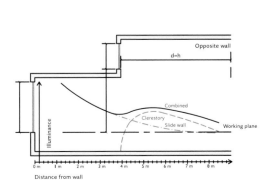

Sawtooth systems

Sawtooth systems are an excellent daylighting strategy when uniform daylight distribution is desired throughout a large classroom or work surface. There is directionality in light distribution under these systems especially on clear days and if the opening is facing south. On an overcast day, however, sawtooth systems provide a little more uniformity than on clear days. In general daylight levels are higher towards the end of the room that faces the opening. The spacing between sawteeth is recommended to be 2 1/2 H, with (H) being the height of the ceiling clearance.

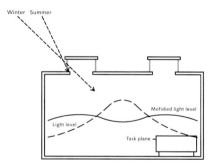

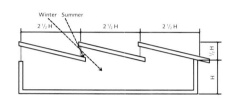

Generic daylight distribution under a sawtooth system with (1) clear sky, aperture facing sun; (2) overcast sky; (3) clear sky aperture opposite sun

Recommended spacing between sawteeth

Roof monitors

Like the sawtooth system, a roof monitor is also an excellent daylighting strategy when uniform daylight distribution is desired throughout a large classroom or work surface. Roof monitors bring in light from above from two opposite directions. Henceforth directionality of light is minimised and uniformity is maximised. Roof monitors can be designed to allow sunlight in winter if desired and block it in the summer when not desired.

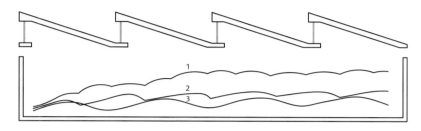

Roof monitors allowing sunlight in winter and blocking summer sun

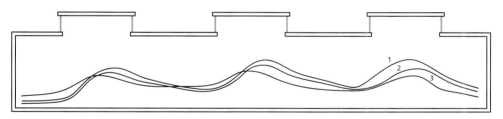

Daylight distribution under roof monitors with (1) monitors facing the sun; (2) monitors at 45 degrees away from the sun; (3) overcast sky condition

Anidolic systems

Anidolic systems collect sunlight falling on an entry aperture and concentrate it on a smaller exit aperture where the receiver is placed. The receiver is a light emitting source or a highly efficient luminaire capable of controlling beam output through well-defined beam spread.

The protruding portion of the system acts as a solar collector and concentrator. It collects large amounts of sunlight through the entry aperture and concentrates it onto a smaller area where the diffuser or distributor is located near the exit aperture. The distributor spreads daylight over a larger area further away from the side wall window.

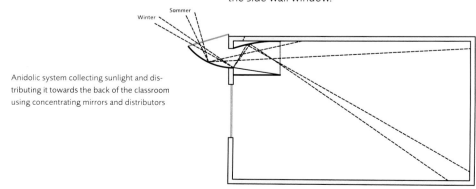

Anidolic system collecting sunlight and distributing it towards the back of the classroom using concentrating mirrors and distributors

Recommendations for visual comfort

Visual tasks occurring in schools range from very small to very large and from simple to complex. There are tasks that may require prolonged periods of concentration and others very brief ones. Minimum recommended illuminance levels for various tasks taking place in a school environment are displayed in the below table according to data from the American National Standard Guide for School Lighting (ANSI/IES RP-3, 1977).

Area			Footcandle	Lux
Tasks	Reading printed material		30	300
	Reading pencil material		70	700
	Duplicated material	Good	30	300
		Poor	100	1000
	Drafting, benchwork		100	1000
	Up reading, chalkboards, sewing		150	1500
Classrooms	Art room		70	700
	Drafting room		100	1000
	Home economics room	Sewing	150	1500
		Cooking	50	500
		Ironing	50	500
		Sink activities	70	700
		Note-taking areas	70	700
	Laboratories		100	1000
	Lecture room	Audience area	70	700
		Demonstration area	150	1500
	Music room	Simple scores	30	300
		Advanced scores	70	700
	Shops		100	1000
	Sight-saving room		150	1500
	Study halls		70	700
	Typing		70	700
Corridors and stairways			20	200
Dormitories	General		10	100
	Reading books, magazines newspapers		30	300
	Study desk		70	700

Illuminance values recommended for performing visual tasks in schools

References

1 Heschong Mahone Group, *Daylighting in Schools: Investigation into Relationship Between Daylighting and Human Performance*, Sacramento, CA: CA Board for Energy Efficiency, 1999.

2 Frank H. Mahnke, *Color, Environment, and Human Response: An Interdisciplinary Understanding of Color and its Use as a Beneficial Element in the Design of the Architectural Environment*, New York: Van Nostrand Reinhold Company Inc., 1996, p.106-116.

3 R. Kuller and C. Lindten, 'Health and Behaviour of Children in Classrooms with and without Windows,' in: *Journal of Environmental Psychology*, No. 12, 1992, p. 305-317.

4 Shelley McColl and Jennifer Veitch, *Full-spectrum fluorescent lighting: a review of its effects on physiology and health*, Cambridge: Cambridge University Press, 2001.

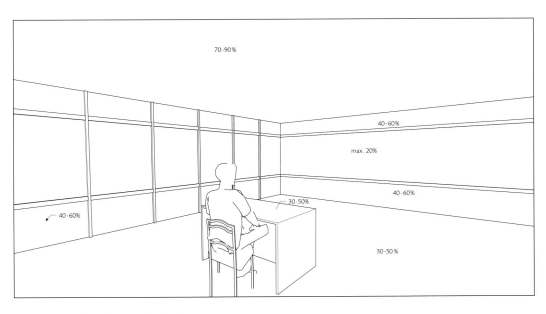

Recommended surface reflectance values for classrooms

Sustainability

Making any building sustainable requires a significant amount of effort in the design stage. But doing this for a new school presents a whole range of challenges specific to the sector: from the partial occupation of rooms to the number of concerned stakeholders.

The task requires much more careful consideration than simply implementing the standard list of low energy building services equipment. A good example of this is the Academy of St. Francis of Assisi, engineered by Buro Happold. This is a city academy in Liverpool which opened in September 2005 and has environmental studies as its specialist subject. As a result, it has exemplary renewable and low energy building services, including 24kW solar photovoltaic panels, solar thermal system for heating water, rainwater harvesting for flushing toilets, intelligent lighting controls and enhanced sub-metering to aid energy management. This equipment is in addition to building fabric measures, which include: a south-facing ETFE atrium to maximise ingress of natural light and passive solar heating and exposed concrete soffits to reduce internal temperature fluctuation and the need for cooling. A national newspaper dubbed it "Britain's greenest school" in recognition of its successful low energy technologies.

One of the first steps in this process is making sure a sustainable engineering design is well-defined and measurable, if is to be of use to the design and construction teams as well as the client. The client may be made up of many groups: the Local Education Authority (LEA), the government or private funder of the project, the school staff and students as well as their parents – all of which will have a voice and so have to be kept informed of progress. The design team can develop the school in a positive and productive manner only after it is clear who makes up the client group and who within that group is able to make financial and operational decisions.

The design team then has to agree with the client a definition of sustainability for the project and create a method of assessment to measure this throughout design, construction and operation. The process is most effective when the overall sustainable target is understood by all the parties involved at the earliest possible stage. It means design and educational decisions for the school can be made in an integrated, sustainable and supportive way, but also means most of the design choices will be influenced by engineering knowledge of sustainability.

Keeping sustainability to the fore throughout the design process means the building services should become the last resort for cutting carbon dioxide (CO_2) emissions. All the issues associated with sustainability – maximising the amount of natural light by aligning the building appropriately with the sun path, minimising the amount of soil removed from site, considering refurbishment and re-use of materials before a new build (which inevitably consumes more energy in creating the new materials used), and the effect of materials and building form on the internal environment and energy consumption – all must be thoroughly examined before specifying low energy buildings services equipment.

Many other issues are of great importance to schools. For example, air quality and noise levels should be assessed to make sure occupied areas are away from polluted and noisy areas on the grounds of preserving the health – and concentration – of building users.

With transport one of the biggest emitters of CO_2, significant attention needs to be paid to developing a travel plan. Transport and civil engineers must consider the travel methods used by staff and students each day and assess the sustainability of this against the agreed sustainability target.

This has to take into account many factors, such as the catchment area of the LEA, the optimum number of schools that an area can support, the anticipated student population of each school, the location of each school, the availability of different forms of transport and the potential for additional, more sustainable travel options. Civil engineers can then take the travel plan and develop it to ensure the roads, pathways and bridges within the school site, and beyond if necessary, are constructed in a sustainable way. This means minimising the amount of soil removed from the site and specifying the use of recycled materials where possible.

Having incorporated all these issues in the building form, the team must specify building services with a low environmental impact. So, water use should be minimised by the selection of low or zero usage fittings and by collecting rainwater for re-use in non-potable functions such as urinal wash down or toilet flushing. Artificial lighting should be provided with daylight controls and presence detectors.

South-facing passive solar ETFE atrium.
Academy of St. Francis of Assisi, Liverpool,
Buro Happold

23.76 kW photovoltaic panels system.
Academy of St. Francis of Assisi, Liverpool,
Buro Happold

Internal views of ETFE atrium. Academy of St. Francis of Assisi, Liverpool

Ventilation design should first try to use the natural movement of the outside air into the school building by using the rising warm air leaving the classrooms, or the prevailing winds, to draw the fresh air into the rooms. Where mechanical ventilation is necessary or desirable, there are a number of techniques to minimise the energy it requires, including heat recovery or drawing in fresh air through earth tubes that use the relatively stable earth temperatures to cool or pre-warm the air entering the building. Again, the need for cooling can be reduced through sympathetic IT equipment specification, which can operate at higher temperatures or have lower heat gains.

Energy consumption should be limited by all these choices, but once the maximum potential of this has been achieved, then the source should be considered. The national grid can provide power from renewable sources, but alternative localised power sources using wind, water or photovoltaic can also be assessed, along with the option of local power generation using gas-fired combined heat and power (CHP) units. Biomass and thermal solar heating can be used to reduce the CO_2 emissions resulting from the heating and hot water demands of the building, often at surprisingly low costs.

All these measures can be supported by pupils too, which helps meet broader sustainability goals. By not hiding this equipment in the building fabric and running campaigns on their usage, great support for the school and its sustainability goals can be garnered.

Measuring the effect these innovations have on CO_2 output, water and electricity consumption and rainwater harvested – data that is simply retrieved from the building management system and can be relayed to pupils via plasma screens around the school – is a good way of gaining pupils' support. This helps educate pupils about the design of their own building and therefore illustrates the impact of all buildings on the environment. Thus, the building is helping the educational process and wider sustainability issues by raising awareness with the consumers of the future.

The final issue in ensuring that the building performs well for the users and the environment is how the building is used. Its systems should be designed to be simple to use for both the occupants and the facilities management and all parties should receive training and support, preferably on an ongoing basis to assist with the operation of the building over the first year or two.

The building services engineering should be the last issue, in terms of sustainability, to be tackled after refurbishment, location, orientation, layout, form, function and operation have all been considered – all topics engineers can contribute positively to. This should provide a school building that reflects the educational needs of the students and allows the staff to teach in a sustainable but still comfortable environment.

Outdoor Spaces

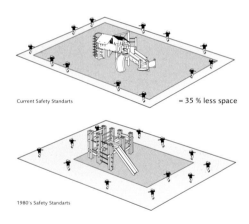

The amount of outdoor play space allocated per child is roughly the size of a parking stall.

Current Safety Standarts

= 35 % less space

1980's Safety Standarts

Since the 1980s safety standards have increased the no-encroachment zone around equipment by 35% and lowered the height of equipment. This leaves less room for non-equipment play.

Outdoor play spaces can contribute to children's healthy development and learning in important ways. However, changes in society have increasingly limited the capacity of the outdoors to contribute to the educational experience of children. The following describes four crucial aspects that should be addressed when designing outdoor play spaces at childcare centres and schools.

Space: One of the prime rationales for children's use of outdoor play spaces is for gross motor play (for example, running). Yet recent studies have found that gross motor movement is decreasing among young children, contributing to obesity in school children. A 2003 study in Yorkhill hospital in Scotland found that children aged three to five spent about 20 minutes a day in vigorous activities.[1] This amount is less than half the 90 minutes of physical activity recommended for children's healthy development.[2] Lack of outdoor space is commonly cited as the reason why children do not go outside to play. We know that denser play areas exhibit more aggressive play and less cooperative play, and educators often struggle to rotate the number of children using one play space.[3] Since the groups have to take turns using the outside space it is not freely available to children whenever they want it.

What to do? Be sure that space has been maximised for children's use. A comprehensive study of outdoor play spaces in Canada found that each child should be allocated 13.5 m² of outdoor space.[4] This number is almost twice as much as space allotted to each child enrolled at present in childcare in North America. Yet the researchers contend that ample spatial provisions are required for the diversity of experiences needed outside for their development while respecting safety standards.[5]

Challenge: Increasingly strict safety regulations pertaining to play equipment have hampered the ability of outdoor play spaces to contribute to vigorous gross motor activity. Stringent safety standards have helped to produce play equipment that is lower in height and less challenging than previously designed equipment. This may account for why a study of children using outdoor play spaces at childcare centres found that 87 percent of the time they were not playing on the equipment.[6] In studied spaces where non-conforming equipment was removed, children resorted to climbing the fences.

What to do? Some safety standards pertaining to children's outdoor equipment are voluntary and devised for commercial reasons to promote international trade rather than developmentally rich play.[7] These standards enable manufacturers to market and sell play equipment in different countries rather than designing it for a specific context. However, children need to take risks to develop, so be sure that you discuss with parents, educators and others involved with the project what constitutes an acceptable risk. Also keep in mind that the expensive equipment that is touted as safer by aggressive sales representatives has never been proven to be safer than older equipment. Additionally remember, children can gain challenges from other sources than equipment – big hills to climb up or, if allowed, trees to climb. These elements are not as highly regulated as equipment.

Things that change. Outdoor play spaces should not be separate from the educational experience because they can play a unique role in the process of developing knowledge. While many outdoor play spaces are characterised by asphalt, they can potentially provide contact with living things like plants and animals, which can powerfully express seasonal cycles. Organic matter is in a state of flux, changing with time, and thus contact with living things can promote both memory and language acquisition. In a Canadian study, children spoke more with each other and for longer durations when they encountered worms or bugs.[8] Likewise, contact with plants and animals can not only enhance cognitive development, but encourage imaginative play and stimulate empathy.

What to do? There are plenty of interesting and hardy plants for children's outdoor play spaces. A very accessible BBC website identifies plants that are easy to grow, that will stimulate senses and that attract butterflies.[9] Another good source is *Plants for Play* by Robin Moore. In this book, Moore considers the tactile, auditory, olfactory, visual and play value of different types of plants, and makes suggestions for specific plants for specific play use.[10]

Things that can be changed. We know from the past 160 years of studying children that they need spaces they can manipulate and create as their own.[11] Unfortunately, an increased emphasis on academic readiness and testing has devalued the importance of play at childcare centres and schools. Yet the outdoor play environment is an ideal location for providing this type of play because it can contain sand, dirt, mud,

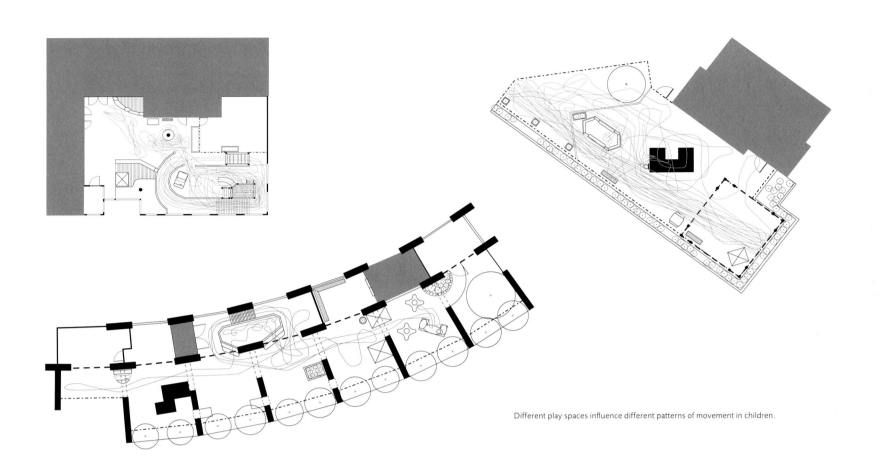

Different play spaces influence different patterns of movement in children.

water and other loose parts that can be easily shaped by children. Interacting with the physical world lies at the heart of play. Play is when the integration of knowledge allows for possible alternative worlds, 'which involve "supposing", and "as if" and enable us to function in advance of what we can actually do in our real lives.'[12] Play can be an activity performed alone or by groups of children – building the foundations of social play, such as cooperation, required in adulthood.

What to do? Provide plenty of manipulable material and utensils (such as shovels and buckets) that can help shape these materials. Recycle objects like cardboard boxes or plastic pools with holes for children's creations. A crucial dimension to utensils and other loose parts is ample, accessible storage. If your school or centre is located in a dense urban area you may encounter complaints that the play space looks messy, but every effort should be made to maintain these messy zones for children's play.

School gardens

The inventor of the kindergarten, Friedrich Froebel, was one of the first teachers to use gardening as part of children's education. During the 1840s he created gardens in his original kindergartens throughout Germany. By the late 19th century in Europe and North America gardens were incorporated into school yards to provide children with important life skills, as well as introduce them to the economic profits of agriculture. In Sweden, Austria, Germany, Belgium and Russia gardens were mandatory at schools, while in England teachers salaries were often determined by the productivity level of their school garden. Technological advancements in agriculture, the development of grocery stores, and an increasingly test-oriented academic curriculum made small-scale hand gardening virtually obsolete, so by the late 1930s many schools abandoned the gardens in their yards.

Yet 75 years later we are witnessing a school garden revival. In the UK alone, over 15,000 schools have expressed interest in school gardening activities. School gardens provide experiences with nature and its processes that are now absent from the lives of many children.

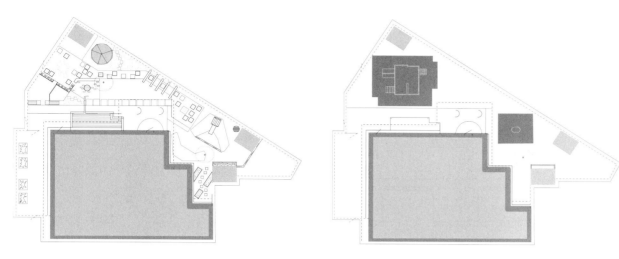

Plan views of the same play space and the same money spent. The design on the left offers change and ample movement for children. The design on the right has only equipment and rubber matting that offers less change and challenge.

Children, and also adults, have forgotten about the miracle of growing food from a small patch of land. Getting involved in gardening not only revives this enchanting process but fosters unique learning opportunities. Gardening not only creates hands-on learning experiences regarding the basic precepts of ecology, but the act of gardening and its fruits can be combined with art, reading, writing, science and even social studies. For example, a school in Chicago uses their wetland garden as part of a writing programme; combining gardening, observation and reflection that are expressed in a daily journal.

This play space often becomes a house for children using their imagination | Here vegetation has been incorporated into the play structure | A garden arbour designed for a child's scale

School gardens vary in type from food to wetland to ornamental gardens, so thought should be given to determine which type of garden would best suit a specific school yard. Funding outside the normal school budget is also necessary to pay for seeds, soil, tools, storage and fencing. The Growing Schools Programme at Teachernet.gov.uk lists over a dozen sources of funding to start a garden at your school. Garden activities that link to learning objectives are also imperative. While researchers have just begun to understand the role of gardens in learning, we do know some critical aspects that should be considered when creating a school garden.

Multiple involvement. School gardens should not only involve children and their teachers, but maintenance people, administrators, staff, parents and neighbours. Knowledge about gardening cuts across all career fields, so you very likely have an expert at hand who can provide valuable information as well as enthusiasm. Multiple involvement will not only help maintain the school garden over the summer months, but can bring a sense of community to the parents and the school as a whole. This was one of the findings from 'Grounds for Action,' a study of school greening programmes conducted by Evergreen Canada. This study also found that 81% of the survey respondents indicated that their school garden enhanced the aesthetic and social dimensions of the school yard.

School gardening has a long history.

Food gardens are extremely popular in school yards, but they are best accompanied by pollinator meadows. The main elements of a pollinator meadow are flowers and wild grasses. These plants attract pollinators, such as butterflies, beetle, flies, moths, bats, birds and ants that are critical to the success of vegetables, fruits and grains. A pollinator meadow will not only ensure the healthy development of food plants, but will extend childrens ecological knowledge about gardens. To ensure pollinator attraction, plants should be selected based on a range of bloom times and their different shapes and colours. Visit Kidsgardening.com and the U.S. Forest Service website[13] which provide names of pollinator plants and the types of pollinators they attract, as well as educational activities for children.

The benefits of a school garden can often be lost on people who think you can only learn from a book. In order to document the educational contributions of your garden it is important that you evaluate the school garden and garden programming at the end of the year. As of now, there is thankfully no standardised test for school gardening programmes, so its important that you measure and demonstrate learning performance in other ways. Learning Through Landscapes, the UK's National School Grounds Charity, has developed a Measuring Success pack for school gardens.[14] This package allows for an evaluation process that can help you measure the learning taking place in your own school garden.

References

1 J.J. Reilly & A.R. Dorosty, 'Epidemic of obesity in UK children,' in: *The Lancet*, 354 (9193), p.1874, 2004.

2 *Health Canada's Physical Activity Guides for Children and Youth* www.hc-sc.gc.ca/hppb/paguide/child_youth/index.html, accessed September 2004.

3 S. Herrington and C. Lesmeister, 'The Design of Landscapes at Child Care Centres: Seven C's.,' in: *Landscape Research*, vol.31, no.1, 2006, p.63-82

4 A.G. Maufette, L. Frechette & D. Robertson, 1999, *Revisiting Children's Outdoor Environments: A Focus on Design, Play, and Safety* Hull, Quebec: Gauvin Presses, p.8, 39.

5 Ibid, p.39.

6 S. Herrington, C. Lesmeister, J. Nicholls, K. Stefiuk, *An informational Guide for young children's outdoor play spaces: Seven C's* Also available at: http://westcoast.ca/playspaces/outsidecriteria/index.html, accessed August 2006.

7 S. Herrington and J. Nicholls, (forthcoming) *Outdoor Play Spaces in Canada: The Safety Dance of Standards as Policy. Critical Social Policy.*

8 Herrington, et al 2006.

9 British Broadcasting Corporation International version, *Gardening with Children*, www.bbc.co.uk/gardening/gardening_with_children/plantstotry_index.shtml, accessed August 2006.

10 Robin C. Moore, *Plants for play : a plant selection guide for children's outdoor environments*, Berkeley, California: MIG Communications, 1993.

11 See the work of kindergarten inventor Friedrich Froebel as it relates to the outdoors in S. Herrington, 'Garden Pedagogy: Romanticism to Reform,' in: *Landscape Journal* 1, vol. 20, no. 1, 2001, p. 30-47, and S. Herrington, '*The Garden in Froebel's Kindergarten: Beyond the Metaphor*. Studies in the History of Gardens and Designed Landscapes,' in: *International Quarterly*, vol.18, no. 4, 1998, p. 336-338.

12 T. Bruce, *Time to play in early childhood education*, London; Toronto: Hodder & Stoughton, 1991, p. 59-60.

13 www.fs.fed.us/wildflowers/pollinators/index.shtml

14 www.ltl.org.uk/about/newsarticle.asp?NW_ID=53

PETER HÜBNER

Designing Learning Landscapes

The word 'school' means both the building and the institution, both of which come laden with preconceptions as to what school was, is and should be. To avoid clashing with traditional building typologies, we have chosen the term 'learning landscape' for the school building because a 'good school' should have more of the attributes of a landscape than of an institution. In school as an institution, education in whatever form should not focus solely on the accumulation of knowledge but rather on encouraging independent acquisition of learning and life strategies. Only by these means will young people gain the competencies they will later need in life and career. All children enter the world as active explorers, curious and hungry for knowledge and it is important to keep alive and foster this potential. This appetite for learning should be sustained and nourished in the learning landscapes where our children spend the biggest part of their young lives. The question is how to provide places which ensure an optimum sense of well-being and encourage eagerness to achieve.[1]

Learning landscapes can only be successful if new educational insights and the results of brain research are integral to the normal school day and become the foundation for architectural planning. In many places this would entail replacing outdated school building regulations according to which a school building still generally comprises inflexible rows of classrooms off long corridors and, apart from a few designated areas, offers no opportunities for an open educational concept. The – quite interesting – school building regulations of South Tyrol might serve as a model here.

A typical school corridor. Long corridors like this with rows of adjacent classrooms are found in many school buildings.

Here, the central hallway is not simply for access but also offers space for work groups. The school was designed as a 'little village' with class 'houses' around a 'market square'. Janusz-Korczak School Überlingen, plus+ bauplanung, 1999

From the outside this building doesn't look like a school. It could just as easily be an administrative building. School complex Im Birch, Zürich-Oerlikon, Peter Märkli, 1999–2004

Approval is withheld for any school design which does not offer educational enrichment. The reference parameters here are not classrooms measuring 60 m² as in Germany but an allowance of 4 m² per pupil, organised into areas which creates more flexibility.

Loris Malaguzzi, founder of the Reggio educational philosophy, states that: 'The other children are the first educator, the second the teacher and the third the environment!' In our architectural practice, plus+ bauplanung, our experience from having designed 25 schools so far has taught us that this statement is true if the architecture offers a stimulating environment. But spaces can also be 'bad teachers' if they are impersonal and difficult to identify with or if pupils are subjected to barrack-like buildings with long corridors and rows of adjacent classrooms constructed from cold and non-sensual materials such as concrete, steel and glass. Here, we prefer natural materials and sunny spaces flooded with as much light as possible and maybe green areas with plants and trees providing the basic natural necessities of life.

There are frequently two serious problems to overcome: firstly, too little fresh air circulation, which means that pupils usually lose attention after 20 minutes and remain unable to concentrate without a regulated supply of fresh air. Secondly, there is often insufficient provision of sound-absorbent surfaces because there is insufficient sound-proofing provision in the building regulations. This makes it difficult for teachers and students to understand one another and is to the particular disadvantage of pupils with language dif-

The old building of the Montessori Secondary School in Potsdam was remodelled between 2000 and 2010 on their own initiative.

ficulties. If possible, the whole classroom ceiling should be provided with sound-absorbent cladding. Inadequacies like these hinder rather than support a free learning environment.[2]

On the one hand, rooms must certainly offer the purely physical background conditions like air, light and warmth. However, they should also free people from external constraints, encourage individuality and fulfil the need for a 'refuge.' Man cannot survive without clothing and shelter. Even small children will build themselves dens and nests by throwing blankets over chairs so they can crawl beneath them and hide. Rooms should communicate; they should embrace and caress all the senses. Schools need individualised learning places. This means that form and aesthetics should not be foremost in driving the planning process. Instead, buildings should be designed which will accommodate methodologies that transcend teaching from the front of the class in 45-minute-cycles. Learning concepts which encourage enthusiastic pupils to acquire knowledge for themselves through project work, free learning and silent studies in groups of broadly differing sizes can produce astonishing results. Even old buildings can be re-organised in a way which promotes forward-looking teaching as the Montessori Secondary School in Potsdam, for example, clearly shows.[3]

Learning spaces always work best in a lively, busy environment of 'creative disorder' rather than where an inflexible, restraining mentality of front-facing straight lines and unyielding right angles prevails. A modern characterful learning environment must, above all else, excite, inspire, liberate, individualise and release all our inherent potential. Every child has a zest for action which will flourish only in an exciting environment and which finds no outlet when 'confined to barracks' in stereotyped box-like classrooms. In Japan, for instance, new schools are built with extraordinarily interesting, open layouts in which I was personally impressed by the lively pleasure in learning taken by the pupils. The architect, Kazumi Kudo, designed the Utase Primary School with the participation of teachers and pupils in a very intensive planning process.[4]

The Protestant Comprehensive School in Gelsenkirchen (see p. 218-221), designed by plus+ bauplanung at the beginning of the 1990s, is a model for a different type of school. Its generous, sometimes two-storey rooms are flooded with light, and plenty of wood, glass, water and plants have been used both inside and out. Several people have remarked that, having already walked through the entire building, they have arrived at the rear entrance and asked the way to the Protestant Comprehensive School. Because it presented such a different appearance from conventional schools, they had not realised it was one, which is probably the biggest compliment we could have received.

Making schools more flexible

Unfortunately, it is still the norm to build schools with long corridors and rows of adjacent classrooms thus cementing a conventional approach to schooling. Forward-looking education, however, requires as a starting point interior structures divided into larger and smaller areas, within which three or four classes make up one organisation unit or cluster.

In the Utase Elementary School, Chiba City, Japan (Kazumi Kudo, 2005), the classrooms have no corridor walls, allowing classrooms to be configured in many different ways.

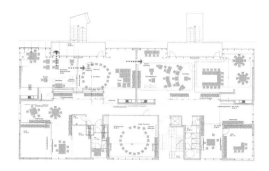

A board system fitted to rail allows the classroom to be organised in different ways; movable partitions facilitate different room sizes. Internationale Friedensschule, Köln, plus+ bauplanung, 2008

Depending on the type of school, various learning scenarios may run across classes and year groups. These schools should have versatile access paths which are not used simultaneously as emergency escape routes. Instead, escape routes can be provided externally via the façade. There are then countless options to differentiate classrooms: there might be a gallery, a bay, a kitchenette or a garden. It is also important to release pupils from the blackboard and create considerably more adaptable furniture systems. Flexible classrooms might have triangular tables, for example, which cannot be arranged in rows but which can be freely combined to accommodate one, four or six pupils. In addition, flexible walls or movable boards facilitate the presentation and discussion of project work and displays. There would also be exhibition areas and variously designed gathering places for different numbers of pupils to eat and learn together and for individual and group work.

Designing around user needs

For architects this means focusing their energy and creativity to create landscapes in which it is not always the constraints of the load bearing structures, fire safety, acoustics, aesthetics, lighting and ventilation that are the first priorities. It becomes more important to set aside the separation of traffic routes and useful areas to produce totally flexible usable spaces. Areas like these are seldom found, mainly for fire safety reasons. However, even if they require the installation of expensive sprinkler systems, these spaces are worth every penny when you consider their potential benefits and long term usage.

Vital learning spaces like these can be organised basically anywhere, even in old buildings. When modernising existing buildings, however, it is not enough simply to renovate the façades, windows and doors. It is much more important to undertake innovative alterations to produce new spatial structures which encourage different teaching models. Monotonous rows of identical classrooms should be broken up. A practical example: in a conventional row of adjacent classrooms, the corridor wall of individual rooms could be removed to provide special purpose and presentation areas. Usually this only works if emergency escape routes can be installed externally making the corridors freely usable. In this way, schools with long, dark corridors can be turned into lively learning environments. An example is the remodelling of the Heinrich-Nordhoff Comprehensive School in Wolfsburg, where the three storeys were totally gutted right down to the load bearing structures and a central two-storey gallery and multi-purpose area was installed under a glass roof. Class escape routes pass through the façade and along external balconies around the building.

Participation

The participation of the users always plays a very important role. Our practice, plus+ bauplanung, has carried out many projects in partnership with users and it has become clear every time that building is a deeply social process. This means that the architect must listen to and take seriously the opinions of those who will use the rooms and need to feel comfortable in them. Within a very short time something very fascinating occurs: a completely different relationship evolves between user and architect: a bond of mutual trust. Using models and drawings, designs for a new school building are developed with the future users, i.e. teachers and pupils, in a number of workshops in small groups, each under the guidance of an architect. The plans are jointly discussed and modified until a very specific solution has been found which is then translated into buildable designs by architects and specialist consultants.[5]

The floor plan shows how four classrooms can be combined to form one organisational unit with versatile working spaces. In the classrooms are areas to which individual pupils or small groups can withdraw to work on specific projects. Campus Klarenthal, Wiesbaden, plus+ bauplanung, 2010

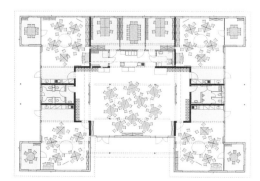

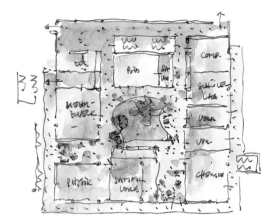

In this renovation project, escape routes have been provided on external wrap-around balconies leaving a central multi-purpose area. Heinrich-Nordhoff Comprehensive School, Wolfsburg, City of Wolfsburg, moderated by plus+ bauplanung, 2010

By locating the emergency stairways outside, the internal corridors become useful spaces which can even be furnished. Internationale Friedensschule, Köln, plus+ bauplanung, 2008

Participation processes: A new school project is planned with the future users, i.e. teachers and pupils, in several workshops under the guidance of an architect using models and drawings.

It is also very important that all those involved understand the complexity and difficulty of the building project and recognise that there are always many solutions which are filtered down to find a 'good' one. From this process emerge 'expert owners,' who develop an intense relationship with their building. The participating users identify with, appreciate and care for their buildings. The surprising thing is that buildings communicate these sentiments even to those who have had nothing to do with the building process. People are quite simply moved by such 'speaking' architecture – even if they know nothing about its evolutionary history. Virtually no vandalism or graffiti are found on schools like these.

It is amazing that all these flexible, alternative room structures, assembly areas, meeting points, exhibition and refuge areas, which will ultimately become the learning spaces of the future, have proven to be affordable even for the public sector and are not an exclusive model for private institutions. Budgets of private establishments are indeed often smaller than those of public institutions. Furthermore, complex planning is not usually reflected in the actual building costs. An oblique angled structure is no more expensive than a right-angled one because the cubic capacity doesn't change. Concrete by the cubic metre, chipboard and glass by the square metre all cost the same, irrespective of how they are used.

The same spaces are built but they are merely configured in a different way – perhaps a bit distorted or slanted. With relatively little change a completely new world can be created. Every corner does not have to be the same colour, for instance, and concrete does not always have to be exposed. There should be lots of light, wood, plants and water.

Any building in which people spend a great amount of time should provide a natural living space. The architecture shouldn't intrude but should foster unconstrained personal expression. People learn better in a comfortable environment.[6] The question that decides everything is how much creativity the architects are prepared to use to find solutions and whether they can translate these solutions into a built reality.

References

1 The book *A Pattern Language* examines in just 1300 pages how typical building projects have been accepted by their users and gives lots of tips for the design of learning landscapes. Christopher Alexander, *A Pattern Language: Towns, Buildings, Construction*, Oxford: Oxford University Press, 1977.

2 Claudia Jacobs, ‚Das Wunder von Allach,' *Focus Schule*, No. 6, 2009, p. 28–29.

3 The headmistress of the Montessori Secondary School describes in detail the structural alterations in: Ulrike Kegler, *In Zukunft lernen wir anders: Wenn die Schule schön wird*, Weinheim: Beltz, 2009.

4 Kazumi Kudo, *Gakko wo tsukurou* (Let's make a School), Tokyo: Toto, 2004.

5 All the phases of a participation process for the Protestant Comprehensive School, Gelsenkirchen, are described in detail in: Peter Hübner, *Children Make their School: Evangelische Gesamtschule Gelsenkirchen*, Stuttgart: Edition Axel Menges, 2005 (bilingual German/English edition).

6 Peter Blundell Jones uses 30 projects to present participation processes and their built results, in particular youth centres, kindergartens and schools, and demonstrates the amazing correlation between the well-being of the users and their living environment. Peter Blundell Jones, *Peter Hübner: Building as a Social Process*, Stuttgart: Edition Axel Menges, 2007 (bilingual German/English edition).

SUSANNE HOFMANN

Schools and Kindergartens under Reconstruction

It is inevitable that, when educational concepts and policies radically change, even solidly built schools and kindergartens have to be renovated. The poor scores achieved by German schoolchildren in the OECD PISA tests prompted a heated debate about how the state school system might be improved and, as a result, German schools and kindergartens are undergoing a range of very different reconstruction programmes. Many schools are now opening all day, which means that children are provided with lunch in newly built refectories and supervised during the afternoons. Kindergartens are also increasingly required to take on a teaching role, offering children a preschool education and preparing them for school life. The spatial reorganisation of children's day centres is therefore essential to foster group activities and provide areas of refuge for individual children. In schools, formal front-of-class instruction is giving way to group work but the classrooms are to be retained, thus creating a need for additional rooms. Moreover, schools and kindergartens are important focal points in the social life of their immediate neighbourhood. Children spend a large part of their day here, but their parents also make a substantial contribution to the life of the school and kindergarten. In city areas with a highly segregated population where language barriers and cultural differences sometimes produce problems, schools and kindergartens provide an opportunity to make contact and integrate. The capacity of children to socialise readily also offers adults the chance to mix more freely. Architecture may assist this process and act as a social catalyst if all interested parties and users of the building are involved in its design and are thus given the opportunity to identify with 'their school' or 'their kindergarten.' Several schools and kindergartens consider this part of their social and educational function with the architecture of their establishment in a valuable supporting role. Italian and Swedish school reformers have suggested that a room with a stimulating atmosphere becomes a 'third educator' after the class group and the teacher. A sensitive architecture, which addresses all human senses and can be experienced physically, is helpful in this respect. It also enables the user (in this case the children attending the school or kindergarten) to identify with the institution by encouraging a rational, emotional and, most especially, a personal bond with the school or kindergarten. Children therefore feel they have a second home, and they are able to accept their educational institution as part of their new home environment. It is only too easy to underestimate the users' appreciation of spatial and atmospheric qualities and, in most cases, little value is attached to the spatial ambience as perceived through the senses. Tremendous inspiration may be drawn from the potential to translate the fantasy worlds of those outside the architectural profession.

Although plans may often be socially ambitious, budgets are usually constrained within narrow limits mostly not sufficient to allow for changes to the structure. In some cases it is not economically feasible to make even minor alterations to the fabric of the building, so many reconstruction projects have to be completed within a narrow framework but to maximum effect. In such cases intensive preparatory work is essential in which the ideas of the users are recorded and translated into an architectural design. The result is realised as a cost-effective building project, which also has to comply with statutory and technical building regulations. This assumes a highly experimental design approach. Examples of this process are to be found in three projects designed and built by the 'Baupiloten' of the Technical University of Berlin.

The 'Baupiloten' are a changing group of students. As part of their architectural studies, they develop independent building projects under professional guidance and supervision, and plan all construction phases themselves, from the design through to its realisation, within the constraints of a limited budget. In the process, the 'Baupiloten' encourage future users of their buildings to participate in the design phase. As trainee architects the status of the students is very similar to that of the users; they are even close to the children in terms of age. Their impartiality and curiosity and, not least, their constant critical assessment of their own position, make for an inspiring collaboration.

In 2003, the Erika Mann Elementary School in Berlin-Wedding was modernised. The pupils, ranging in age from 9-13 years, produced collages of fantasy landscapes in a workshop entitled 'The path through the garden of the future,' giving convincing concrete expression to the architectural future of their school. Inspired by these lively drawings and the visions and wishes of the children, the 'Baupiloten' tried to interpret moods and atmospheric effects and to define them more precisely in further collages and spatial models. Future uses and functions were also taken into account and the results subsequently realised as prototypes. The children were invited to test and re-evaluate them. It was absolutely essential that all these designs

should be legible and, above all, immediately comprehensible. They introduced an ephemeral sensitivity intended to inject a playful light-heartedness into the stark severity of the school building. A 'school committee' comprising representatives chosen from all classes from year 3 upwards took on the role of the clients throughout the building process.

The district of Berlin-Wedding is an urban social hot spot with more than 50% unemployment. 85% of the parents of the children who attend the Erika Mann School are of non-German speaking origin and pupils come from 25 different countries. Its transformation into an all-day school was intended to help the children overcome language and cultural barriers; and the wide range of facilities available in the building were designed to provide an education centre for all neighbourhood residents. Parents and teachers were therefore actively involved in the building process. The orientation of the school towards theatre and music also had to be taken into account as the building transformed to become a 'Children's Neighbourhood Centre.' The project was supported with resources from the Federal Government's urban regeneration programme: the 'Socially Integrative City'. Nevertheless, the budget was very tight and it was not possible to make massive changes to the fabric of the building. The broad corridors and hallways of the school house, built in 1914 by Berlin city councillor Ludwig Hoffmann, provided sufficient space to accommodate additional work and leisure areas, and room was also found for new cloakrooms. However, a prerequisite was the use of non-combustible materials to comply with fire regulations.

The students and schoolchildren created the 'World of the Silver Dragon' to form the basis of a playful and expressive architecture. As they enter the building, visitors are greeted by changing small exhibitions of the children's work on the theme of the 'World of the Silver Dragon'. A gallery on the ground floor and in one of the stairwells presents a constantly changing display of the children's current work. The further you go into the school building the more strongly you feel the spirit of the Silver Dragon: a spirit which changes, resonates, glows and shimmers. On the ground floor, in the world of 'star dust diving,' plants grow under violet light above yellow-green lacquered metal furniture, providing the imaginary dragon with a place to sleep. On the first floor in the 'breath of gentle air,' the breath of the dragon becomes perceptible between the light translucent veils of the ceiling and the shimmering textile wardrobes. The second floor houses the 'throne on the beat of the wings,' where groups of four children sit on folding seats in the crook of the dragon's wing to read, work and chat. Finally, on the third floor you can 'fly with the dragon.' The children learn

Start of the 'Silver Dragon Worlds' project:
Collage workshop with the children of the
'School Committee'

The hallway of the Erika Mann Elementary School in
Berlin-Wedding before and after conversion in 2003
with its inviting foldable seating.

in small study groups between luminous metal dragon tails. The main stairwell has become a versatile musical instrument and the dragon can dance and jump along the 'Giant Humming Trail.' The reconstruction captured the imagination of the children to such an extent that they were able to feel and describe the presence of the dragon. Their identification with the school was also so great that, years after the renovation work, nothing has been defaced or destroyed.

For their second project in 2004–2005, the 'Tree of Dreams' Kindergarten in Berlin-Kreuzberg, the 'Baupiloten' followed a similar approach. In this case the cost limit for renovation work was even lower than it had been to reconstruct the school. Children attending the kindergarten range in age from 2–11 years. They produced pictures and models to depict their visions of a 'Tree of Dreams.' The youngest amongst them were not yet able to express themselves in language but were able to communicate through their pictures: the 'Tree of Dreams' would be their companion and playmate. The images and wishes of the children again served to inspire the work of the 'Baupiloten.' They designed structures and shapes representative of a tree, offering protective nooks and crannies to snuggle into. The 'Tree of Dreams' encourages children from a wide variety of cultural backgrounds to come together. As they arrive, the tree greets them in their 14 different languages. It works like a mythical creature that has become real, stimulating the children's imagination and social skills, and encouraging them to play and communicate in smaller or larger groups. It glitters and glows, moves and makes noises. Its leafy roof reflects natural light deep into hitherto insuf-

The corridor in the kindergarten in Berlin-Kreuzberg prior to the reconstruction.

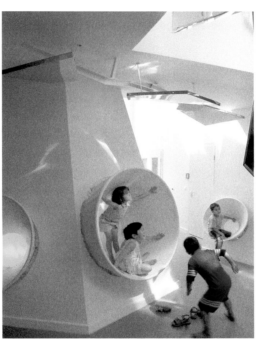

After the reconstruction: The children romp in the flowery bowers and swings of the 'Tree of Dreams.'

The children choose their favourites from the preliminary designs submitted by the 'Baupiloten.'

ficiently lit corridors, its leaves rustle as if the tree is 'giggling.' The 'Tree of Dreams' even 'snores,' inviting the children to share its dreams. They are able to explore and experience their world with all their senses, make new friends and chat to one another.

In another refurbishment project in 2005–2007, the 'Taka-Tuka Land' Kindergarten in Berlin-Spandau, the 'Baupiloten' were given the opportunity to change the spatial organisation of the building. In the course of essential renovation work to this kindergarten, originally built only as a temporary solution, the façade was restructured to provide a play space for the children, and the existing room sequence was broken up to create intercommunicating group spaces. The kindergarten was named after Pippi Longstocking's 'Taka-Tuka-Land' as featured in Astrid Lindgren's children's novel of the same name. The children and their teachers presented their visions of 'Taka-Tuka Land', which were to form the basis of their new daily environment,

incorporating musical bridges, little huts, a merry-go-round of blossoms and the throne of shells belonging to Pippi's father. The 'Baupiloten' again drew inspiration for their designs from these ideas and by observing the movements, communication and daily routines of the children. Through reconstruction, the school building becomes Pippi's ancient oak tree; in its hollow interior 'lemonade' is made and flows like a river, along which seven activity stations are provided for the children. For example, you can see visitors to 'Taka-Tuka' approaching from a distance through the large panoramic window where crystals reflect the midday sun and form the 'glittering cave' of Lindgren's story. The children can wait for their parents in the yellow glow of 'lemonade' and display their works in the Lemonade Gallery. The focal point is Lemonade Island: on this yellow platform the children can romp, hide and lose themselves in this lemonade world. The 'lemonade river' breaches the rough bark of the oak tree at its last activity station. Nooks and crannies are provided in the walls of the building and bark of the tree where the children can climb, hide and snuggle up. The play space within the façade is softly cushioned with luminous yellow fabric, and tarpaulin covers offer protection against all weather conditions.

The kindergarten building is interpreted as Pippi Longstocking's ancient oak tree in which lemonade is made. The children can experience the 'lemonade' spatially at seven activity stations.

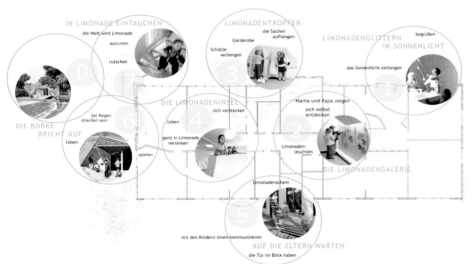

The children present their visions of Taka-Tuka Land.

The Taka-Tuka Land Kindergarten in Berlin-Spandau before and after renovation, view from the garden

The children's reactions during the design phases and after completion of the three projects confirmed how important it had been for the design work to take explicit account of the atmospheric effects produced by the architecture. It was also essential to ensure that these effects were monitored and reflected throughout the building process. Because the children had been so closely involved in the design process, they were able to identify strongly with their newly created environment.

Nurseries and Kindergartens

The term kindergarten which originally derived from the notion of the school as a metaphorical garden, alludes to children as unfolding plants, being nourished and nurtured with care and love in a plant house or a nursery. Along with this are biblical allusions to the lost innocence of Adam and Eve in the Garden of Eden. The German educational pioneer Friedrich Froebel (1782-1852) almost certainly invented the term; he imbued the kindergarten idea with a faintly mystical quality believing it to be a symbolic representation of nature, a sort of microcosm of the world, reflecting the positive aspects of a diverse milieu.

Today the nursery or the kindergarten is viewed in a less sentimental way. These terms usually refer either to full daycare, for young babies to children up to the age of five or six, or to part-time education for early years. The framework for these institutions is a highly controlled, rigorously evaluated environment, which often focuses on the health and safety of children over and above their social and educational development. It is in this context that the design of the building and its external play spaces take on a critical role in helping to pacify or stimulate children as is appropriate to their needs.

There is no real difference in terms of their overall aim between the kindergarten, the day nursery or the nursery school. However, each has a particular meaning in its context. The word kindergarten is used as a generic term in Europe and Japan and has particular resonances bringing to mind the somewhat mystical, craft based Steiner school system. In Denmark and Sweden the term relates specifically to facilities for children between the ages of three and five. In the USA it identifies the preschool class attached to elementary schools; nursery schools by comparison are sometimes referred to as 'childcare centres' or 'early learning centres'.

There is in addition a sometimes bewildering range of part-time early years care and education facilities, as well as add-on services to the basic childcare offer. For example, Germany's Kindertagesstätte (children's daycare place) often includes before and after-school facilities for older school age children in the form of a Kinderhort. It is felt that school children should benefit from an alternative environment, when formal education is over for the day. They return to the safe, play-orientated environment of the preschool, perhaps the place they attended as young children, albeit in a separate securely controlled zone of the early years building.

In France, state-run nursery schools are usually called écoles maternelles, whilst privately run nursery schools are known as jardin d'enfants. The state sector, which has grown gradually during a 90-year history, now serves over 95% of children aged three to five. Local authorities are required by law to provide pre-primary education if it is requested. France also operates other daycare provision, such as crèches, which cater for under threes, écoles maternelles for children aged 3-6 years and garderies that provide after-scholl services.

In Italy, preschool education is provided in both public and private nursery schools. Since the creation of the scuola maternal statale in 1969, attendance has risen steadily; at present 90% of children aged three to five attend full-time, sometimes six days per week. Although quality varies from region to region, preschool is widely accepted. There is a clear perception amongst most parents that their children will fall behind in developmental terms, if they do not attend.

Politicians in the UK have at long last recognised the need to catch up and build affordable new childcare throughout the UK. However, there is a tendency to use the school as the context for early years provision. Although there are some good facilities integrated into schools, this approach is generally an economic exigency. With its play based ethos, and the need to ensure that the scales and textures of the early years environment are appropriate for young children, it is important to recognise the specialised nature of early years, and make purpose designed environments, which are totally separate from the school. Here we have only featured examples, which are innovative child-centred exemplars of the highest quality; young children deserve nothing less.

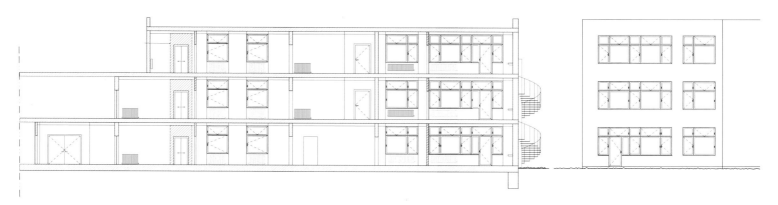

Section and elevation

Entrance foyer with wardrobe, featuring the fox graphic, earthy brick wall feature and broad sliding doors | Ground floor wardrobe | Homebase for 3-4 year olds, with cushion storage and soft plinths all at child height | The rabbit image indicates the ground level

Kita Sinneswandel

Berlin, Germany

Architect	Baukind, Berlin
Pupils	65
Building area	750 m²
Average classroom	34.6 m² ('homebase')
Parking spaces	15
Build cost	1 million EUR
Completion	2013
Year group system	3 age-related groups

A building which provides a coherent narrative structure through design

Often the easiest job for an architect is to be given a greenfield site, a blank canvas so to speak, where he can do as he wishes without constraint. If you take that freedom away, introducing conditions to which he must respond, arguably it becomes more difficult and more expensive. So for example, a site which is in a historic setting may limit the imagination because there are so many planning restrictions. Alternatively the architect may have to work within the confines of an existing building, and convert it from the inside with the challenge to create something stimulating and child-orientated. The constraints of a tight budget create equal challenges.

1 Entrance foyer

2 Child WC

3 Group room 1 + 2 (per age group)

4 'Snoezelraum',
  controlled multi-sensory environment

5 Counselling room

6 Climbing and physical adventure room

7 Children's restaurant

8 Rest and relaxation room

9 Staff room

10 Office

11 Personal conference/meeting room

 Existing building

Demolished

New building

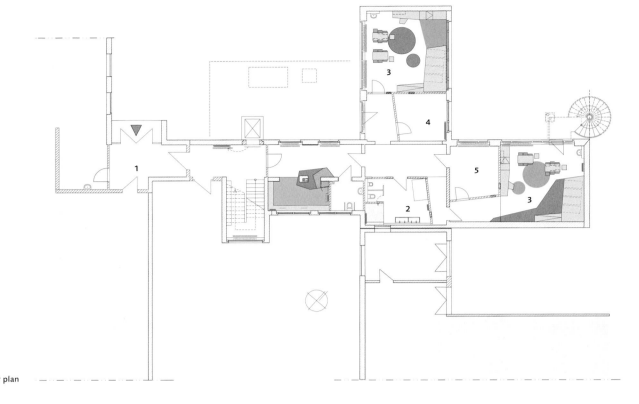

Ground floor plan

It is fair to say that all of these restrictions existed when the specialist Berlin-based architectural practice, Baukind, was commissioned to transform an existing school building (the former Helen Keller School in Berlin-Charlottenburg) on three storeys to accommodate 65 children, most in full daycare, and many of them deaf or with impaired hearing. The new nursery is completely bilingual, using spoken German and German Sign Language. The challenge was to create an intelligent building, one which was of course functional and safe, but also a coherent sequence of spaces to which the children themselves could relate and learn from.

The accommodation required included six homebases (ten children in each), an art studio and a large children's restaurant. On the ground floor the youngest children aged 1-3 years find an environment which is in warm earthy colours, violet, with brown to red shades, evoking the soil in which the tree is rooted. This symbolises the roots of a tree, perhaps the mythical tree of life. A so-called 'Snoezelraum' provides a cosy environment that stimulates and soothes all senses at the same time. More vibrant yellows and oranges are adopted for the middle level which is for the children aged 3-4. Here, the wall and floor graphic melt into each other to give a dramatic zig-zag edge to the room. On the top third level bright blue and green colours are used, this area being dedicated to

the oldest children aged 5-6. This colour orientation is clearly a narrative structure which refers to the base, the middle and the top of this most fundamental element of nature's structures. Both colour concept and animal characters were developed together with Atelier Perela.

The orientation is given further legibility with the use of animal images, the worm and the rabbit around the roots, the fox and the deer, animals which represent the part of the tree trunk which is still grounded but already stretching and growing in height, and the upper branches and canopy of foliage which is represented by the squirrel and the owl. This provides a clear sense of orientation, one which exudes safety

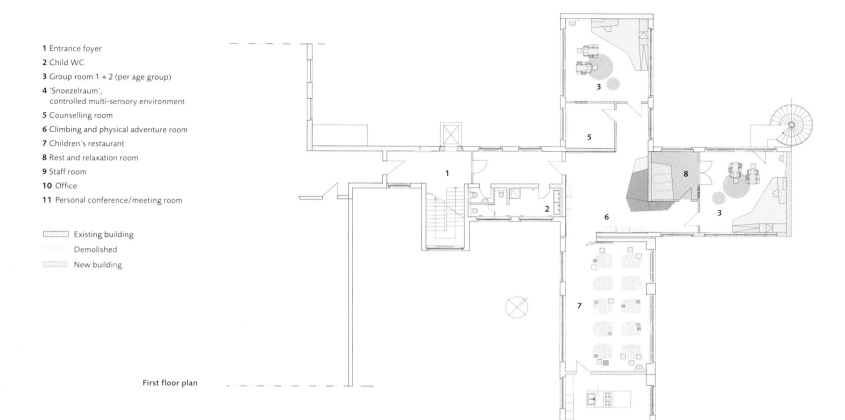

1 Entrance foyer
2 Child WC
3 Group room 1 + 2 (per age group)
4 'Snoezelraum',
  controlled multi-sensory environment
5 Counselling room
6 Climbing and physical adventure room
7 Children's restaurant
8 Rest and relaxation room
9 Staff room
10 Office
11 Personal conference/meeting room

▨▨▨ Existing building
░░░ Demolished
▨▨▨ New building

First floor plan

Washrooms are positive, colour coordinated spaces | Restaurant in use with different scales tables and stools, which also act as constructive play toys after lunch

and security, but also challenges the children to go out and explore. The narrative is given clarity when the children themselves go out into the forest with their adult carers and have the narrative structure explained to them. All animal graphics are simple elegant designs verging on the abstract, thus eschewing the over-explicit anthropomorphism of Disney-type imagery.

The children's restaurant celebrates the ritual of coming together of everyone to eat and share this fundamental communal event. It is furnished with purpose designed furniture which is scaled to each age range. Tables and stools are not only used for lunch, they also function as play pieces, giant robust building

blocks which can be tipped up and used for all sorts of imaginative play. A large sliding door optimises the space and ensures flexibility. A true learning environment for play which is flexible, spatially transformative and elegant. All furniture has been designed by Baukind. This multi-functional furniture creates a platform for playing and also incorporates adequate storage space, which alleviates the mess of toys.

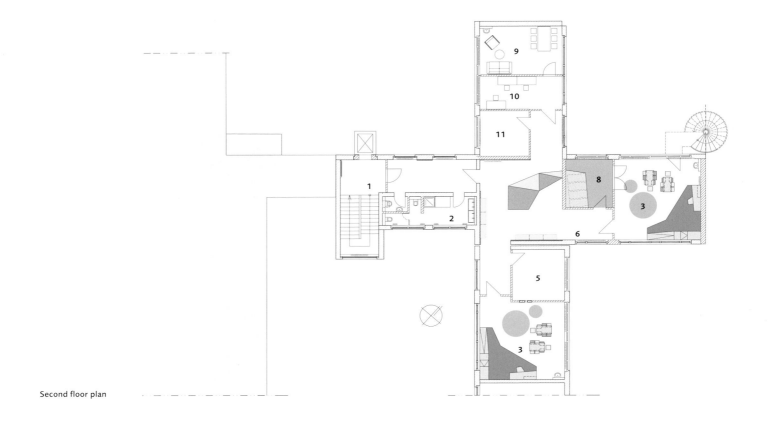

Second floor plan

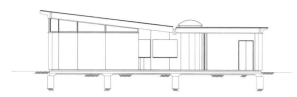

Northwest elevation

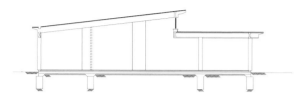

Southwest elevation

Sections

Northeast elevation

View of the back yard, with the circular meeting room on the left and the oval nursery in the centre | The complex form of the building creates a number of different play spaces | View of the corridor, note the splayed ceiling beams showing the building's underlying structure, and the wall hung tapestry. The girls remember their visit to the butterfly house during the previous week | The child-scaled door adjacent to the children's play kitchen gives children a sense of ownership.

Cherry Lane Children's Centre

Hillingdon, London, UK

Architect	Mark Dudek Associates
Pupils	60 children aged 3-5; up to 50 aged 0-3 years
Building area	80 m²
Average classroom	65 m² serving 35 nursery age children
Parking spaces	10
Build cost	620,000 GBP
Completion	2011
Year group system	2 integrated age groups of 0-3 and 3-5 year olds

A building which uses early years research to develop an appropriate child-orientated architecture of play

The principles behind this kindergarten in an impoverished community in West London are firstly to shape an environment which is in tune with children's natural rhythms of play, and secondly to deliver an ambitious project on a very tight budget.

The most characteristic pattern in children's play is the free flow, from activity to activity, transforming as it goes. Through observational research the designers have been struck by the levels of inventiveness children bring to this play, using the environment of the kindergarten, both inside and outside, as a touchstone for their developing relationship with the wider world. In keeping with this pattern, each child can develop his or her personal routes through the play spaces,

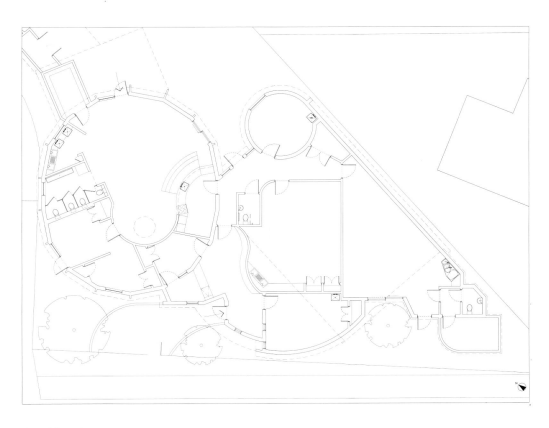

Ground floor plan

indeed through the wider environment of walkable journeys to and from the kindergarten. Movement through the various spaces rather than confining children within a single room is one of the key design parameters.

A further dimension of this play was the concept of complexity. For most children a complex scene invites curiosity and awareness much more readily than a simple, easily read architectural scene. Equally a playroom with corners and hidden places will hold more fascination for the young child than a straightforward and easily passable one, while too much complexity will leave children bewildered and lost. At Cherry Lane this means complexity in plan and in section; corridors

are winding rather than straight, room features such as ceilings and fenestration are variegated, the building's structure is evident rather than hidden away.

Within the framework of this spatial complexity, it is important to provide quiet spaces within which individuals or small groups of children can play undisturbed. Hence the spaces are choreographed by a number of specific child-orientated features, such as a child height door, the stage area (with a theatrical curtain and city mural as the backdrop), the wet play spaces all of which enable the children to relate better to their environment. Use of natural materials with views out to the green surroundings promote connectivity to the natural world and of course the direct

access to the external play spaces encourages free flow between the inside and the outside wherever possible.

The material qualities of this building are soft rather than hard, extending to the very shape of the building itself. Warm yielding materials such as cedar cladding and soft, mellow fabrics for the seating, drapes and wall hangings were used. Rooms are never square, the main nursery is oval, the entrance and circulation curves and twists its way between the two main built elements, meeting rooms are either circular or triangular in shape. Fluidity, spatial complexity and a green naturalistic tempo make this a building of immense pleasure, an authentic learning environment.

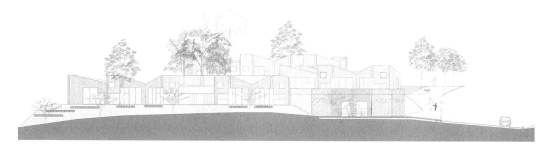

West elevation

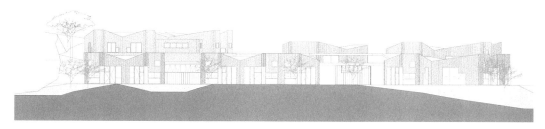

South elevation

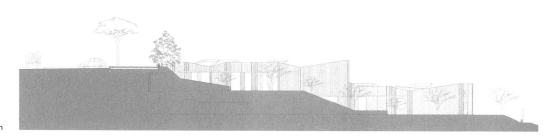

East elevation

The form of the building encloses courtyard spaces sheltered from the sun | The curvilinear shapes of the modular units become a single coherent building

San Antonio de Prado Kindergarten

Medellin, Colombia

Architect	Ctrl G Estudio de Arquitectura, Medellin and Plan B (Federico Mesa), Medellin
Pupils	300 aged 3 months to 5 years
Building area	1,500 m²
Average classroom	56 m²
Parking spaces	0
Build cost	1.8 million USD
Completion	2011
Year group system	18 age-related groups, 18 children per classroom

Combines spatial variation with efficient modular construction

The idea of a modular classroom or in this case a kindergarten classroom is not a new one. It is estimated that savings of up to 50% of the manufacturing costs are possible by making the majority of the building off-site in a clean factory environment. The units can then be delivered to site on the back of a lorry, either in kit form or as pre-assembled units all ready to be lifted onto the only on-site element of the construction, the foundations and below ground drainage. In some ways, pre-fabrication is ideal for school sites which have six-week summer vacations, thus avoiding the disruption which the traditional build processes will bring.

The problem with the modular approach is that the pre-assembly idea, predicated on cheapness alone, usu-

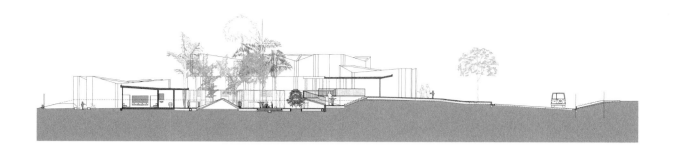

Sections

ally means that architecture is largely absent from the equation. The parts are usually constructed of repetitive box-like units, 3.8 metres wide and a maximum of 8 metres in length, so that they can fit onto a lorry for transportation to site. There is little possibility of varying roof shapes or eccentric plan forms which may appeal to children. The form will be dull and uninspiring as a consequence lacking the complexity and playfulness of an authentic kindergarten architecture.

There is a further problem which comes with all of this, an important sustainability principle, namely thermal mass: because of their factory construction, usually a steel or timber frame for rigidity during transportation is required. To keep everything as transportable

as possible lightweight insulated infill panels are used for the walls and roof. As a result the buildings lack the embodied thermal performance of a dense material like stone or concrete. This makes the enclosed environment inherently unstable, with a notable tendency to be very hot in summer and, unless ventilation is extremely efficient, stuffy and uncomfortable in winter.

At the Kindergarten in Medellin, a team of two architectural practices has created a classroom module to deliver the promised expansion in primary school places required in this area of the Aburra Valley, high up in the Andes Mountains. Looking for an architecture which would fit into the natural topography, they chose a variegated, almost plastic plan form, without compro-

mising on the basic modular requirement for repetitive units. Each classroom module is designed around one or two standard templates at most. The units comprise of two parallel long walls with four angled and gently curved corner units at asymmetrically splayed angles. Each pair of units fits together back to back with a fully openable wall panel to enable group learning. To create an organic natural effect using modular components is not easy. But here the designers have effected an organic feel which is totally complimentary to the landscape. Using pre-fabricated concrete units they have skilfully achieved sufficient variation in the architecture to create an easily constructable building all in thermally efficient concrete which is truly poetic.

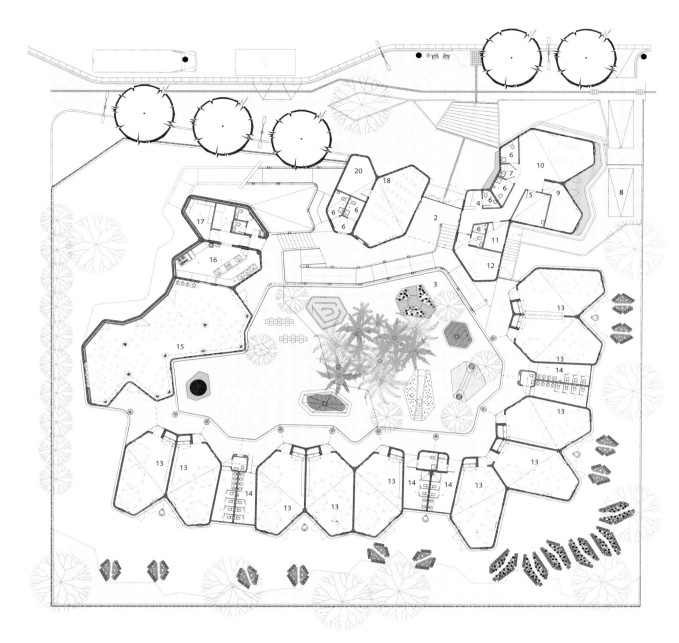

Ground floor plan (access level)

1 Entrance court
2 Entrance foyer with stair to first floor area for babies
3 Courtyard for meetings and informal play
4 Reception desk
5 Administration block
6 Toilets
7 Kitchenette
8 Staff work area
9 Head of Centre
10 Main consulting room
11 Storage of teaching resources
12 Nursing room
13 Classrooms
14 Children's bathrooms
15 Cafeteria
16 Kitchen and services
17 Storage
18 Auditorium
19 Balcony
20 Technical services
21 Toddlers
22 Sleeping
23 Loading zone

Typical classroom with radiating light | Views of the classrooms

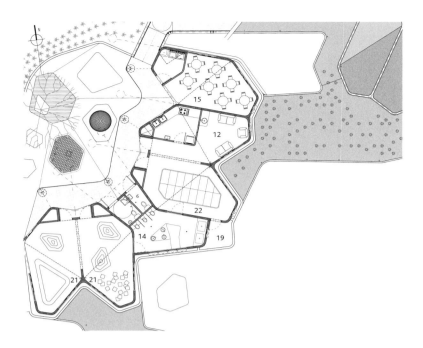

First floor plan (level +1.5 m)

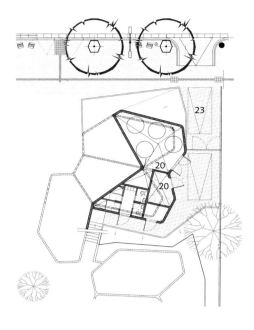

Basement plan (-1.5 m)

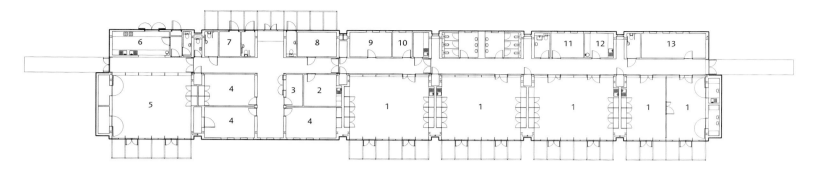

Ground floor plan

1 Activity room
2 Staff room
3 Reception
4 Multi-purpose/training room
5 Community café

6 Café kitchen
7 Groundsman's office
8 Plant room
9 Manager's office

10 Parent room
11 Quiet room (2-4 years)
12 Nursery kitchen
13 Quiet room (0-2 years)

Colonnade from the rear, a pavilion in a park-like setting | View from the street, an enclosed protective façade with secure vertical windows and Douglas fir cladding | Interior views of activity areas opening onto children's garden and allotments beyond

Lavender Children's Centre

Mitcham, Surrey, UK

Architect	John McAslan + Partners, London
Pupils	90 aged 0-5 years
Building area	990 m²
Average classroom	4 activity rooms 68 m² each
Parking spaces	20
Build cost	1.42 million GBP
Completion	2005
Year group system	Age-related activity areas for babies

A largely pre-fabricated research project to produce a high quality template for future childcare buildings which will be easy to manufacture and construct

Developed for the Greater London Borough of Merton, this 90 place nursery is part of a larger 500 million GBP 'Sure Start' programme being developed throughout England at present. It is unusual to have such a high budget for a childcare building, however, a lot of area has been squeezed from what is essentially a 1,400 GBP per square metre construction budget. When the commission was won in 2003, the development team approached its procurement as something of a research project. Working in tandem with structural engineers Arup, the architects have adopted a largely pre-engineered system build approach to the needs of the childcare community. The result is a highly engineered kit of parts which were essentially bolted together on site having been pre-fabricated in

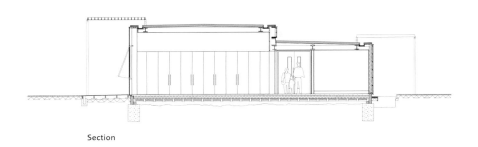

Section

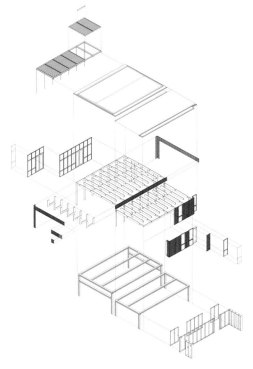

Elemental axonometric

a factory, thus reducing costs and saving construction time. It is a system which could, with a bit of tweaking, be adapted to other sites. The engineer describes it as like a giant Lego kit, an appropriate concept for a nursery.

The prevailing site condition, noisy on the east side and quiet on the west, suggested the clear linear layout with offices facing the road creating an acoustic and visual barrier and children's spaces at the back. They overlook some run-down allotments which are nevertheless valuable green space and which will eventually be transformed into a wild garden. The building is set up as a series of inter-connected timber pavilions distinguishable from the front by panels of

different coloured glass in the tall windows, a colour coding which is carried through into the play spaces behind. If the front is closed and discreet, the rear is the opposite. It is predominantly glazed with timber louvers opening onto an external timber deck, a sort of colonnade between the activity areas and the outside play spaces, the interface between the safety of the interior and the challenges of the great outdoors. Sun sweeps around the elevations and filters through the louvers, the quality of light and shadow is one of the many distinctive features of this simple but inspired building.

Cladding panels are of Douglas fir, chosen for their durability and weathering qualities. The almost fili-

gree structure gives the building a delicacy which is very unusual for a children's environment. There are touches of quality throughout, but is subtle and refined, an architecture which respects the sensitivities of young children, providing a neutral backdrop for the drama and colour of their own activities. The need to protect this elegant structure with high metal fencing and banks of CCTV cameras is one of the unfortunate drawbacks of the times in which we live (the previous childcare building was burnt down). The temptation to treat this as a fortress has been resisted, however, and given time, the community element of the building will assume the original intention, to provide a focus for the families of this deprived urban community.

Site plan

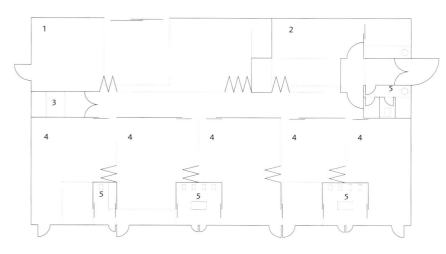

Ground floor plan   1 Multi-purpose area
                    2 Teachers' room
                    3 Bathroom
                    4 Classroom
                    5 WC

Sondika
Kindergarten

Sondika, Bilbao, Spain

Architect	Eduardo Arroyo, No.mad arquitectos, Madrid
Pupils	30 aged 0-3 years
Building area	450 m²
Average classroom	65 m²
Parking spaces	Parking available at school building on same site
Build cost	400,000 EUR
Completion	1998
Year group system	0-1,1-2, 2-3 yrs. in age-related groups of 8, 12, 10

An economical building which provides a sophisticated environment for very young children

The form of the building is a simple rectangular block. Most of the roof is flat yet its linear form is punctuated by a number of over-scaled dormer rooflights which gives the external appearance one of spatial variation within the strict geometries of the box. The architects describe this as a 'multi-faceted geometry', which relates to the surrounding mountainous landscape, reflecting blue light off the topography onto the shiny metallic roof finishes. The building glows in the morning sun, magnifying winter sun into and around the vicinity of the site. The effect gives children a real sense of excitement as they approach in the morning. Once inside, the roof-scape feature has a further positive effect. Each activity area, which is dedicated to children of different age, has its own distinct spatial quality, with higher and lower roof lines to enhance

Elevations

Cross sections

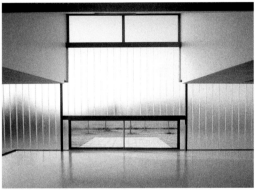

Rear façade in the twilight with roof scape projects and semi-translucent horizontal wall/window glazing system | South elevation, the framed glass faced with child- and adult-scaled doors out | View from a south-facing activity area towards the woods beyond | Low-level child height window is balanced by its high level twin. Adults are denied the views the children have, unless they get down to child level

the spatial drama of this deceptively simple interior. There is a sense of calm order, yet it is never boring. From the activity areas, children can stare at the landscape through a continuous glass wall, which wraps around the accommodation. Inside the children's activity areas, moveable partitions in mirrored, etched or transparent glass, further enhance the feeling of spatial transparency and variation. Yet for the most part, the transparency is only available to children, since above child height, the partitions become solid. It is a privilege that the children recognise is theirs within this child-orientated environment. The extent of glazing on both of the main façades is, according to the architects, a key feature of the offer made to children who come here. Where many children's environments close the users off from the surroundings, here the

architecture ameliorates subtly between the inside and the outside; children can see out, yet they are never on show, an effect which is down to the carefully choreographed orientation. Clear views are towards the countryside to the south (with a north-facing glazed façade which provides protection from the hot sun). Whereas the glazing to the south is in semi-transparent highly engineered solar glass, to give shade and controlled views on the hot south façades. The architects describe this connectivity the building has with its surroundings with a metaphor from nature, that of the 'marsupial bag'. This they say quite rightly is a unique place in nature where the baby has the possibility to contemplate the outside world, from a privileged and protected place. It is a sensitive image for both protection and a sense of the outside world. The re-

sult is an effective faculty for very young children, at an extremely modest price. With its highly glazed front and rear façades, the building stands out from the surrounding main school façades to create a distinctive aspect, a fitting presence on the school campus, and an example of architecture which can really make a difference to its very young users. It is neither patronising, avoiding Disneyland type references, which can often be found in buildings for the very young, nor does it use overtly modern architectural styling, for its own sake. There is a sense here that the architects have taken the psychological needs of the children seriously, to create a mature and subtle form of architecture.

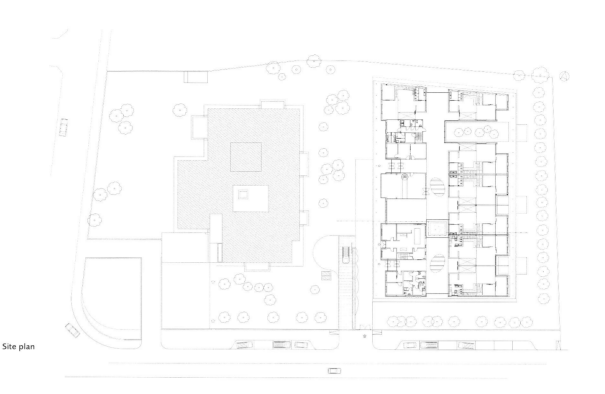

Site plan

Views of covered colonnade providing a natural extension to the interior space out into the gardens | Night view | The central square with views to the courtyard garden, a little bit of outside space captured within the building

San Felice Nursery and Preschool

San Felice, Reggio Emilia, Italy

Architect	ZPZ Partners, Milan
Pupils	42 toddlers 1-2 years, 80 children 3-6 years
Building area	2,300 m² (incl. large kitchen)
Average classroom	18 m²/child (nursery); 11 m²/child (preschool)
Parking spaces	46
Build cost	2.34 million EUR
Completion	2000
Year group system	Age-related groupings in homebase areas

Employs an open and advanced curriculum which has evolved to utilise the environment as 'the third teacher'

Across Europe and the USA there is an on-going period of transition for many educational systems and the environments which support them. Experimental structures are built to deal with a changing educational emphasis, not always with complete success. Generally the architecture must follow the experiments within education rather than it happening the other way around, education following architecture. In some early years systems, such as in the UK for example, there is little recent tradition of state-funded preschool provision upon which to draw for inspiration and guidance. It is not surprising therefore that we all try to draw on the best experience from long standing successful systems which appear to synthesise an educational/care vision with a strong and

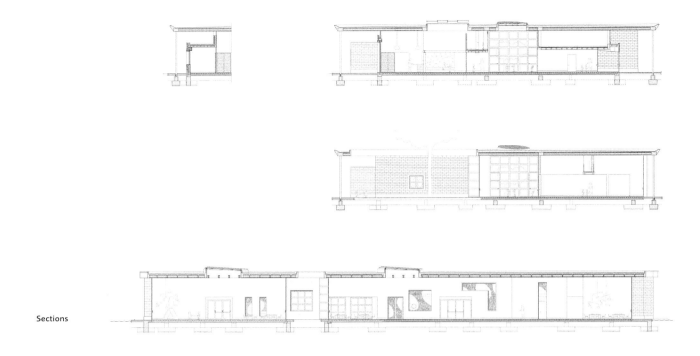

Sections

coherent environmental strategy. One of the most frequently cited examples of such a system is the world
reknowned City of Reggio Emilia Child Care Service,
better known simply as 'Reggio'.

To provide some background to this exemplary system, represented here by its latest projects designed
by ZPZ Partners, we need to go back to 1969 and the
creation of the Scuola Materna Statale, the Italian system of universal early years care for those who want
it. Since then, attendance has risen steadily to the
point where 95% of the children in Reggio Emilia aged
3-5 attend full-time, sometimes six days per week.
Although quality varies from region to region, childcare attracts a large number of votes and is therefore

viewed as an important political expedient. The constitution to protect young children has been national
law in Italy since 1973. However, its general principles
are more precisely defined by the regional administrators and the system is regularly up-dated. One particularly important aspect of the 'child's constitution'
is the requirement that all new facilities are developed
by a multi-disciplinary group comprising local coun-
cillors, architects and pedagogic experts. Modena
distinguishes its child friendly planning strategies by
making them friendly for both boys and girls. The
view that the city is a male-orientated space, predominantly given over to the convenience of the car, is at
the heart of this philosophy. A multi-disciplinary commission – involving teachers, architects, engineers,

solicitors, social workers, psychologists and police
representatives – has been established to influence
the layout of the city and send reminders to adults of
the desire for a child-orientated culture. One of these
projects, for example, introduced street signs which
could be read and understood by young children.

This initiative begins in Modena's kindergartens,
which extend their activities into the community to
become a focus for that community. Parents are given
responsibility and encouraged to organise events
within the kindergarten building at the weekends,
even engaging those who do not have young children themselves. Parent classes and pre-natal groups
meet in the kindergarten rather than in the hospital

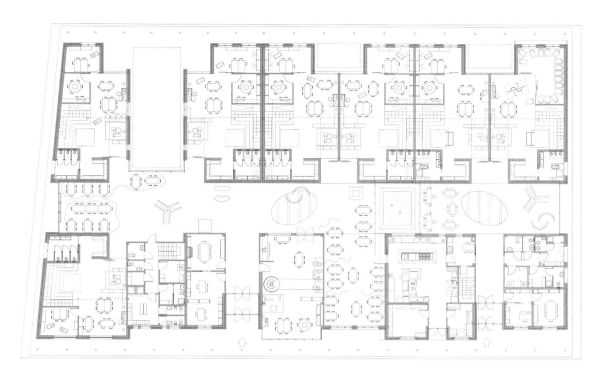

Ground floor plan

or at home, so that insecure parents are supported discreetly during this life changing event. It is recognised that whereas mothers and grandparents might have provided support, knowledge and reassurance in former times, there is now a knowledge gap which is increasingly being addressed through childcare services. Thus a central square is placed at the heart of each childcare centre. This terminology is a deliberate reminder of the urban spaces in Italian cities whose primary benefit is to encourage social interaction. So the central enclosed space is analogous to the public meeting place; here parents, teachers and children make contact with each other, thus fulfilling one of the primary functions of kindergarten life. Within the centres there is a particular emphasis on this idea of

relations, and how they shape the future citizen. It is a concept which is central to the educational philosophy and is based on the development of a long standing child centred philosophy, where the environment is conceived as a complex hybrid, constructed not by selecting and simplifying the elements, but through a fusion of distinct poles (inside and outside, formality and flexibility, material and immaterial), which creates rich and complex conditions.

In the San Felice project, although externally the building appears simple, with a big green flat roof which oversails the orange masonry walls below, within the building you find a rich and vibrant atmosphere which supports activities but never restricts them. The

'homebase' areas are clearly delineated for the age-related groupings for children ranging from 1 year olds to 6 year olds. There is a respect for the individual age ranges with each containing its own range of activity corners, a physical climbing area, a soft corner, an art/wet area and a general play and activity zone. Within this there is also a bright and spacious children's toilet room. The double-height spaces each have their own staircase up to the mezzanine sleeping area on the upper level. It has the feel of a self-contained family apartment, social but small enough to feel cozy and safe for the youngest children. However, the relations children develop are intended to be wider than this small family group. So the central square, which in this example is a more elongated shape, provides the

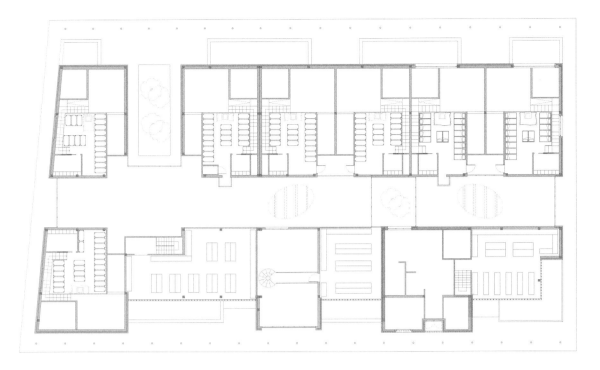

First floor plan

Light plays on the surfaces, an important constituent part of nature which is communicated to children through their environment | Views of activity area with stairway up to mezzanine sleeping area

venue for a range of communal activities where older and younger children can mix together. For example, there is a central dining area with an attached kitchen where good food is prepared but which is also visible to young children through windows from the square. The important social role eating has within Italian society is continually underlined, with children joining their older and younger friends around the dining table. There is very little eating which takes place within the homebase areas. Similarly there is a music room and an art room, suitable for older children but open and visible to others, so that art and creativity are at the centre of school life. And finally there is ready access to the outside play throughout the building, emphasising this notion of inside/outside polarities.

The inner activity areas are discrete but always visible from other communal areas. The illusion of privacy within an open environment is a balance achieved by the subtle definition of different areas and different spaces. Slightly dropped or raised ceiling planes with oval or rectangular cutout rooflights make the ceiling planes as interesting as the floor planes. There is a sense of freedom of movement between the different areas of the building, yet at the same time children are made aware of what is and what is not their own territory.

All of the Reggio projects are experiments in creating children's spaces which incorporate the pedagogic system in a precise way and its reflection as

aesthetically harmonious interior architecture. This is achieved within the context of a clear form treating the architecture as background to the children and their activities. It is spacious, elegant and decorated in a restrained manner so that architectural simplicity is never overwhelmed by the artwork or the activities that take place within. It is a fascinating environment for children providing a balance between social and private spaces in a coherent architectural style.

Site plan

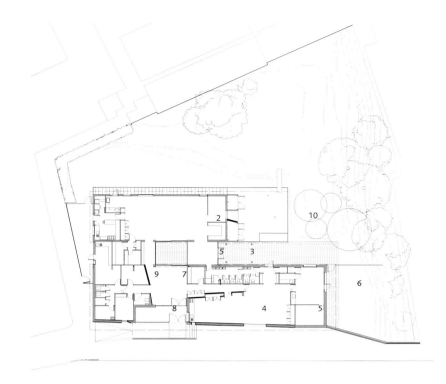

View of the stone wall and horizontal roof plain from the street |
View from the courtyard looking towards the covered outside play
area and storage cupboards | Views into the main activity area show-
ing the even coulorless clearstory lighting

Hoyle
Early Years Centre

Bury, Northwest England, UK

Architect	DSDHA, London
Pupils	40 aged 0-5 years
Building area	435 m²
Average classroom	80 m²
Parking spaces	0
Build cost	695,000 GBP
Completion	2003
Year group system	3 age-related groups 0-5 years

Centre for children with learning difficulties with a distinctive architectural
strategy appropriate to its confined urban site

The design is predicated on a detailed understanding of
the existing context, taking cues from the urban scale of
a worn-down public housing estate built in the 1960s. In
addition, working closely with the present head of centre,
the design extends the concept of 'building upon qualities'; by seeking to understand more detailed aspects of
current childcare practices which work for children and
carers, then extending these principles into a completely
new environment for care and education. Through this
osmotic process, an architecture has emerged which is
new and inspiring, but at the same time one which has
familiar qualities. This enables the users to feel comfortable and at home in their new setting. It is a subtle balance. The building form is a pavilion built into a secure
enclosed courtyard. The courtyard provides a natural

Sections looking north

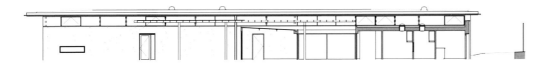

Section looking west

heart to the school, encouraging a sense of well-being and belonging which is focused on the garden. The flat plain of the roof extends out into the garden, which thus has a practical dimension providing a large area of covered outside play area. This powerful architectural device has a symbolic effect, encouraging children to go out and explore, through its expressive horizontality. This effect is further accentuated by the use of clearstory glazing. The roof appears to float above its heavy stone walls. There are integral external storage cupboards and full-height openable window door panels throughout which further extend this rugged inside/outside quality. A new steel frame supports a profiled metal roof approximately 800 millimetres above the walls of the original nursery building. This raised height is infilled with new clearstory glaz-

ing. This principle was extended to the areas of new build to allow for continuous natural light to all areas which is almost devoid of glare. There is little applied colour within the building, rather the intention was to provide an even, almost neutral backdrop for the children and their artistic output. This approach to the architecture is taken further with the use of natural materials throughout. The external enclosure of insulated stud is clad with dry stone walling to the street which builds on the qualities of an existing drystone garden wall. Render is used elsewhere on the garden elevations. The plan is split into two, providing the main nursery accommodation for 3-5 year old children on the west garden side and younger children on the east street side. The two wings are divided by a glazed courtyard and library which seems to draw the

garden into the building's heart. This architectural clarity is calming and helps young children to orientate themselves in the institution. This small building was part of a UK government initiative to encourage imaginative thinking about design for early years and special needs. The development sought to create a distinctive centre for other early years providers within a run-down and dislocated urban quarter adjacent to the M66. The notion of building 'signature architecture' as part of a regeneration strategy was unusual in the locality and has had a galvanising effect on the community at large; the building has become something of a reference point for early years institutions across the region and a source of pride amongst many people in the area.

Site plan with existing Spitalgate School to the right

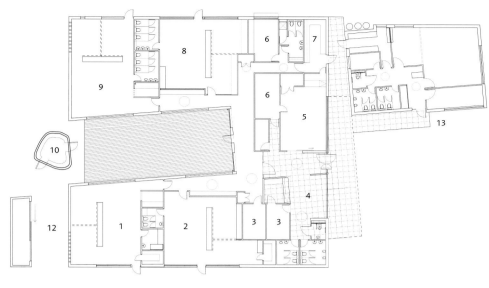

Ground floor plan

1 Babies	8 2-3 years
2 1-1.5 years	9 3-4 years
3 Offices	10 Story room
4 Entrance area	11 Play court
5 Training room	12 Baby garden and storage
6 Staff	13 'Sure Start' centre
7 Kitchen	

End façade at the highest point of the building with child height coloured optic windows | The entrance court with the coloured 'Sure Start' building detached from the main nursery | View from the courtyard looking towards the children's cloakroom area | Activity area | Courtyard with picket fence

National Day Nurseries Association

Grantham, UK

Architect	Mark Dudek with Michael Stiff and Andy Trevillion, London
Pupils	100 preschool children aged 0-4 years
Building area	1,200 m²
Average classroom	120 m²
Parking spaces	12
Build cost	1.2 million GBP
Completion	2003
Year group system	Age-related homebase groupings

Distinctive tapering plan and section to reflect organic growth of children

The National Day Nurseries Association is a charitable organisation responsible for the welfare and support of private nursery providers. They commissioned the architects to work on two of their new regional centres, which combine both private and public childcare support services within this deprived urban community. The building combines private and public funding to provide a balanced high quality environment on a site adjacent to the local state primary school. Part of the provision includes a 'Sure Start' centre, with spaces for training and support to adults within the community. This is a speculative model for early years which attempts to integrate welfare and education services in a new way. The centre at Grantham is predominantly for preschool age children and includes the provision of full daycare for up to 100

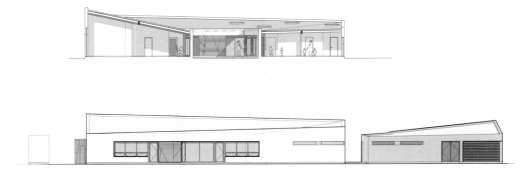

West and south elevations showing the subtly tapering roofline

Cross section through courtyard and children's activity areas

children. Here, the NDNA's remit also includes training and outreach work for its members. There is a study and seminar area which is used by the local university, training future care workers. The end result is a complex building with a main nursery section comprising units for children in groups aged 0-1, 1-1.5 years, 1.5-2 years and finally preschoolers aged 3-4 years with administration all organised around a tapering play corridor (with children's cloakrooms) which leads onto a secure U shaped play courtyard. This is the interface between all age ranges, and provides a theatrical space for a variety of activities. Included is a detached free form 'story-room' which helps to terminate the open end of the courtyard. It is a reference point for children within the main building, a special place for special times. The design develops the

constraints of the room schedule by adopting a metaphor of growth. The idea is that as children grow, so the building should grow; this was taken as a key design idea, with the gentle tapering of the building's form in plan and in section. At its lowest and narrowest point, there is the baby room, an intimate enclosed zone appropriate for the youngest and most vulnerable; the children's activity rooms are ranged in ascending age order around the courtyard, so that the final room for the oldest preschool children is a lofty spacious area, symbolically encouraging children to be more active and adventurous. It gives a subtle twist to the entire building form, within the framework of tight budgetary constraints. The possibility to be different with the new generation of childcare buildings is often limited by both the constraints of the budget and

limited aspirations of many client bodies involved with the development of these buildings. It is often viewed as a hospital type environment with a strong emphasis on security and functionality. This approach tends to exclude the possibility of fantasy and imagination. Here the designers have introduced a clever twist to the design which has a subtle effect on those using the building. There is something not quite right about the rooms, yet this spatial twist is one which switches children onto the space where they reside, often for long periods of time. It is a 'home from home', yet it is also an inspiring place, elegant and designed with the perceptions of young children in mind.

Site plan

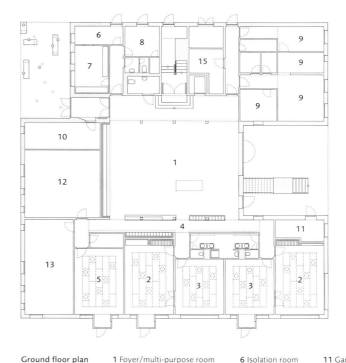

Ground floor plan

1 Foyer/multi-purpose room	6 Isolation room	11 Garden storage
2 Children 0-2 years	7 Office	12 Storage
3 Ancillary room	8 Staff room	13 Services
4 Wardrobe	9 Kitchen	14 Closet
5 Therapy room	10 Strollers	15 Terrace

View from the street | External covered play court on the east side adjacent to the children's garden | Bay window detail | Central first floor courtyard and external staircase

Kindergarten Jerusalemer Straße

Berlin, Germany

Architect	Staab Architekten, Berlin
Pupils	180 aged 0-10 years
Building area	1,280 m²
Average classroom	60 m² each for 12-14 children
Parking spaces	0
Build cost	3.45 million EUR
Completion	2002
Year group system	Year age groupings 0-6 years

A three-storey building for children with distinctive bay windows and internal courtyards creating a modern architectural language of play

Berlin town planning constraints dictated a three-storey form for this new daycare centre. This would be very unusual for an early years building within the UK and deemed to be unsafe. However, here it seems to work well, providing an economical high density solution which through its clever manipulation of form appears on the outside like an urban villa, whereas on the inside it has a light, spacious feel with its subtle volumetric play between solids and voids. At no point does it feel institutional, rather it is an ordered yet playful environment, as if it has been devised by a child manipulating a set of Froebel play blocks.

The architects admit to designing a building for play. There are clear practical requirements to provide a

First floor plan

Section north-south

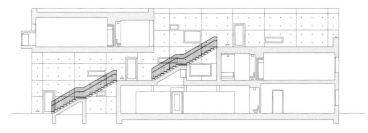

Section west-east

number of self-contained group or activity rooms each of which is age-related with the youngest children at ground floor level and the oldest children on the top second floor, a sense of hierarchy is established. Each pair of rooms supporting the age groupings has its own shared bathroom. Children's cloakrooms are located within the activity areas. The administrative offices and shared group spaces are on the ground floor around the secure entrance loggia.

Within the central core of the block at each level there is a cut out U shaped courtyard or terrace area connected via external stairs to the next level. At the top of the building the terrace appears on the west side and is very open like a roof terrace. The next level

down the terrace steps across to the centre of the building following the staircase down and is much more enclosed. Finally at ground floor the terrace becomes a huge covered play area cut out of the block now located on the east side of the building. It is a natural extension to the children's garden particularly useful on rainy days. Children (under adult supervision) can promenade around the building with confidence; it is readily understandable and highly legible yet holding within it a sense of intrigue, which encourages exploration and extends spatial understanding.

The external treatment supports this legibility by means of coloured render with horizontal banded windows stepping back from the flat-faced façades.

A further element of this composition is the projecting bay windows. They bring a sense of spatial variety, as each balcony/bay is ranged across the three-storey street façades. From the outside they express the sense that this is a building for children as well as for their adult carers. However, the bay windows are also highly functional. Each activity area has one of these bays scaled to the height of a child; smaller groups of children can withdraw from the main activity areas and into their safe elevated little playhouses high above the street.

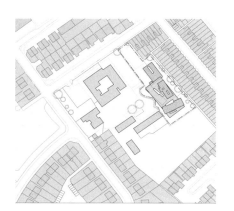

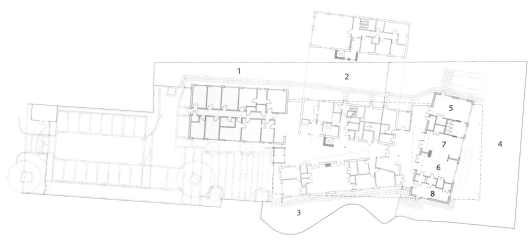

Ground floor plan

1 Block 1: Primary healthcare
2 Block 2: Offices and support spaces
3 Block 3: Family services
4 Block 4: Nursery

5 Preschool children
6 3-4 years
7 Toddlers 2-3 years
8 Babies 0-18 months

Site plan

The building block composition around the main entrance | Rear façade | Main children's activity area showing sliding folding wall panels | Circulation area

Sheerness Children's and Family Centre

Sheerness, Isle of Sheppey, Kent, UK

Architect	Architype, Cinderford
Pupils	50 aged 0-5 years
Building area	1,139 m² (700 m² ground floor)
Average classroom	45 m²
Parking spaces	22
Build cost	2.06 million GBP
Completion	2005
Year group system	Age-related activity areas

A comprehensive range of community accommodations all organised discretely to create several buildings in one

It is important to understand the physical context of Sheerness which is a peninsula isolated from the southeast mainland and with only very few routes helping to bring life and commercial activity to this region. As a consequence the town suffers from high levels of urban deprivation and much child poverty. As a response to this unusual situation, government in collaboration with the North Kent Architecture Centre developed a brief for a new community building which was to be a focus for children and families in the area. The facilities included a family services centre with a children's activity room, a toy library and an SEN room, a primary healthcare pavilion with consulting rooms for local people, and a 50 place nursery. Offices for the government's 'Sure Start' programme were to be housed in a separate block, with ad-

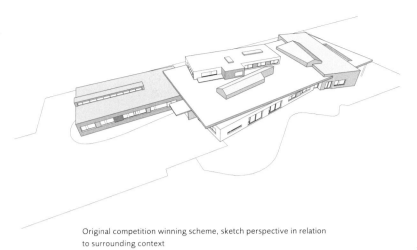

Original competition winning scheme, sketch perspective in relation to surrounding context

Southeast and southwest elevations

ditional community spaces for hire. This complex schedule required a clever architectural response incorporating internal security, clear organisation and sophisticated architectural space making; the trick was to balance security with a welcoming open atmosphere. Architype's planning strategy for the project was to ensure that a clear functional separation was maintained between the various users within the overall framework of a single relaxed community which the architects describe as a 'village'. Distinct uses within the scheme are expressed pavilions, their exteriors painted with warm pastel colours that imprint the building beacon-like on the surrounding landscape. Acting like an arrangement of toy bricks covered over by a single roof, courtyards are formed between the blocks (or pavilions) which are used as the functional

circulation routes and informal social areas. According to the designers, the success of the building lies in the pleasant flow between larger spaces and smaller more intimate spaces, inducing users and visitors alike to feel comfortable and at home. A single shared entrance leads into the circulation spaces. As you move through between the brightly painted external walls of the pavilions, to the calmer colours of the nursery areas, the natural ventilation and generosity of daylight, both top-light and side-light, blurs the distinction between inside and outside. The roof is described as a 'table roof' sliding lightly over the pavilions, shifted off-axis to make the spaces beneath more dynamic, creating dramatic angular perspectives. Light is one of the great qualities of this area, and it is used within the building as an important

modulating device, integral to the perception of space. It floods through rooflights, sometimes angular, sometimes diffused, playfully reflecting off the coloured walls. The interior responds differently to bright sunny days and to overcast conditions. A smattering of coloured glass lights up unexpected corners. Finally mention should be made of the masonry construction, revealed through an exposed panel showing the Planziegel solid clay wall construction. This system reduces cement usage without the need for additional insulation. Lime render and plaster onto the blockwork forms a healthy and breathing construction; this is one of the first time it has been used in the UK, a suitably optimistic detail which sets a caring tone for the future users of this complex structure.

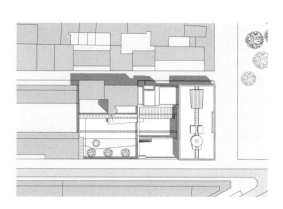

Site plan

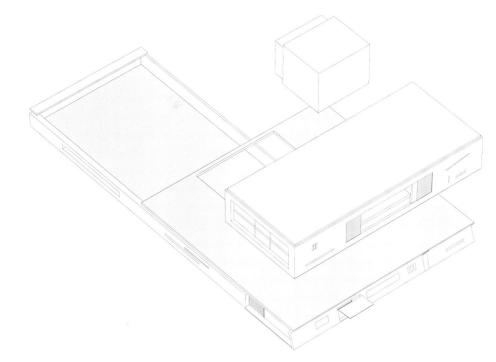

Conceptual isometric view

Children's stage within courtyard with director's block above | View from courtyard illustrates the complex yet legible architectural language | View of children's pavilion floating above the granite base

École Maternelle ZAC Moskowa

Paris, France

Architect	Frédéric Borel Architectes, Paris
Pupils	25-28 per homebase; 8 homebases
Building area	2,000 m²
Average classroom	60 m²
Parking spaces	0
Build cost	2.7 million EUR
Completion	2000
Year group system	3 age-related sections: 3-4 /4-5 /5-6 years

Early years community centre with a distinctive architectural strategy appropriate to its confined urban site

One of the major problems with any educational facility is security and the risk of vandalism when the centre is closed at night and during the weekends. This is of particular concern in high crime areas. Here the architects have made something of a virtue of this practical consideration designing a building which is predominantly closed and secure on its vulnerable ground floor with small windows and shutters, but open on its first floor with large windows and a roof garden. The architects describe this organising principle in child centric terms as a 'fortress-like' plinth; the more open glazed upper level connects visually to the city beyond. This hierarchy is given further expression through the use of materials; there is solid grey granite cladding on the ground floor, with predominantly glazed or white rendered panels

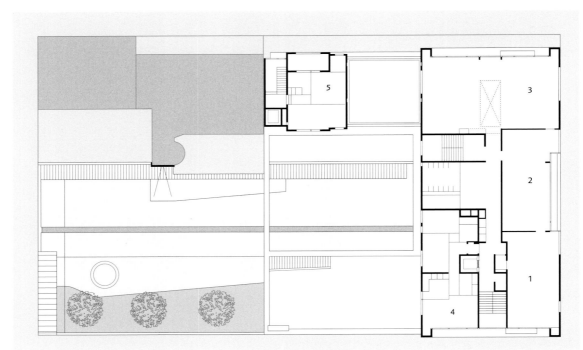

Second floor plan
1 Children's activity (homebase 1)
2 Children's activity (homebase 2)
3 Children's activity (homebase 3)
4 Garden room
5 Director's suite

to the first floor structure, a lighter finish which is more expressive of the openness of the children themselves. This material clarity is carried through into the building's functional layout with all children's activity spaces on the open upper level, and areas for more discreet activities such as sleeping on the closed ground floor. Staircases, lifts and circulation corridors are clearly and simply set out to provide a building which is not only legible in elevation, through the way it looks from the outside, but also in terms of its plan layout. The architects strongly believe that it is important for children to be able to understand their environment. Children learn from everything particularly during the early years, but they must be capable of understanding the place within which they live on the most basic levels. It follows therefore that the coherence

and legibility of the internal organisation, reflected on the external façades, communicates crucial lessons which will contribute to their educational development and sense of well-being. This architecture of clarity is well illustrated in the axonometric study where the three primary forms are described. There is the base with its small expressive windows and security shutters, the first floor main block with its large curtain glazing and a third block, floating enigmatically away from the other two elements, containing the administration offices. The whole assemblage wraps around an inner space, which acts as a semi-public courtyard for social events, and the children's secure playground at all other times. It contains a small cultivation garden where children can plant vegetables and see them grow.

The organising principle can be interpreted firstly as the children's world contained within the first floor block, where they may relate themselves and their emerging personalities to the city beyond the confines of the day-care institution, secondly as the adult world of control and a certain amount of discipline contained within the slightly austere, detached block floating away to the north and thirdly as the base structure, solid and secure and perhaps expressive of the community itself. It all goes to make a building which is immensely practical in terms of the paradoxical needs children have: security and protection from a sometimes hostile public realm on the one hand, and an environment which is open to exploration and imaginative interpretation on the other.

Section

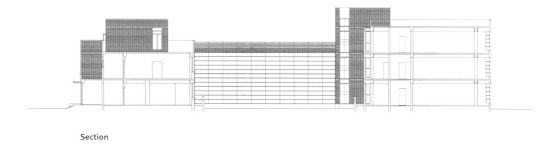

Elevation

Model view | Street façade | Courtyard | Circulation zone | Activity space

Shenyang Xiaohajin International Kindergarten

Shenyang, China

Architect	Shenyang Huaxin Designers, Shenyang
Pupils	180 aged 3-6 years
Building area	3,030 m²
Average classroom	85 m²
Parking spaces	7
Build cost	5 million RMB
Completion	2004
Year group system	11 classes, 3 grades

Education nursery with child-orientated features

As the Chinese economy gears up for the development of its industrial base over the next ten years, the need for childcare is becoming increasingly urgent. Many new childcare developments are exploring an approach which emphasises functionality, with relatively large child numbers, wrapped up in a sympathetic child-orientated architectural form and usually located close to new residential areas. What makes these early years facilities particularly distinctive is their separation from the school; instead they are designed as stand alone institutions. One of the most recent is this 180 place nursery and daycare facility at the entrance to the New Riverside development in the suburbs of Shenyang in the northeastern province of Liaoning. A constrained site has necessitated a tightly organised arrangement which fits well into its semi-ur-

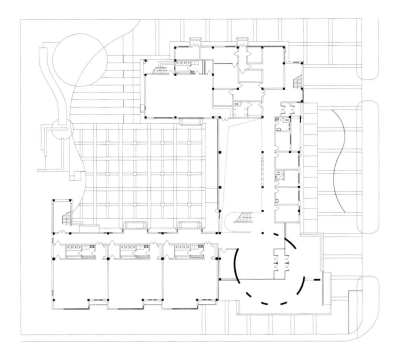

Ground floor plan

First floor plan

ban setting. According to designer Ma Tao, three principle constraints dictated the planning strategy. Firstly the tight site, secondly the need to optimise south light for internal and external activity areas and finally the residential building which blocks the further development of the kindergarten on its northern end. As a result the building was arranged around a courtyard yet only on two sides.

Conceptually, the designer viewed this as an exercise in urban design, describing it as a castle or a toy house. With three storeys of classroom activity areas on the south side and a two storey block on the north side containing two identical classrooms, all stacked one on top of the other it is easy to understand why. The third element is a linking eastern block which acts as the main communal hall just inside the entrance. It is an almost monumental double-height space with gigantic window-roof lights orientated directly onto the courtyard garden. There is a play of large scale set against smaller and smaller scale parts, all the way down to the children's play houses in the activity areas. The choice of façade materials is intended to enhance the idea of the city as collage, with a mixture of red-brickwork and yellow render mingling with large panel bay windows. Other twists such as an elliptical oval shaped access ramp which forms the southeastern corner of the block provides appropriate distractions for the users. This ovoid is directly over the entrance lobby, the concave and convex forms play against each other. The nine classrooms are set out in regular bays each with angled bay windows orientated to the southeast to optimise daylight. There is a sense of rhythm to the façades, with a horizontal emphasis with indented mini balconies, small-scale windows and extract unit feature panels connecting the vertical emphasis of the stacked classroom units. This building illustrates the tentative nature of designing for children in China. It is playful yet serious and functional at the same time. Every child can develop their own particular view of the building, its internal spaces, its external details and its imagery. However, there is something of a mismatch between the architecture and the interior design resulting in some strange junctions and difficult relationships between inside and outside. Yet this should not distract from the fresh vibrant spirit of the architecture itself.

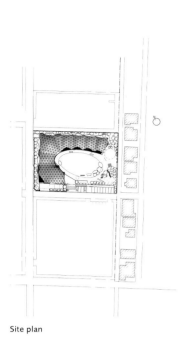

Site plan

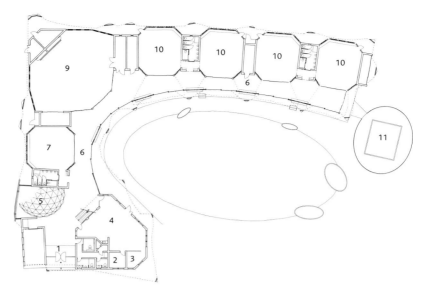

Ground and first floor plans

1 Entrance
2 Health room
3 Principal's room
4 Staff room
5 Library

6 Corridor
7 Communication room
8 Storage
9 Playroom
10 Classroom

11 Pool
12 Conference room
13 Consultation room
14 Data room

The internal play garden framed by the building | High level view showing the entire site with its two-storey entrance block on the left and open-air pool on the right | Interior views

Bubbletecture Maihara Kindergarten

Maihara, Japan

Architect	Shuhei Endo Architect Institute, Osaka
Pupils	80 aged 3-6 years
Building area	1,323 m²
Average classroom	60 m²
Parking spaces	8
Build cost	380 million JPY
Completion	2003
Year group system	Age-related groupings in 20 children classes

Organic, expressive architecture designed with the spiritual well-being of children in mind

The architect describes the building as a continuous wave structure, made almost exclusively of natural timber in the form of short timber beams joined in a 'space frame' structure held together with hexagon shaped metal fittings. Timber is viewed as a traditional material and therefore must be used in its purest form; no laminates are permitted. The zinc roof, like the structure itself, runs down to the ground. The result is a roof covering which has a strong natural atmosphere reminiscent of Steiner architecture from the 1920s. Although the plan comprises four nursery spaces and a large community room, the conventional square or rectangular spaces of most childcare buildings are dissolved into a three-dimensional sculpture of unusual spatial qualities. The sculpture's very structural ambi-

North and east elevations

guity makes its edges stretch out into the surrounding garden suggesting a tree or similar organic form to be found in nature.

As the architect himself has stated, this approach is intended to subvert the conventional cut-off between inside and outside, and the prescribed fixed room form which most childcare buildings have. This highly intellectual vision of a building for children is based on the principle that, as young children play in random patterns, they should be allowed a degree of freedom within their play spaces for random spontaneous play, for chance encounters with others and the ability to change and adapt their environment just as any woodland creature might do. As the roof is both

structurally and spatially independent of the internal spaces and subdivisions, change would and should be expected. The form of the building is a metaphorical comment on this take on childhood. It is also an elegant, unusual form, which has a very strong presence in the city.

This is a building which defies conventional definitions since its walls are integral to its roof plan. In some ways the conventional four space plan is at odds with the expressive free-flowing roof structure. It is a big roof, a single flowing, folding shape drooping down to the ground. There are no roof gutters, and nothing penetrates the single, albeit folded planes of the big roof. The plan (and structure of the roof) twist

and curve around the internal play space, enclosing and sheltering both inside and outside. Although it is predominantly single-storey, there is a two-storey 'pavilion', which provides a large communal entrance with adjacent staff accommodation and on the first floor a conference facility that can be used when the rest of the building is closed off. A large outdoor swimming pool, an important community facility within this humid climate, also provides natural therapeutic play for young children.

Special Schools

The term 'special school' refers to provision for children with special educational needs and disabilities. Due to the stigma attached to these people in the past, very little emphasis was placed on designs which had a progressive or an even vaguely inclusive architectural-educational convergence. In the past, physical deformity and dysfunctional behaviour was viewed as being a social services task rather than an education issue; for a long time it tended to be swept under the carpet. Learning difficulties such as dyslexia were hardly recognised up until the 1980s and autistic spectrum disorder was viewed as being beyond therapy with the confinement of children away from public scrutiny being the only real strategy.

Fortunately, over relatively recent times, this view has changed fundamentally. With the acceptance that special needs children can and should be educated and can be cared for within an appropriate school setting (albeit with additional assistance), what could be described as a new building type has emerged. Since 1994, UK Government policy has been committed to including pupils with special educational needs and disabilities into mainstream schools as part of an ethical view which aims to recognise and celebrate human diversity. Similar initiatives have been implemented across mainland Europe. Where it works well, inclusion benefits all students. However, sometimes it does not function effectively due to a mismatch between facilities in mainstream schools and those required in special needs settings.

On the whole it is a laudable aim to include pupils with special educational needs and disabilities into mainstream schools, to dissolve traditional views and stigmas associated with those who are 'different'. Yet some recent evidence suggests that those students on the more extreme end of the disability spectrum need and deserve their own purpose designed buildings, as much as young children need specific early years settings. Furthermore, special schools can and should provide particular environmental qualities which actively enhance and support the special needs of their users. As design strategies have evolved, a more various range of facilities have been developed to cater for specific needs across the spectrum whilst maintaining strong connections to mainstream education wherever possible.

For example, children in the middle to extreme range of the autistic spectrum disorder, may have tendencies towards physical violence, usually to themselves, and they may exhibit sudden irrational behaviour such as the desire to run away. This requires a particular view of security and safety, consideration for the design of the building enclosure to avoid sharp, hard surfaces is another dimension of the agenda. Research has shown the need to avoid daunting repetitive patterns, as autistic children are also prone to severe concentration problems. The use of a limited amount of colour and an ordered window or door arrangement to create pleasing rhythms within the architecture may help to support their special needs in this respect. Whatever their need, a close and in depth process of consultation with teachers and carers should be developed which is specific to those stakeholders. Special schools are rarely standard designs as you might expect with a primary school.

Today there are many different approaches being developed. For example, partnerships between special and/or mainstream schools located on different sites with pupils and staff travelling between the two schools sharing facilties and skills can be a viable strategy. A better approach is two separate schools which are designed as distinct institutions co-located on the same site. Here there may be opportunities for pupils to share spaces, such as assembly halls, sports facilities as well as teaching resources, without sacrificing the need for the safety and security of a specific building. All mainstream schools are required to consider resources for current and future pupils with special educational needs and disabilities.

For obvious reasons, many of the featured case studies deal with the institution as a self-contained village, completely separate from the mainstream school. The Pistorius School for Disabled Children (pages 96-99) is a case in point. Catering for children with mental and physical disabilities, it accommodates a total of 150 students which all have a personal learning plan, tailored to their specific capabilities. This enables individuals to develop at their own pace, with teachers catering for specific needs. In this situation the presence of children without mental disabilities is viewed as a drag to educational effectiveness. However, the sense of a collective belonging to the larger social group is still viewed as being important. Therefore the school has worked towards larger group events which help students to achieve this sense of belonging to a whole school community.

Pupils with learning difficulties or disabilities gain a great deal from outdoor practical experiences. Especially those who are not physically disabled but have learning difficulties have been found to gain confidence and become more relaxed when working outdoors, which is why the outside areas attached to special schools must be designed with this in mind. Interaction with the natural world, with animals such as rabbits and larger livestock has proved to have tremendous therapeutic benefits.

There are certainly advantages for the whole school community when inclusive strategies and design features are incorporated into an existing school. For example, improvements in acoustic conditions that aid students with hearing impairments will help all students. Improvements to the layout and internal design of shared areas such as corridors will promote positive changes in student behaviour throughout the community. However at this point it is fair to conclude that there is or can be no definitive guide to designing for special needs. The challenge for any design group is to build on the existing knowledge which is usually available as design guidance and/or statutory requirements at government level (such as the requirements of the Disability Discrimination Act, 2004), whilst at the same time treating the community as unique and special as implied by the term 'special school'.

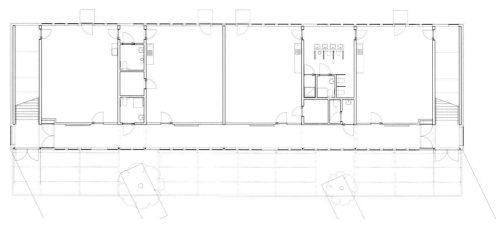

Ground floor plan

Site plan: **1** New building | **2** Play court

Exterior views showing the random window patterning which gives
the functionality of the layout a playful aspect | External landscape
and covered outside canopy | Typical classroom interior with window
wall rhythm to provide space for heating, ventilation and view | View
of first floor access corridor

BSBO De Bloesem School

St. Truiden, Belgium

Architect	VBM Architecten, Heverlee
Pupils	approx. 40 aged 6-12 years
Building area	848 m²
Average classroom	55 m²
Parking spaces	n/a
Build cost	1 million EUR
Completion	2006
Year group system	Special needs groups of max. 15 pupils

An economical system build, which provides functional yet playful building
forms with the use of randomly placed windows

The existing institution is located in the small town of
St. Truiden, Belgium. The site is close to the town centre and is an attractive park-like setting. Initially the option considered was to restore the existing 1950s pavilions on the site and effect minimum disruption to the life
of the institution. However, this was seen as impractical
and too inflexible an approach. Therefore a phased process of replacement was adopted starting with the construction of a two-storey classroom block comprising
eight classrooms arranged in pairs with associated storage and bathroom zones in-between. Close contact between the new buildings and the existing mature landscape was something the client wished to maintain, so it
seemed obvious to the designers that the existing footprint should be followed, replacing the worn-out blocks

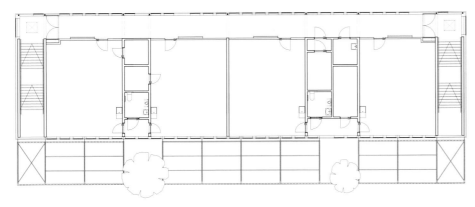

First floor plan

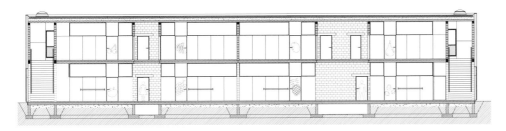

Longitudinal section

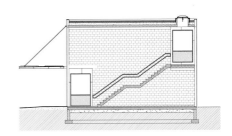

Cross section

with new buildings to benefit from the excellent orientation of the existing blocks. The T form of the existing will be retained and gradually replaced as a series of phased works with the architects preparing a master plan, which maintains the connectivity between inside and outside spaces. Eventually new buildings will wrap round the site edges with an elongated backbone on the street side and 'fingers' extending into the green spaces. The park and the building appear like two interlocking hands, providing spatial intimacy for its users. The school educates children with special needs, including two classes for those within the autistic spectrum of behavioural difficulty. Developing their architecture in close consultation with a team of special needs education experts, the designers noted that one of the key conceptual requirements was to stimulate the users and the need to orientate children with a simple built form, similar to the existing. The use of a limited colour palette inside the new building also facilitates orientation. Basic coding of classrooms with the use of coloured floor surfaces and coloured door icons (different for each room) ensures that the messages the children receive are filtered and not too confusing. However, perhaps the most important aspect of the new environment is what the architects describe as 'randomised rhythms,' a clear theme to be seen on the fenestration design. The windows, which are all the same size, are slipped past one another, either seemingly hanging from the ceiling plane or sitting on the floor plane. They are grouped apparently at random; there appears to be no correspondence between the lower and upper floors, yet despite this seeming randomness, there is a definite rhythm which makes the end result a complex visual harmony. It becomes like an abstract pattern, which is fascinating to follow, yet totally logical and consistent when viewed from inside.

Often when architects work with education experts, the way in which they respond is open to a range of interpretations. The architect's interpretation can end up being in profound conflict with the original intentions of the client who is trying to communicate subtle messages about learning, in a language, which architecturally, is far from subtle. Conceived as a flexible yet repetitive construction system, here the whole design is in harmony with the fundamental views on how these children will learn best.

Site plan showing the two schools with the UCL Academy at the top

Front entrance to the school with garden: Buses arrive via this route and drop the children under the canopy | Model of the school showing each element of the building with the two main wings of accommodation linked at high level by the staff room, the main school hall (with bridge link) and research centre | The drop off area at the front of the building is used as a play and teaching area for life skills such as traffic awareness

Swiss Cottage
SEN School

Camden, London, UK

Architect	Penoyre & Prasad, London
Pupils	230
Building area	7,415 m² (18,000 m² both schools)
Average classroom	60 m²
Parking spaces	45
Completion	2012
Build cost	19 million GBP (for both schools)
Year group system	Age-related groups, 3 form entry for children and students aged 3-19 years

A building which defines a new type of anti-institutional architecture

Swiss Cottage SEN (Special Educational Needs) School is co-located with UCL Academy on a complex site in Camden in central London. It is one of the largest SEN schools in the UK and brings together children with a very wide range of conditions, including severe physical disabilities and autism.

Well known for their expertise in education, Penoyre & Prasad have designed a building distinguished by sophisticated architectural massing which suggests a village of distinctive school departments rather than a single monolithic block. Thus the early years department, can be clearly identified from the outside firstly because each has its own entrance and secondly by its distinctive external play areas, unusually located at rooftop level. This

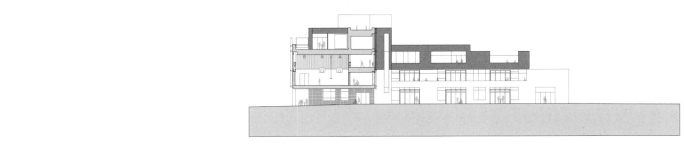

Section and elevation

clarity is further enhanced by a colour language inside combined with a strong palette of construction materials. At street level the entire composition locks together like a giant construction set, an appropriate metaphor for a building which is predicated on the idea of 'learning through play.' The school's ethos emphasises integration rather than segregating by disability type. Here children with different needs are brought together in refined classroom environments which support them with appropriate therapy resources. The whole school is divided into three smaller schools, lower, middle and upper, each with its own dining area. Given that many children will spend their entire school education in this building, providing a sense of identity and progression through the three sub-schools was important. As in the adjacent UCL

Academy, which is a more traditional secondary school, the external pre-cast concrete cladding is coloured differently for each department. External terraces which are a key element of each learning cluster, are treated like outside rooms in their own right with the 'walls' lined either with warm timber cladding or flush glazing. There are over 250 staff in the school. Academic terms are much longer than for mainstream schools as the support that the school offers is vital to the children's families throughout the year. A spacious staff room sits on the top floor of the structure, alongside the research centre, with its own roof terrace. Parking spaces are also provided on site as many teachers travel long distances and the car parking offer is important for recruitment and long term staff retention.

Outside every bit of ground works hard within the confined site. For example the drop-off area for the morning buses, lined with a glass and timber canopy along the length of the building's street frontage, is secured during the school day and used as a play and teaching zone for life skills such as road crossing.

In the construction of two schools with their own innovative approach to education, matched in terms of complexity and difficulty by a site which is bounded by a conservation area, two busy roads and a welter of internal landform issues such as an underground rail tunnel and high voltage power cabling, Penoyre & Prasad have risen to the challenge with deceptive ease.

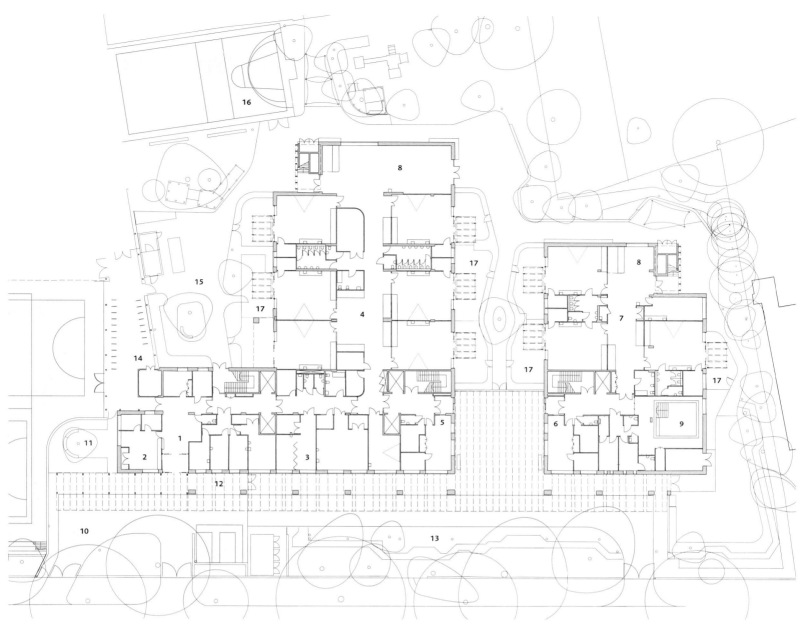

Ground floor plan

1 Entrance foyer
2 Main reception
3 Therapy Suite
4 Middle School
5 School sub-reception
6 School sub-reception
7 Lower School
8 Dining
9 Hydrotherapy Suite
10 Arrival court
11 Visitors' garden
12 Drop-off zone
13 Life Skills area
14 Cycle parking
15 Productive gardens
16 Kickabout space
17 Outdoor classrooms

The external terraces which provide additional break-out space for small group play | Adventure playground with UCL Academy buildings in the background

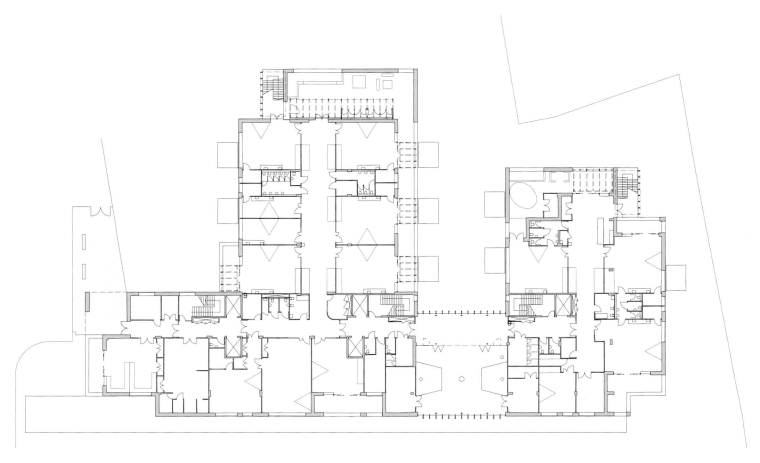

First floor plan

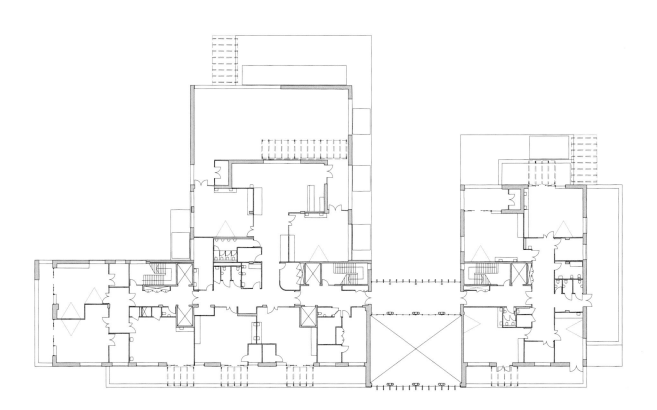

Second floor plan

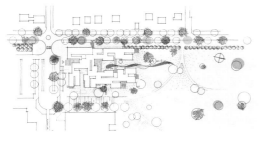

Site plan

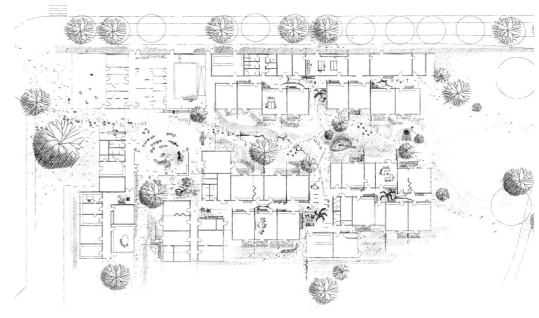

Ground floor plan

Overall view | Southwest façade details | Views of courtyard garden showing retractable blinds

Pistorius School for Disabled Children

Herbrechtingen, Germany

Architect	Behnisch, Behnisch & Partner, Stuttgart
Pupils	150 aged 6-16 years
Building area	4,450 m²
Average classroom	48 m²
Parking spaces	2 for buses
Build cost	10.5 million EUR
Completion	2005
Year group system	6-9 students per classroom

A family house concept in a village of separate buildings

The architects won the commission in a competition run by the municipal government of the Heidenheim district. Their two key ideas were to shape a supportive educational environment and to integrate the school into its natural setting. In consultation with school staff, the initial ideas developed and matured around the concept of the 'family house'. This family house concept provides a sense of the individual school areas, whilst also maintaining its identity as a single institution through a coherent architectural language. The scale and general organisation supports teachers in their role as surrogate parents. Each classroom or 'home' is expressed as an independent entity, whilst physically connected to and being an integral part of the whole institution. Scaled-down furniture, natural timber finishes,

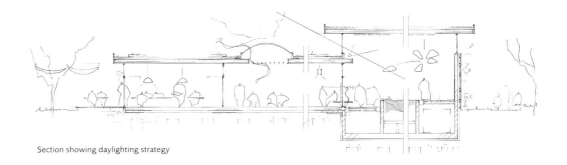

Section showing daylighting strategy

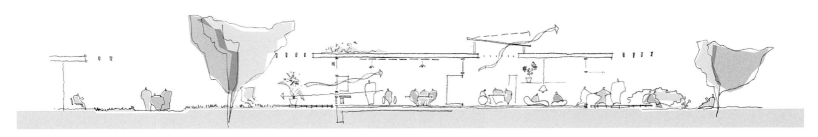

Section showing natural ventilation strategy

red and white desks, sunny wall colours and clean un-cluttered rooms provide a safe haven. The symbolic hearth in each classroom area is a central point covered by a barrel-vaulted skylight that filters daylight into the heart of each individual 'family' space.

However, that is not the end of the story. Since education is essentially a social experience, outside the home, students should become aware of the wider world. The classroom blocks are loosely formed into a U shape, enclosing outside spaces. Here there are ready connections to other adjacent classrooms and internal mini courtyards. From the security of their 'homebases' they can venture out into the slightly less secure yet protected terraces and landscaped mini

courtyards which relate spatially to each classroom. The protective layering extends towards the wider context. For example on its south side, a block of administrative offices are positioned as a buffer to the road, the public world outside. Thus the private realm of the school is separated and protected by the physical shape of the architecture. The communal heart of the complex is the entrance foyer, a village square where children and teachers cross paths during the day and where concerts and plays can be staged.

The horizontally orientated structure is simply articulated in its natural and renewable building materials. It is a composite structure of timber paneled frames braced with reinforced concrete. However, the feel is of a pre-

dominantly timber building, which is appropriate both in terms of the site on the edge of the Swabian forest, and because of the local industry focusing on timber engineering and the production of furniture. Free floor plans without load bearing walls ensure that the building is readily adaptable to a range of different functions and layouts. It is a building which can be easily expanded in the future. For the moment it is a charming and humane environment ideally suited to the practical and spiritual needs of its users. This kind of architecture does not come cheap, probably four times the cost of a traditional school building, however it is a mark of a humane society recognising the special needs of those with little or no voice in society.

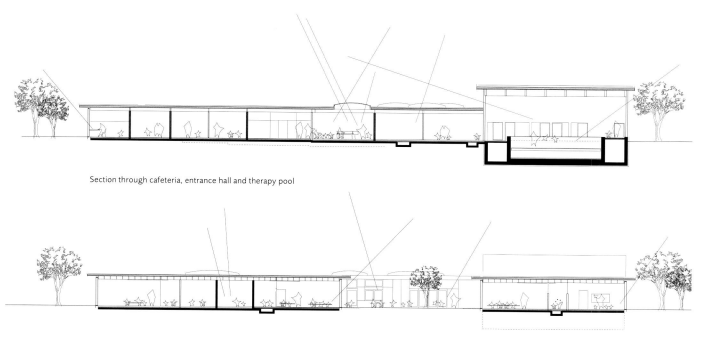

Section through cafeteria, entrance hall and therapy pool

Section through classroom and community spaces

Circulation space with rooflight | Classroom | Circulation area showing structural clarity of roof and wall with strategic use of high level glazing | Therapy pool with lightweight roof floating above space

The technology of the building is worthy of further mention. With its compact, deep-plan pavilion arrangement, the necessity to get both natural light and ventilation into the centre of the development is critical, in order to maintain comfort and assert the light open ethos of its woodland setting. The designers were particularly aware of the ventilation problems surrounding the therapy pool area, with its high air change requirements. They were also careful to avoid the deadening institutional feel of the dark airless central circulation corridor, a common mistake in many schools which adopt a double aspect classroom arrangement.

The cross section showing dining hall, entrance hall and therapy pool is a good illustration of the natural ventilation system at work, which the scheme adopts to counter the deep plan throughout; solar penetration within the hall is controlled yet also facilitated by way of high level automatically opening clearstory windows, to provide a warming atmosphere (with the added benefit of relaxing views towards the forest canopy beyond for those floating in the pool), whilst ventilated rooflights in the adjacent rooms enable the exhaust air to be sucked out by the 'stack' effect (where the surface of the rooflight heats up and attracts the hot air by way of convection).

Similarly, the section through the classroom and community area is aired by a broken roof line with a high level floating linear rooflight over the corridor/circulation zone. This provides natural ventilation which runs through the classroom section from east to west with low level ventilation sucked in through the classroom perimeter windows. Specially designed high level acoustically treated ventilation baffles along the corridor walls are provided so that the necessary separation for acoustic privacy is facilitated without sacrificing the need for continuous ventilation. Perimeter windows are protected from the sun and the rain by a projecting roof line together with extending solar canopies on all south- or west-facing elevations.

This is a mature building which has a sustainability ethos at its core. It is not 'high tech' or obvious in its use of technology, yet it is a technically highly intel-

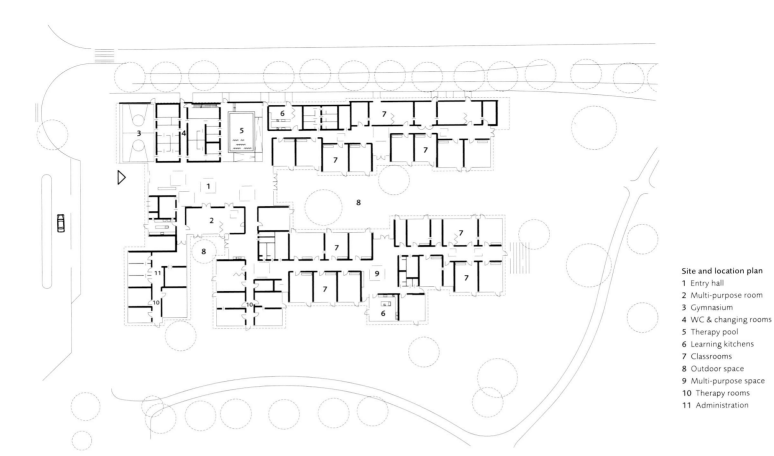

Site and location plan
1 Entry hall
2 Multi-purpose room
3 Gymnasium
4 WC & changing rooms
5 Therapy pool
6 Learning kitchens
7 Classrooms
8 Outdoor space
9 Multi-purpose space
10 Therapy rooms
11 Administration

ligent design which has taken a great deal of development within its system build approach. This is very much a 'touchy, feely' piece of architecture, it almost melts into the background. It marries timber design with the need for privacy and community to create something which is inherently comfortable for its users. The flexible nature of its technology is complemented by the environmental strategy which is sustainable and easy to control locally. The ordered clarity of each and every element on show to the users reinforces the idea of the building as a visual narrative, a lesson in its own right, which orientates and calms its users, so that they can concentrate on the important task of their own social and educational development.

Site plan; the new school is shaded dark, the existing primary school is shaded light

Ground floor plan, entrance area overlooking multi-purpose hall and retreat

Special School
Sursee

Sursee, Switzerland

Architect	Scheitlin-Syfrig+Partner, Luzern
Pupils	45 aged 4-18 years
Building area	2,600 m²
Average classroom	70 m²
Parking spaces	0
Build cost	9 million CHF
Completion	1999
Year group system	Special small ability groups

The architectural treatment creates an open, transparent building

This modern structure could be a stylish headquarters building for a public corporation. In fact it functions extremely well as a school for children with physical and learning difficulties and adapts the requirements of its brief to the existing context. The three open cortiles which puncture the coherence of its glazed façade to the west not only provide light and ventilation but also create a sense of openness inside, promoting the idea of spatial transparency from the outside. It is a simple effect yet also one which represents a distinctive approach to this building type. It is open and closed at the same time, secure from general public access, yet displaying its life to the surrounding city streets and adjacent primary school, rather than hiding its functions away from view, as is often the case with special schools.

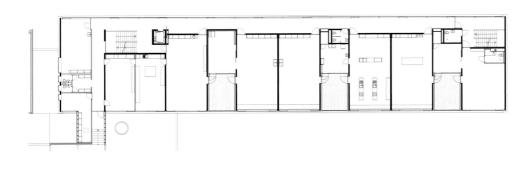

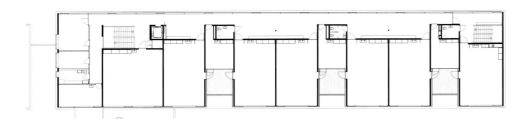

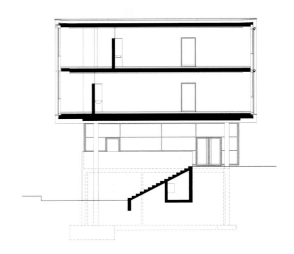

First and second floor plans with open double-height courtyards (shaded)

Cross section showing linking stair between lower and upper levels

Façade to lower level outside sports area | Elevation from upper entrance court showing the three double-height cortiles cut out of the glazed block | Corridor interior | Classroom interiors

In fact the relationship this special school has to the existing school with which it shares the site is an important one. Rather than closing itself off from the primary school the design endeavours to encourage actual physical contact between the two. Not only does it share external play areas, with a lower entrance play court and an upper area for sports (both linked by a broad connecting staircase beneath the new building), it actually shares the sports and multi-purpose hall, both visually and physically. The architecture therefore acts formally to encourage contact between the two schools. The school's main entrance at the north end of the new block hooks onto the existing school's hall, and provides direct access to bleacher seating which overlooks activities in the multi-purpose hall by way of openable windows/doors. The highly glazed en-

trance is also used as a gallery for the work of the students which is visible from the outside. This provides a setting where both 'sides' can, from time to time come together and celebrate the shared experience of education and social interaction. Other shared spaces on the ground floor further extend this concept of compatibility, with a library and what the architects describe as a 'retreat', a sort of soft lounge area where students can chill out and relax outside the confines of a formal school setting. Above ground floor the special school retains its own autonomy by emphatically separating the main teaching areas from the ground floor shared social zones. On the first floor, there are practical teaching areas, workshops for arts and crafts and the schools' demonstration kitchen. There is also a small staff kindergarten and teacher's rooms. On

the second floor there are classrooms with smaller therapy rooms interspersed along the length of the block. The open double-height courtyards mentioned previously encourage a spatial flexibility with students sharing areas and maintaining visual and verbal connections between the two levels of accommodation. This contributes significantly to the social coherence of this relatively small learning community. The complex sectional drawing shows how the new building runs along the site slope, accommodating the site level change between the upper outside play area on the west and the lower court on the east. The design also incorporates a large basement storage archive for the city, a further representation of its functional and spatial dexterity.

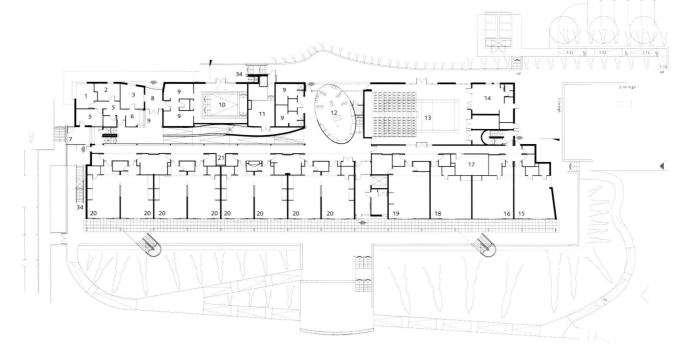

Ground floor plan

1 Head teacher	9 Changing	17 IT suite
2 Medical room	10 Hydro therapy pool	18 Food tech
3 Administration	11 Plant room	19 Profound and multiple
4 Lobby	12 Library	learning difficulties (PMLD)
5 Parents' room	13 Sports/dining hall	20 Classroom
6 Reception	14 Kitchen	21 Calming recess
7 Parents' terrace	15 Music and drama	
8 Entrance lobby	16 Design tech	

Rear façade and main entrance | Elevation to playing fields |
Central access ramp | Sports hall with 'bleacher' seating

Osborne School

Winchester, UK

Architect	Hampshire County Council Architects
Pupils	170 aged 11-18 years
Building area	3,646 m² (723 m² boarding)
Average classroom	49.5 m² (8-10 pupils)
Parking spaces	56
Build cost	5.9 million GBP
Completion	2003
Year group system	Inclusive MLD/SLD/PHLD keystage groups

Split section exploiting site topography with 'light' two-storey classroom
block and 'heavy' communal spaces at back

The general layout of this secondary special school for children with complex learning difficulties relates to the site constraints with a railway cutting and city water main to the western boundary and a primary Romano-British cemetery to the south. The sloping site suggested a two-storey solution would be more efficient and cost effective than the traditional single-storey convention for this building type; that presented an unusual challenge for a school dealing with special needs. Special schools usually adopt a single-storey form for obvious accessibility and safety reasons. Here the compact planning has resulted in a much more integrated solution which is nevertheless negotiable and user friendly. The new buildings run in a linear form along an existing narrow terrace with levels relating closely to the topography to minimise its

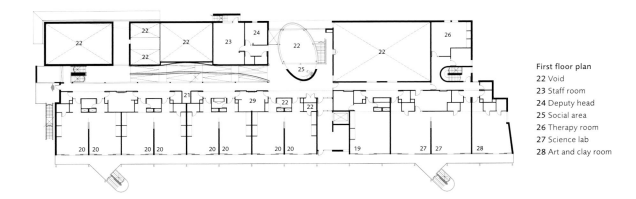

First floor plan
22 Void
23 Staff room
24 Deputy head
25 Social area
26 Therapy room
27 Science lab
28 Art and clay room

Cross section east-west

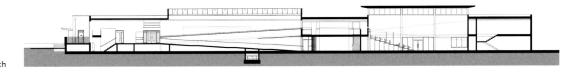

Longditudinal section south-north

environmental impact. The cross section is organised in three parts, a two-storey classroom block facing the playing fields, a central circulation spine which is a double-height volume along most of its length and a more solid rear block which acts as a shield to the railway line. A low key but clearly legible entrance brings the visitor directly into the main circulation spine. From the mid-level foyer, the layout of the whole building is apparent. A long top-lit ramp dominates the south end of the plan and leads to a double-height elliptical library at the centre; it breaks the linearity of the rest. Glass blocks bathe this space in diffuse light on even the dullest of days. The hydrotherapy pool and main hall to the west can be accessed independently for community use. Classrooms on both levels connect directly onto the playing fields to the east. First floor

classrooms open out onto a continuous balcony. Crucially this secondary means of escape allows the main circulation spine to be open and barrier free. The stairs, ramps and large central lift animate the interior and provide opportunities for life skills and mobility training. General teaching areas are paired and interconnected with sliding doors for flexible use. Hygiene and toilet facilities are dispersed along the access galleries for convenient and direct access. This arrangement has eradicated bullying and graffiti which was commonplace in the former school building with its dark unsupervised corridors. Interior finishes are simple and robust with a limited palette of colours to allow the school community to take ownership with their own displays of colour and creativity. The building axis is orientated north to south and a deep 'brise soleil' to

the east controls solar gain and glare; the central rooflight is glazed with high performance solar control glass with opening vents which are interlinked to glass louvers to the south and west façades providing controllable fresh air on the hottest days. The building envelope is externally insulated and employs the thermal mass of solid PFA block walls and a central concrete ramp core to modulate internal temperatures. All classrooms are naturally cross-ventilated; large rectangular sunpipes provide stack ventilation and daylight to the rear of the ground floor classrooms. Elsewhere maximum use of natural daylight is utilised to achieve good lighting conditions and optimum energy conservation. The ecological theme is further emphasised with a new loft area ('roost') built in to provide a home for indigenous Piperstrelle bats.

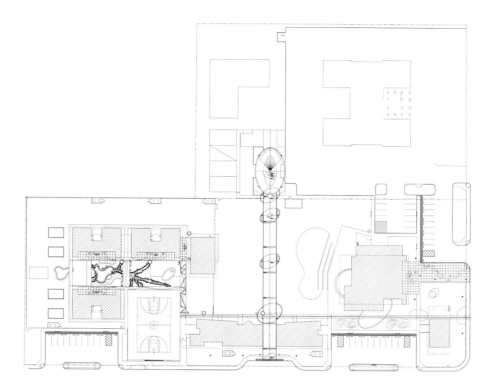

Site plan

Pavilions are carefully positioned around the campus | Main entrance |
Open areas between the buildings with linear dry stream beds | Over-
hangs and canopies provide shade

Feather River Academy

Yuba City, California, USA

Architect	Architecture for Education – A4E, Pasadena
Pupils	175 aged 11-17 years
Building area	2,303 m²
Average classroom	90 m² (flexible and divisible)
Parking spaces	43
Build cost	7.25 million USD
Completion	2005
Year group system	Needs-related small groups, mixed ages

Comprehensive consultation with the users throughout the design

Feather River Academy is a public high school oper-
ated by the Sutter County Superintendent of Schools
Office for at risk youths from grades 7 to 12. Current
enrolment comprises approximately 100 full-time students and 75 independent students who attend part-
time for specific study sessions. Students referred
to the FRA have either been expelled from district
schools, sent by the courts due to their low level crimi-
nal activities, or are assigned by the probation service. All students have severe discipline issues.

As academic performance is almost always related to
one or other of these dysfunctional groupings, students with low or deficient credit ratings may also
end up here, to re-adjust their performance through

Elevation administration

Section administration

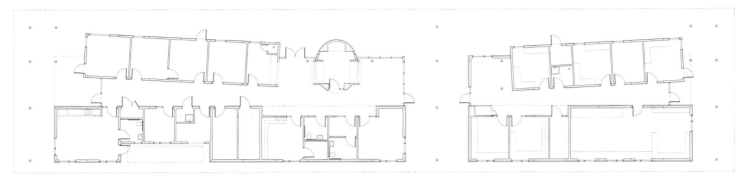

Floor plan administration

intensive tutor sessions. The children served by FRA are the most at risk in the community and many feel they are disenfranchised from society as a whole. Designing the new buildings required a fully therapeutic environment to support a spectrum of mild to severely damaged individuals together with a low key and inobtrusive but effective internal and external security system.

The decision to appoint Architecture for Education was made because of their pioneering work in developing schools inclusively. The design process incorporated action workshops with staff, students, community agencies and other key stakeholders. This approach was critical in developing a learning envi-

ronment which students and staff would be proud of and to which they would feel a sense of ownership and belonging. One might also speculate on the need to consult as a form of practical research into a building type, which is barely understood.

Following three years of planning and construction, the school finally opened in the fall of 2005. The accommodation is set out in campus style, forming what can be described as a 'learning village'. On a flat 1.6-hectare site, the complex programme of accommodation intermingles and knits together the various programmatic components right across the site. The architecture itself is characterised by a series of linked single-storey pavilions with dynamic folding roofs;

overhangs and canopies capture outside spaces, making the play between inside and outside an essential aspect of the learning experience. The programme comprises classrooms, multi-purpose rooms, administration areas, a building for special educational needs, a greenhouse for educational and therapeutic planting and an Internet café. The external site amenities include learning gardens, formal and informal playing fields, an outdoor stage, covered arcades, parking and multi-purpose activity courts or plazas. Classrooms are paired around a shared resource area and various outside spaces extend the learning environment out into the landscape, which was a critical requirement coming out of the consultation.

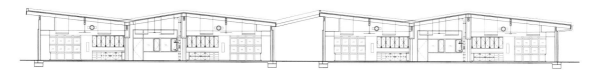

Elevation classrooms

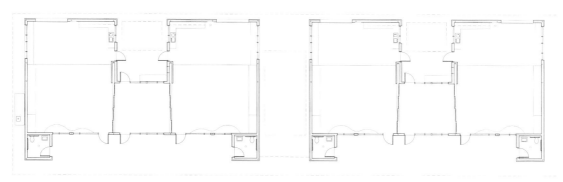

Section classrooms

Partial floor plan classrooms

Feather River Academy serves an academic community enrolled three to four years below grade level. Understandably perhaps, students suffer from low self-esteem and require constant one on one counseling and periodical supervision from the probation services. Staff and administration personnel strive to meet the needs of each child individually in a more intimate high school setting than is the norm. Their aim is to return students to their home districts as normal, fully functioning, and most importantly, caring members of the community who will subsequently be able to contribute to society. For this the external environment has an important role to play; for example, the open areas between the buildings have linear dry stream beds that come to life during the

winter months, a garden planting programme fosters students' understanding of the agricultural qualities of the community, which is facilitated by the careful positioning of the pavilions around the campus; in addition, antique farm equipment from pioneering farms throughout the county is carefully placed around this special landscape for learning.

It is important to recognise the intensive period of development work with the end users and other stakeholders, which contributed to the success of the final design. These were not just issues relating to practicalities such as room layouts and adjacencies that were discussed in detail; also, more complex aesthetic design aspects were implemented as a result of this

consultation, such as the desire for a varied roof line, perhaps an outdoor theme reflecting the local mountains and Pacific Bird Flyway.

Some projects are included in this book because they are stylish architectural statements, which make students feel they are part of a modern technological world. This project is not one of them. It is low key and relaxed in style, a perfect match for the semi-rural setting. However, the school is a complex and well-worked design, which complements its sensitive functioning to provide a truly therapeutic environment for the 21st century.

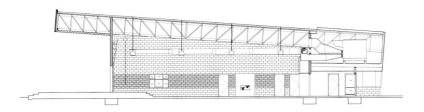

Elevation multi-purpose hall

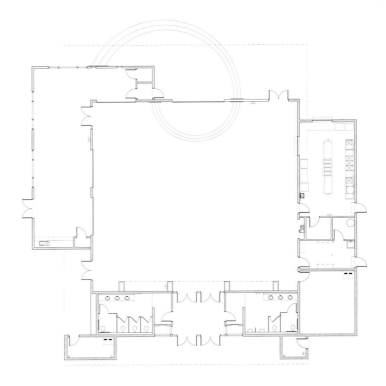

Floor plan multi-purpose hall

Section multi-purpose hall

Circulation area | Multi-purpose hall | Typical ICT rich classroom |
Break-out space connected directly to cultivation areas

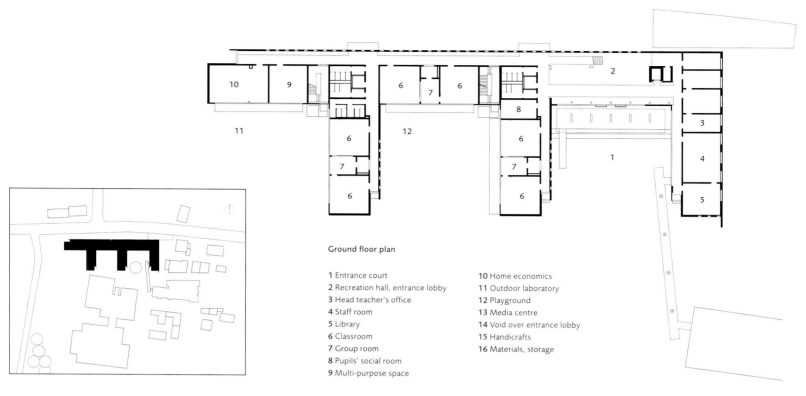

Ground floor plan

1 Entrance court
2 Recreation hall, entrance lobby
3 Head teacher's office
4 Staff room
5 Library
6 Classroom
7 Group room
8 Pupils' social room
9 Multi-purpose space
10 Home economics
11 Outdoor laboratory
12 Playground
13 Media centre
14 Void over entrance lobby
15 Handicrafts
16 Materials, storage

Site plan

Typical south-facing windows showing alternate open and fixed glazed panels with projecting solar shading canopies | View of laboratory courtyard showing alternate three-storey wings and main block of accommodation

Special Pedagogic Centre

Eichstätt, Germany

Architect	Diezinger & Kramer Architekten, Eichstätt
Pupils	220 aged 6-15 years
Building area	4,700 m²
Average classroom	65 m²
Parking spaces	6
Build cost	8 million EUR
Completion	2001
Year group system	Traditional 3 form entry classbase system

The use of modern architectural style with applied colour to accentuate particular circulation routes through the building

This three-storey structure is organised in a serrated E shaped plan. It has a solid back wall creating a visual and acoustic barrier to the main road on the north, and three wings of accommodation, which form enclosed court-yards to the south. Each court has a particular function: there is an entrance court, secondly a playground dedicated to younger children and finally a 'laboratory' play yard for outside experiments and sheltered small group activities on sunny days. This is a particularly important aspect of the pedagogic approach.

The use of materials in this building is carefully choreo-graphed to provide a strong visual and sensory environ-ment, which aids orientation for the students. This is complemented by an emphatic colour narrative used

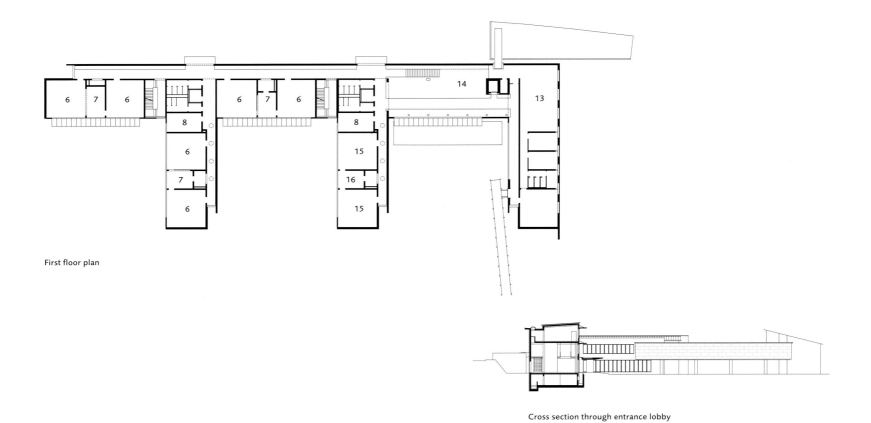

First floor plan

Cross section through entrance lobby

Entrance lobby with strong colours on the walls acting as visual clues for partially sighted students | Typical classroom interior with desks orientated towards the electronic white board

to good effect in the main circulation areas, the entrance lobby and main staircases; it is a type of colour/form language which is aesthetically controlled yet sends out clear messages to those students who might be partially sighted or physically limited in other ways. The message is that strong colours signify staircases and therefore may be a potential hazard; yet at the same time they are part of the everyday pleasure of life and should be utilised and enjoyed whenever possible.

The articulation of each façade is a sophisticated interplay of solid and void, with alternately recessed and expressed windows. On the south there are broad bands of glazing with fixed solar shading and openable windows in three continuous bands of fenestration. On the north there is an almost solid three-storey façade, which is punctuated by large bay windows. These bays provide occasional break-out areas and echo the internal planning as they correspond to the north/south corridor links within. It is a mature architectural language, which treats young children with respect and care because they can 'read' the building from the outside.

The internal architecture is just as carefully controlled as the external façades. On entering there is a large double height activity area with a grand staircase and lift. Adjacent but on the first floor there is a media centre. The lobby area is a place for meeting, for hanging out and for occasional assemblies and community meetings. It is lit up internally at night, colours radiating a welcom-

ing visual message across the courtyard and beyond. Classrooms have a similar spatial clarity. Each is paired to another classroom. Each pair has its own entrance/cloakroom lobby and a small group room so that pupils can on occasion withdraw from the main teaching group. The use of beech chairs and storage containers provide a much-needed hint of colour and texture within these areas. Because student numbers are limited to 12 per class, and all corridors are wide enough to provide access for two wheelchairs, there is a welcome sense of space. It is generous and calm to provide a perfect environment for play and learning.

Primary Schools

Primary schools have sat alongside secondary schools as one half of the basic state educational structure since the widespread introduction of statutory schooling around the end of the 19th century. Primary schools are given a specific section, as they are distinct from the secondary school on account of the age ranges they cater for. A primary school usually functions for children aged 5 or 6 to age 11, and unlike many secondary schools, they are small, intimate and located close to the residential areas they cater for. Children will tend to stay in a single classroom for much of the school day. It will act as a sort of homebase, they will only leave it for physical exercise, assemblies and specialist lessons such ICT and music.

This well-understood and conservative building type will usually comprise of paired classrooms so they can share toilet and storage facilities. In addition, there will be a limited range of facilities shared by the whole school. The contemporary dimension, which makes the primary school innovative and different, is community access. Most primary schools have been located on the same site for generations, and usually they have generous site areas and a prime strategic location at the heart of things. It therefore makes sense for additional services such as early years facilities, health and adult training to be co-located. Sports halls provide the opportunity for adult evening classes; even playing fields can be used for local community events such as the annual school fete. These facilities are now being added on to many existing primary schools as extensions or new stand-alone buildings within the existing school site.

When new primary schools are built, it is usually to service a new housing development as families leave the traditional urban city centres for the suburbs. For example, the Mary Poppins Primary School in Berlin (pages 124-125) is a central component of the infrastructure for a new residential zone currently under construction. A key feature of this development is the retention of a large meadow, which has been enhanced to serve as a green 'lung' for the new residential community. The school is situated between the housing and the meadow, to serve as a symbolic gateway for the children and families who will use the meadow for recreation during the summer months.

A theme often raised when consulting with school users, particularly children, is the desire for building forms, which are more expressive and non-rectilinear than traditional primary school buildings. Architecture which is fun, colourful and legible, is an aim which is difficult within tight budgetary constraints and the conservative attitudes many designers bring to these commissions. At the Burr Elementary School (pages 128-129), the designers have managed to address the practical issues with a building which appears from a distance to be a conventional two-storey rectangular block. However on closer scrutiny the basic form is given an exciting twist by the introduction of curved semi-oval cutouts. Like a piece of half eaten cheese, the building is imbued with a spirit and vitality which is expressive of children themselves. It shows a new vibrant attitude for the next generation of primary schools.

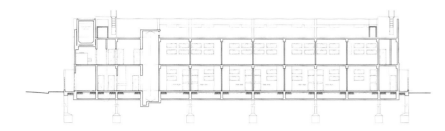

Longitudinal section

Cross section

The courtyard play area with the main entrance on the left and the play hall on the right | View from the street with super graphics spelling out the school's name in graffiti style | Detail showing the toilet block with blue graphic design illustrating the function to children | Corridor at first floor level with children's art displayed on the walls

Kingston International School

Hong Kong, China

Architect	Kwong & Associates, Hong Kong
Pupils	250 aged 5-11 years
Building area	800 m²
Average classroom	26 m²
Parking spaces	3 for cars, 2 for coaches
Build cost	17.2 million HKD
Completion	2001
Year group system	Paired classrooms for 12 age-related classes

An economical layout with a rooftop play area and a perimeter wall integrated into the building design to create a secure yet attractive compound

The plan and overall form of this school building is deceptively simple. It comprises a two-storey linear block surrounded by a high wall rendered in smooth white stucco. Classrooms are large yet basic, each with its own pupil toilets, a pair of sinks and always with windows orientated towards the west. Internal circulation is via a single 1.4 metre wide corridor on the south courtyard side. There is a general office at one end of the corridor with the entrance and a play hall at the other end, the only element which breaks the linearity of the classroom block.

The way in which this basic composition has been articulated is, however, very sophisticated. The architecture strikes a subtle balance between, on the one hand, the idea of the neutral canvas, and on the other, an inspir-

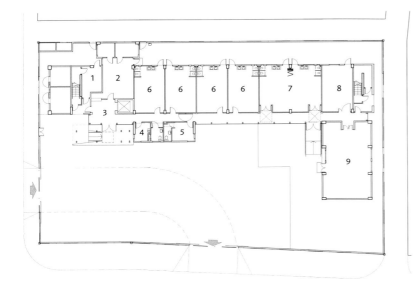

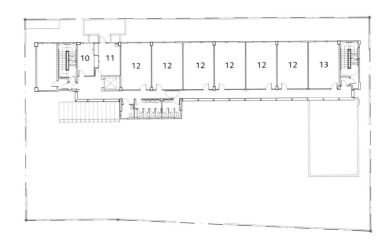

Ground floor plan	1 Kitchen	6 Classroom (kindergarten)
	2 General office	7 Drama room
	3 Entrance lobby	8 Music room
	4 Sick room	9 Indoor playhall
	5 Supervisor office	

First floor plan	10 Meeting room
	11 Staff office
	12 Classroom (primary school)
	13 Library

ing totally modern signature building. Internally, care has been taken to ensure that the building does not dominate the users. All the walls of the classrooms and virtually every surface of the external play areas are intended to act as a backdrop to the artistic endeavours of the children. The architects have not been precious about their building, indeed children are encouraged to assert their creativity with their own work covering virtually every surface. The result is an architecture of colour and simple elemental form which is intended to stimulate young minds without overwhelming them. It is both exuberant and controlled, a suitable place in which children can play and learn and where users can have a great deal of control over their environment. As this is an environmentally conscious design, only wood from managed

renewable sources was specified as the primary material for internal cladding and doors in circulation areas and classrooms. Natural ventilation is used as much as possible and all air conditioning equipment is CFC-free. In addition the client required that the building be flexible enough for three different uses, either as a primary school, a kindergarten or as a childcare centre. In the end it is a combination of all. Each of these uses requires different facilities to be provided, therefore the building has been designed as an infinitely flexible structure with no load bearing internal partitions. A particularly important consideration was the scale of children. Every stair has a dual-height handrail for big and small users, and low level windows provide views out for the smallest child. Every door has a high and low vision panel so

that they can see and be seen when moving around the building. Hinge guards cover dangerous door openings. Ultimately the whole structure is intimate and small in scale, without ever being patronising to its users. Externally the building asserts itself within its somewhat bland setting. The school announces itself with quirky graphics inscribed on the street wall, which promise an experience of education which will be fun and creative. All the windows on the busy Waterloo Road elevation are small, in order to mitigate against traffic noise. The building is an attractive, functional and economical structure which has become a landmark statement about the primacy of education and the importance of young children within this new community in Kowloon Tong, Hong Kong.

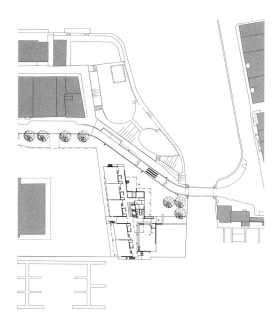

Site plan

Ground floor plan

1 Entrance	5 Lobby
2 Foyer	6 Storage
3 Classroom	7 Library
4 Corridor	

Montessori Primary School

De Eilanden, Amsterdam, The Netherlands

Architect	Herman Hertzberger, Amsterdam
Pupils	280 aged 4-12 years
Building area	1,333 m²
Average classroom	47 m²
Parking spaces	6
Build cost	1.5 million EUR
Completion	2002
Year group system	Special Montessori age-integrated system

Integrated into a housing block to form an urban school at the heart of the community

For a long time Herman Hertzberger has been designing schools which are closely related to the local community. He has pioneered the notion of the multi-storey villa form which optimises the tight site constraints of building in a city like Amsterdam. However, it is the first time he has actually combined a school with a housing block to create a new highbred form of school architecture. It is an approach which is more usually seen in the provision of early years centres, smaller, more distinctive buildings than the typical primary school, which can sit comfortably with housing or other more commercial facilities.

Located on one of the most attractive sites in Amsterdam, the block is surrounded by water, as the name

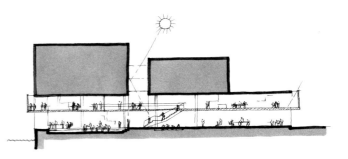

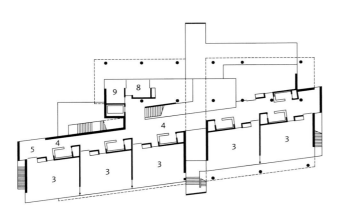

Conceptual sketch section

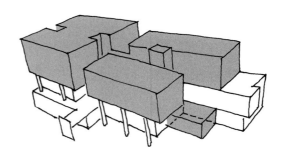

Axonometric drawing

Second floor plan
8 Offices
9 Void

View of rooftop playground with local housing in the background | Front elevation | Interior view of main entrance hall 'central plaza' showing the first floor gallery decks | Classroom with low level windows

De Eilanden suggests. Included as part of a complex of eight high cost homes, the school was carved out of the two ground floors of this exclusive urban living block. So rather than having a free-standing institutional form entitled 'the school', pupils attend an institution which is integrated and subsumed into the housing block, with all the cost benefits and the advantages this bestows, not least of which is the possibility to share this marvellous site with another user. However, the architecture of the school is not quiet and conservative (like the housing above which was designed by a different architect). Rather it seems to slip out from beneath the housing at every opportunity, with bays, stairs, porches and play areas extending the accommodation from out beneath the skirts of the red brick housing blocks above.

Access to the building is from the lower school hall. This double-height hall is the focus of school activity; passing the main auditorium you enter into this so-called urban plaza, which visually connects upper and lower level and provides a flexible gathering space, a communal hall, an indoor play area or a space to hang out. The architect's sketch shows the concept of the bisection, with sunlight reflected down into the heart of the plan, beamed in from the deep cut along the centre of the block, magnified by the use of highly reflective ceramic tiles on the wall surfaces. The design somewhat resembles an ocean liner, with walkways and stairs to create a beautiful promenade of routes in and around the teaching accommodation. The school's ten classrooms are ranged across the rear south-facing façade,

each with its own wet zone outside the classroom which shows as a widening of the corridor/circulation area. Some of the classrooms have decks and balconies, which act as escape routes as well as extended learning areas outside the classroom. It is a playful yet highly disciplined form of architecture which avoids the institutional feel of many school buildings. The limitations of building next to the housing has forced the architect to adopt clever devices to ensure the school is never too constrained by its partner accommodation. Thus he created a building which is contained but generous and full of modulated light, producing an all the more dramatic spatial experience.

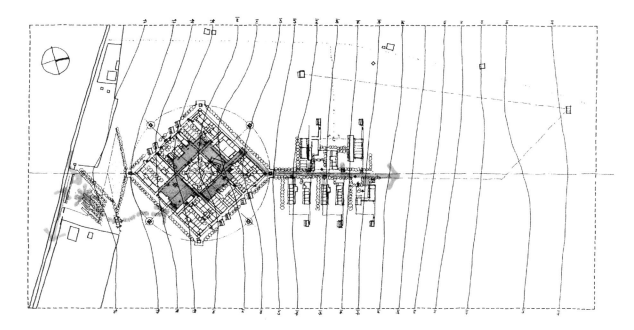

The master plan

Students enjoy the shade on the solid stone plinth | Views of the infant school courtyard during the opening ceremony | Classroom interior

Druk White Lotus School

Ladakh, India

Architect	Arup Associates, London
Pupils	750 aged 4-18 years
Building area	1,776 m²
Average classroom	61 m²
Parking spaces	General parking zone at the base of the village
Build cost	n/a
Completion	2002 (first phase)
Year group system	Single form entry integrated groups

The school has a spiritual ethos, apparent in the building's site organisation and integrated environmental strategy

The school is located in the village of Shey, approximately 16 kilometres from the main town, Ley, in the centre of the Ladakh valley. Sometimes known as 'Little Tibet', Ladakh is an ancient kingdom set high in the Indian Himalayas, close to Tibet's western border. This remote high altitude desert is cut off by snow for around six months of the year, with winter temperatures dropping as low as –30 degrees C in some areas. In summer the hot sun and snowmelt bring the rich fertile valleys alive.

The population is mainly Buddhist, with a minority of Muslims and Christians; for centuries, monasteries were the centres of learning and the focus for the community's practical and spiritual needs. The Drukpa Trust, a UK-registered charity under the patronage of His Holi-

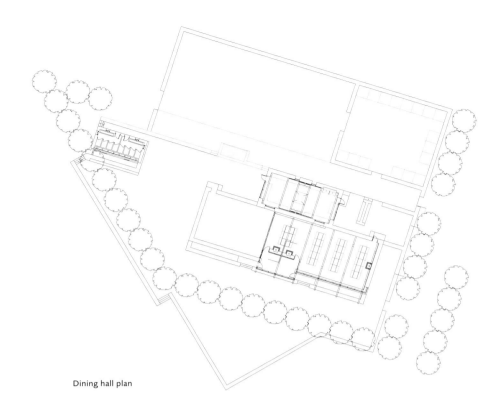

Dining hall plan

ness the Dalai Lama, has initiated the creation of the Druk White Lotus School, which will eventually cater for 750 mixed pupils from nursery age to 18 years. Although the project is a local initiative, it has an international context, with funding from charitable donations in the UK and Europe as well as the local community. Arup Associates and Arup, the engineering arm of the London based consultancy, have developed an environmental strategy, which has wider implications for sustainable design research and practice. Arup had several reasons for becoming involved in such a specialist community project located in this remote part of the world. When Arup first visited Ladakh at the Trust's invitation in 1997, they were impressed by the ambition of the project and by the need for such a school locally. When findings of

field research evolved as the design progressed, it became clear that this work could contribute significantly to the development of appropriate building technologies both here and elsewhere in the world. Every year Arup gives leave of absence to an engineer or architect from the design team to be resident on site, to act as an 'ambassador' for the Trust and to assist the local construction team and client committee. The project was presented at the September 2002 Earth Summit in Johannesburg.

Located close to the River Indus and its surrounding irrigated fields, according to the designers, the gently south-sloping, south-facing site will be steadily developed from open desert into a humane, well-scaled envi-

ronment for children and teachers, this being an important resource within which the local community can work comfortably. The environmental strategy takes particular advantage of the unique solar position of the high altitude (3,700 metres) site to be energy self-sufficient. In addition the site strategy aims to ensure an entirely self-regulating system in terms of water and waste management. There will be gardens and extensive tree planting as a result of this irrigation system; the related water infrastructure is drawn from a single borehole by a solar-powered pump. With the site encircled by peaks rising to over 7,000 metres and overlooked by two important monasteries, the master plan aims to achieve a unique sense of harmony with its surroundings. The complex is organised within a nine square grid arrangement and

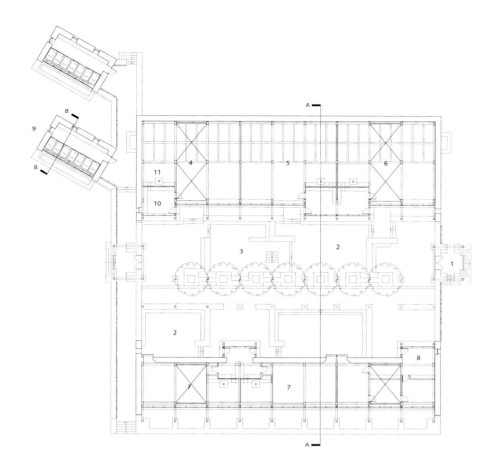

Nursery and infant school plan
1 Entrance to courtyard
2 External teaching spaces
3 Water point and play
4 Nursery
5 Lower kindergarten
6 Upper kindergarten
7 Year 1
8 Teachers' spaces and administration
9 Solar-assisted VIP latrines
10 Air lock and lockers
11 Warm/quiet corner

Student in multi-purpose hall | The multi-purpose hall, a movement lesson in progress | Timber roof under construction | Roof makeup from below

surrounding circle of a mandala, a symbolic figure of particular religious significance. There are four principal areas, interconnected by way of a spine type route but not occupying the full extent of the site. The first is the site entrance and bus drop-off from the road to the south, which gives pedestrians access to the second, the daytime teaching areas. The third element along the spine is the residential accommodation for some pupils and staff rising to the north. The fourth area, comprising the water and energy infrastructure, is located separately alongside a service track to the west.

Typically, single-storey buildings are arranged around a series of primary and secondary routes in a plan which is not unlike a small village or local monastery, tightly planned and enclosed around shaded courtyards, in stark contrast to the surrounding open desert landscape devoid of shelter from the bleak conditions. Within the daytime teaching area, which is orientated 30 degrees from south towards east to favour the morning sun, stands the recently completed nursery and infant school courtyard. Also accommodated in the daytime teaching area will be three further teaching courtyards for the junior and senior schools, the computer and science laboratories, a library and community resource facility, art studios, an open-air assembly courtyard and a large multi-purpose hall. To the north along the residential spine will be a medical clinic, vocational training workshops, dining hall, kitchens and the residential accommodation. The nursery and infant school provides three large teaching/play studios for nursery and kindergarten years, two further classrooms for year 1 children, and a small suite of rooms for the head of schools and administration. These spaces are organised in two single-storey buildings arranged around an open, landscaped courtyard that will be used for external teaching during summer months and may eventually be covered with awnings made from parachute fabric, which is readily available locally. A water point is provided for wet play, and deciduous trees are planted for shading. Just outside the teaching courtyard there are two innovative, solar assisted, dry latrine buildings. All classrooms are entered from the courtyard via a lobby (containing children's lockers for shoes), which provides a thermal buffer. The courtyard is planted to provide a canopy

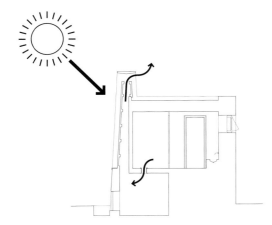

Section through VIP (ventilated improved pit) latrine. The dark south-facing façade, with the solar flue, draws air through the cubicle and pit, preventing fly and smell problems.

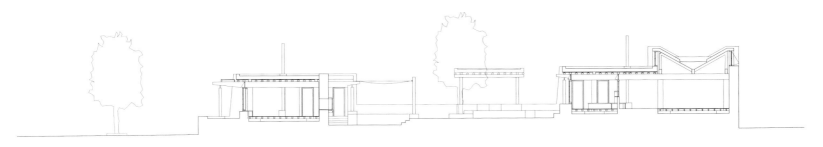

Section AA of nursery and infant school courtyard

covering of foliage with wet play and external teaching areas beneath both solid and flexible coverings to extend teaching space and reflect the extreme temperature conditions across the climatic cycle. Each classroom has a quiet warm corner with a small stove on a stone floor. There are timber floors everywhere else, and white-painted mud rendered walls are provided to maximise teaching flexibility in clear uncluttered spaces. Each courtyard has a pair of detached solar-assisted VIP (ventilated improved pit) latrines arranged along an external walkway crossing one open end of the courtyard.

The key aspects governing the structural design were earthquake loading, durability and appropriateness. The kindergarten buildings have cavity walls on three sides

with granite block in mud mortar as the outer leaf and traditional mud brick masonry for the inner leaf; this gives increased thermal performance and durability compared to the rendered mud brick walls commonly used. The heavy mud roof is supported by a timber structure independent of the walls to provide the earthquake stability. The large spans needed in the classrooms, combined with the open glazed south-facing façade and the high weight of the roof makeup, required large timber cross sections and steel connections to ensure that they resist seismic loads and to warrant life safety in the case of an earthquake. These were difficult to procure locally, so the structural framing plan and connection details for the future phases have been altered to reduce timber section sizes.

The client's brief to develop a model school was ambitious, not only in terms of 'hardware' such as energy and site infrastructure, buildings, material resource use, but also in 'soft skills' such as building up competency in the local project management team, establishing a cost database and in optimising the use of local resources. All these initiatives aim to support the whole project as a demonstration of a new approach to teaching in such a unique rural community. Ultimately, this is far more than a school in the conventional sense, it is more of a village, with everything designed to complement the major infrastructure initiatives, water and energy management in the most positive way.

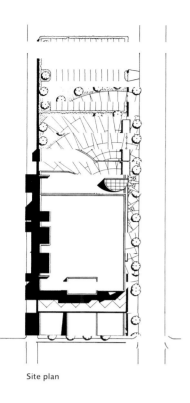

Site plan

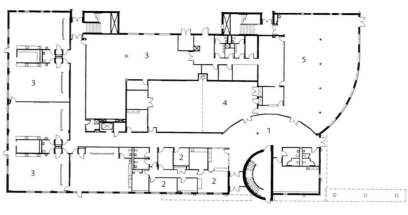

Ground floor plan

1 Lobby	6 Classroom
2 Offices	7 Science classroom
3 Kindergarten	8 Gymnasium
4 Multi-purpose space	9 Library
5 Cafeteria	10 Computer laboratory

Little Village Academy

Chicago, Illinois, USA

Architect	Ross Barney Architects, Chicago
Pupils	688 aged 5-13 years
Building area	6,637 m²
Average classroom	84 m²
Parking spaces	23
Build cost	7 million USD
Completion	1996
Year group system	Age-related 2 form entry

Compact palazzo style form which occupies a single urban block located at the heart of the inner city residential community

This is a constrained urban site measuring 36 x 120 metres of which 720 square metres comprise parking spaces. The school is in the form of a three-storey rectangular block which takes up a large part of the available site area. The walls of the school are hard up against three sides of the surrounding streets like a palazzo in urban Rome. Nevertheless the compact plan incorporates a varied range of accommodation including 20 traditional classrooms with specialist science and computer rooms, a dining area at ground floor level, a kindergarten and community room. There is a library which is articulated architecturally with walls and roof projecting beyond the lines of the urban block. It is open to the local community after school hours, which comprises many recent immigrants with a poor grasp of English; it is a symbolic statement about the

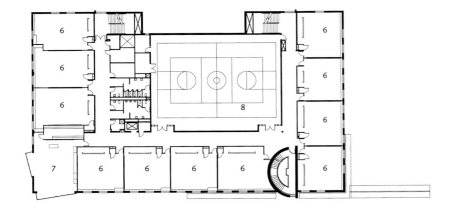

First floor plan

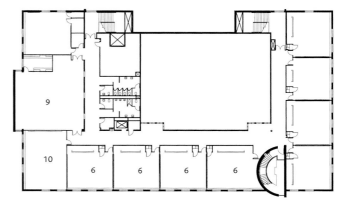

Second floor plan

Sunlight filled main circulation stair with sundial | Solid red brick block enlivened by projecting bays, third floor library in the foreground and sundial staircase towards the end of the long façade | Library interior benefits from high level lighting and solid walls with full-height corner windows for views | Science laboratories with translucent walls giving an even, natural light

importance of education, like a beacon visible to passers-by from the surrounding streets.

The perimeter block form is in local red brick with a recessed loggia to the west, playgrounds for the kindergarten on the south and a small play plaza for the main school to the north. The arrangement provides a powerful civic presence, yet with a number of architectural flourishes which add a twist to the otherwise austere form. Apart from the library picked out in shimmering white metal cladding, there is a dramatic tapering staircase tower clad in coloured geometric tiles, an important access and social meeting point within this vertically organised school. Inside the stair tower there is a sun motif in the form of a semi-circular 45 degree rooflight; the back wall features a sun dial calibrated to the angle of the sun radiating from above. The motif is echoed on the external street courtyard with the axis mundi graphically set out in coloured floor tiles; according to architect Carol Ross Barney, the sundial refers to the role of the sun in Aztec culture and has become an important local landmark.

The advantages of the planning strategy are firstly that it allows a very high density with economical circulation between classrooms. Outside there is no left-over space, its perimeter edges act as secure buttresses against the outside world. Paradoxically the proximity of classroom windows and doors to the street gives it an immediacy to the local community, which is welcoming to outsiders, yet in a controlled way. The cafeteria and gymnasium are well-used community facilities as are the many adult evening classes which run in classrooms on the ground floor. Perhaps more importantly, it is an extremely economical layout both in environmental terms and in building costs. The heavy external envelope and internalised plan form make good sense in this region which experiences extreme temperature ranges across the seasons. The drawback of the tight planning is that much of the internal circulation areas on the ground and first floors have only restricted levels of natural light. However, good artificial lighting and bright reflective finishes help to reduce this problem. Everywhere there is evidence of thoughtful pragmatic design decisions which have created a building of immense practical value both to the local school children and its disparate community of adult users.

Section through circulation zone

End elevation showing the lightweight structure over the circulation

Typical section through classrooms

Street frontage, more traditional brick structure relates to Victorian terraces surrounding | Rear playground façade with continuous first floor louvers | Ground floor classrooms with mini courtyard space | Circulation space

Ranelagh Multi-denominational School

Dublin, Ireland

Architect	O'Donnell + Tuomey Architects, Dublin
Pupils	250 aged 4-12 years
Building area	1,142 m²
Average classroom	69 m²
Parking spaces	0
Build cost	n/a
Completion	1999
Year group system	Age-related single form entry

Located on a confined urban site, the school relates closely to its surrounding context to create a 'home from home' model school

Many school authorities look to create large schools located on out-of-town sites. As a result the facility is often distanced from the local community, children need to travel, there is a loss of intimacy. Here the thinking was to create a small building located on the same site as the previous run-down school right in the midst of the residential neighbourhood. It was to be fully integrated into the working class neighbourhood from which the majority of its pupils are drawn.

Due to the limitations of the site, a two-storey building was required providing four classrooms on each level. Internally the simple plan with its eight north-facing classrooms is given a distinctive quality with the circulation spine overlooking the playground to the south. It

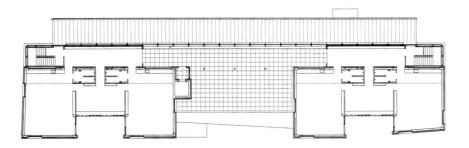

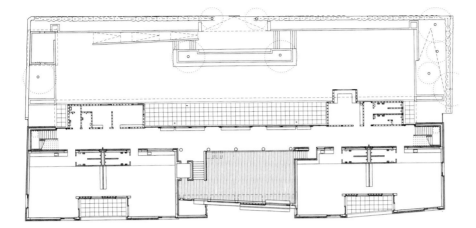

Ground floor plan

First floor plan

has staircases at each end with a lift in the centre. The circulation zone is intended to be more than a functional movement space and is generously proportioned with seating, display areas, coathooks and drinking fountains. It is a street for children, a social mixing area for the youngest to the oldest children as they move from classroom to playground.

The building occupies the upper north side hard up against the street. The south side is open with a small play yard which is surrounded by a landscaped fence to provide protection from the sun and privacy from the terraced houses across the street. The wrought-iron perimeter fence is a remnant of the previous school, whose gate still forms the entrance at the rear. Whilst the north-

facing elevation, hard up against the street, is relatively closed with one window per class puncturing the brick façade, the south side is much more open and transparent with a full-width glazed and shuttered window running along the entire width of the building at first floor. In contrast to the solid masonry construction of the classroom block, this circulation area is made with lightweight timber to provide the maximum area of glazing. The contrast between solid and lightweight architecture is practical and gives an interesting spatial twist to the building.

Classroom specification was tightly prescribed by the Department of Education. However, colour was used as a form of coding throughout the building. The floors are coloured lino, in classrooms yellow, black in wet areas,

terracotta in corridors and blue in teachers' rooms. The unplastered blockwork walls are also coloured. The inside faces of the external classroom walls are white. The walls to corridors, bathrooms and adjoining classrooms are painted in strong earth colours, red, blue and green. Taken from Italian frescoes according to the architects, they are vibrant and strong, yet complementary to each other and to the naturally coloured untreated materiality used elsewhere. In 2005 this school received the prestigious RIAI Architecture Award.

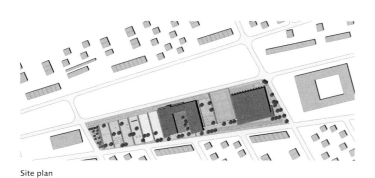

Site plan

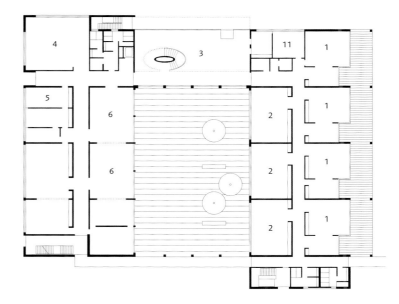

Ground floor plan

1 Preschool	**8** Classrooms grade 3
2 Classrooms grade 1	**9** Classrooms grade 4
3 Entrance hall	**10** Handicrafts
4 Media/library	**11** Storage
5 Headmaster's office	**12** Classrooms grade 5
6 Assembly hall	**13** Classrooms grade 6
7 Classrooms grade 2	

North-facing street façade | Courtyard with walkway to sports hall | Interior showing generous circulation area using natural materials and modulated lighting effects

Mary Poppins Primary School

Berlin, Germany

Architect	Carola Schäfers Architekten, Berlin
Pupils	600 aged 5-11 years
Building area	3,000 m² (not incl. sports hall)
Average classroom	65 m²
Parking spaces	3
Build cost	10.3 million DM (not incl. sports hall)
Completion	2000
Year group system	Traditional 3 form entry classbase system

A central community primary school with detached sports hall integrated into the master plan for a new residential zone

The school is a central component of the infrastructure for a new residential zone currently under construction. The site is the former military airfield of Gatow on the west bank of the River Havel, Berlin. A key element of this development is a large meadow which has been retained and enhanced to serve as a green 'lung' for the new living area. It connects the existing lake to a new park. The meadow and park are bounded by a strip of new housing. The school is situated between the housing and the meadow, to serve the children and families. It is very much at the heart of this new eco-friendly community.

The detached volumetric of the housing and the school help to structure the public open spaces, pro-

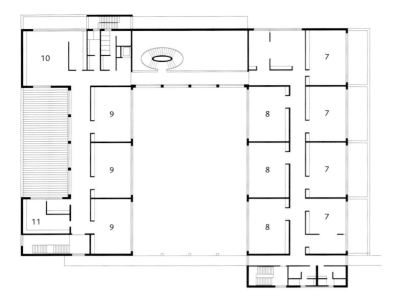

First floor plan

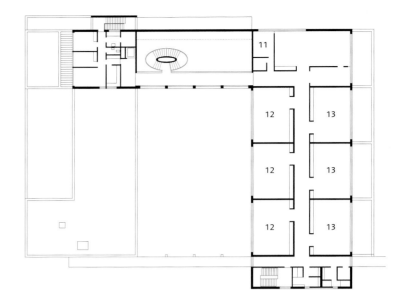

Second floor plan

viding views across and between the solid structures. The primary school itself is a U shape with the three built sides forming a courtyard which is open to the south. The three-storey structure forms a protective back to the street on the north side, with a ground floor pedestrian link partly enclosing the courtyard and connecting the east-west axis across the site. This provides links to a sports hall in the east with football pitches and a more traditional playground area to the east. The sports hall is a shared facility, utilised by the school students during the day and the community at night.

Within the school, accommodation is in the form of a double-sided corridor on the two east-west wings

with classrooms organised in suites of four from pre-school on the ground floor through to grade six on the third floor. The implication being that the older the child, the higher he or she will be positioned in the building. The teaching administration, staff areas and media/library are at ground floor level within a self-contained 'adult' block in the west wing. The entrance itself is an impressive three-storey volume with a gallery bridge link on the two upper levels. It is all connected by an oval feature staircase which creates a dramatic event of moving up and down the building.

The architectural treatment is predominantly 20th century 'Bauhaus' modernist with flat roofs and white rendered walls. Colours are subdued, instead the ar-

chitects have chosen to use materials in their natural state with timber windows, ceiling and wall panels and the subtle use of side and top lighting in circulation and communal areas to create a muted yet striking building. Clearly the architects have taken the issue of way-finding seriously, with circulation areas which are highly modulated spatially, becoming narrower and wider as required and lit to the best dramatic effect. This is a robust structure built to resist the impact of future generations and a building which has an emphatic public presence within the community.

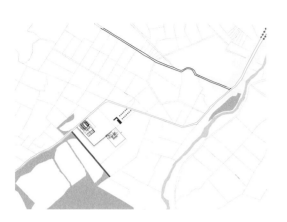

Site plan showing orientation

Key section through courtyard

External view of the classroom 'dens' with their own gardens | View looking towards main entrance with perimeter security fencing integrated into the architecture | Vision panels in corridors | Internal view showing classroom work area with rooflight | Multi-purpose hall

North Kildare Educate Together School

Celbridge, County Kildare, Ireland

Architect	Grafton Architects, Dublin
Pupils	245 aged 4-12 years (12 with autism)
Building area	1,200 m²
Average classroom	76 m², 96 m² for children with autism
Parking spaces	18 staff, 6 for staff for children with autism
Build cost	5 million EUR
Completion	2002
Year group system	Single form entry with attached autism unit

The school has an integrated education policy with a fully integrated unit for autism and communal social facilities

Set in an isolated semi-rural location, this school takes as its three defining constraints firstly the need to integrate a significant autistic unit into the functioning of the main primary school plan, secondly the requirement to create a defensive building which would resist the possibility of vandalism outside school hours, and thirdly to build economically and robustly without sacrificing architectural quality. These constraints have not only been addressed here, but the end result is a building which has a strong and positive civic presence and a highly efficient form.

The single-storey plan is tightly contained around an internal courtyard garden which forms a wing of classrooms orientated to the southwest sunshine and and an autistic unit contained on the southeast corner. The main

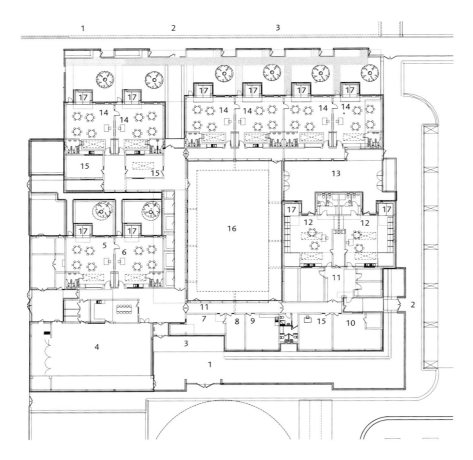

Ground floor plan
1 Main pedestrian gate
2 Autistic unit entrance
3 Main entrance
4 Multi-purpose hall
5 Junior infants
6 Senior infants
7 Administration
8 Principal's office
9 Staff room
10 IT room/library
11 Autistic unit entrance hall
12 Autistic unit classroom
13 Autistic unit playground
14 Classroom (grades 1-6)
15 Resource room
16 Courtyard
17 Classroom 'dens'

entrance, administration and multi-purpose hall are on the northwest (roadside) of the plan. Each classroom has its own access out to the playing fields at the back. Circulation wraps around the inside courtyard on three sides, connecting the classrooms and the autistic unit to the main entrance. According to the designers, this courtyard is the main focus for the school, which over time will grow rich with flowers, plants, trees, bird and insect life. Each classroom also benefits from its own mini courtyard on the outer perimeter of the plan, with teaching areas orientated southeast or southwest. In each of the school classrooms, there is a 'den,' a unique study carrel, which allows for individual and small group study when appropriate. There are also dedicated play corners and attached changing areas which give the

classrooms their own self-contained feel, like an individual school within a school. The autistic unit has its own separate courtyard play area accessible directly from the teaching areas. This all weather play area, with its outdoor toy store, connects these spaces directly into the central courtyard. There is a sense of spatial layering here which has been carefully manipulated to maintain the client's desire for integration. The building maintains a subtle balance between control and democratic open movement. For example the grouping of principal's office, staff room and the library is deliberately organised to monitor the entrance/reception area. Parents wait to collect their children in the entrance courtyard, which is separated from the bus and car set-down area by the perimeter fence which is in turn embraced by the flanks

of the building so that it feels like an integral part of the architecture rather than an afterthought.

Wherever possible natural materials have been used, red brick around the base of the walls, timber windows, terracotta window sills, birch plywood paneling with a coppercoated roof which aid the visual and tactile understanding children have for their environment. The main external wall finish is rendered blockwork which gives the building a sculptural quality. This effect is enhanced by the variegated roof-scape, which undulates across the flat landscape giving the interiors a diverse spatial quality.

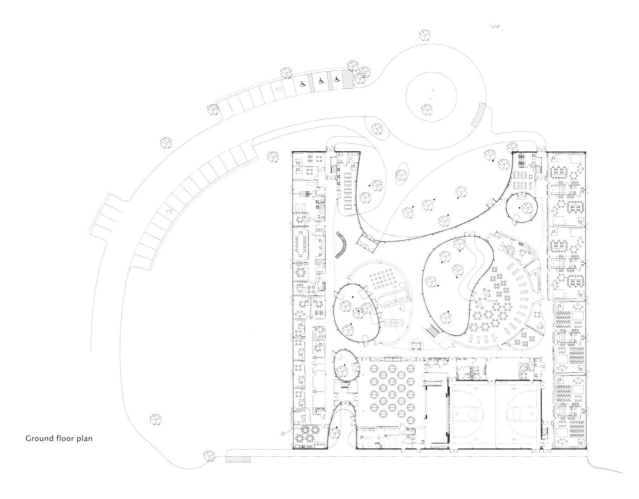

Ground floor plan

Aerial photograph shows coherence of conceptual ideas | Entrance court with rusticated wall in foreground | Corridor between the courtyards | Reception area with rock bench

Burr Elementary School

Fairfield, Connecticut, USA

Architect	SOM 'Education Lab', New York
Pupils	496 aged 5-11 years
Building area	6,500 m²
Average classroom	79 m²
Parking spaces	60
Build cost	12 million USD
Completion	2004
Year group system	4 form entry, 22 students per class

Compact plan with feature courtyards to provide an economical yet appealing layout

Two issues which frequently emerge when consulting with school communities are firstly the issue of physical connections between different departmental areas, which is a staff concern and secondly the desire for buildings with more expressive freeform plans featuring circles and other organic shapes to make the experience of education more fun; this latter issue is usually raised by pupils. These two competing aims are usually in direct conflict with each other.

At the Burr Elementary School, the designers have managed to address both wishes in this distinctive new school building. From a distance, the form is a double-height rectangular block (with some upper mezzanine levels), evoking a smart, highly glazed

First floor plan

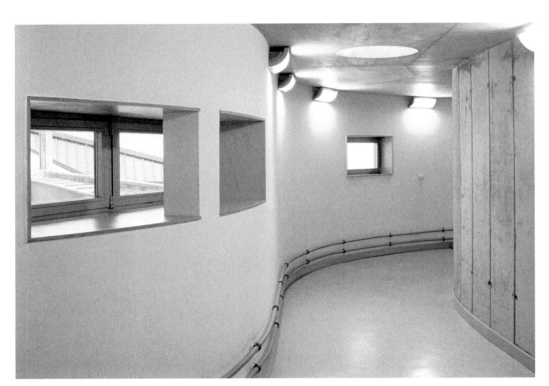

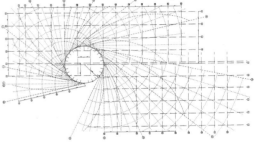

View of the main entrance from the public courtyard | The geometry of the concept is apparent on every façade; this is the rear and servicing side of the building | A corridor becomes a meandering playful route between conventionally organised teaching spaces | Conceptual sketch

be read as a series of moments which are both partial and whole. The architect describes it in his own more poetic language: 'The sunflower is a metaphor and a symbol of organic growth. The light of the sun makes its form, it is the source of its life. Education, knowledge, is the light which illuminates children's minds. The nature of ourselves depends on the quality of education we have received.' Clearly, whatever symbolic reading one places on this, the fundamentals of the educational process have been used as a representation of optimism and a purposeful future for its pupil body. Unlike many schools, it rejects the purely functionalist dictum of education as a social discipline, rather it seems to be suggesting that education is also about self-discovery, a sense of belonging to a community based around an idea of collective faith; there

is even a degree of anarchy embodied within the labyrinthine spaces between its rooms. In the architect's own words, it is like 'a big family house', with numerous places in which the pupils can hide and create their own sense of mystery. This is no place for the casual visitor, and its architecture recreates the complexities of the city with its walkways, passageways and cul-de-sacs. It must be a great place to go to school. The school's schedule of accommodation called for a mixture of large- and small-scale spaces with some 40 classrooms, but there is also a curriculum emphasis on the creative disciplines with art/workshop spaces attached to each classroom group. There is a multi-purpose hall for 500 (which can be used as a synagogue), a dining hall and two kitchens for meat and milk, in accordance with Jewish traditions. All of the rooms

are shaped to fit the exigencies of the overall form yet they are in the main completely functional spaces. Classrooms are linked and each has its own external terrace so that students can enjoy views of the forest beyond. All rooms are connected by way of a sinuous twisting corridor, arguably the only area which does not need to be straight. This school design is a one off, an icon, made for its special context, part memorial, part futuristic sculpture. It commemorates the lost children of Berlin, yet celebrates their future within the framework of the new Jewish community in the city. Its curving fragmented forms must make attendance fun, education as a form of play. Perhaps more school designers should be given the freedom to design a school in such a way, so that it becomes far more than the ubiquitous 'machine for learning'.

Perspective with pond

View across the pond | Children play in the snow in front of the new classroom | Interior views of the classroom

Mossbrook Primary School

Norton, Sheffield, UK

Architect	Sarah Wigglesworth Architects, London
Pupils	Aged 5-11 years
Building area	200 m²
Average classroom	146 m²
Parking spaces	20
Build cost	350,000 GBP
Completion	2003
Year group system	Groups as small as 12 and as large as 76

Government funded project exploring innovative prototypes of classroom design

Located on green belt land to the south of the city, the designers recognised this gift of a site, a wooded copse overlooking a pond bounded by an existing sensory garden. They decided to submerge the new building within this natural environment as much as possible. Slightly detached from the main school campus, the new classroom develops its own distinctive architectural language and finds new ways to exploit the rich natural environment. The building is full of intelligent and thought-provoking details which are oriented towards the perceptions of children rather than adults. For example within the entrance lobby, the workings of a toilet cistern at the back of the adjacent WC cubicle is revealed behind its Perspex casing. There are vision panels in the walls and the floor which permit close observation of physical and nat-

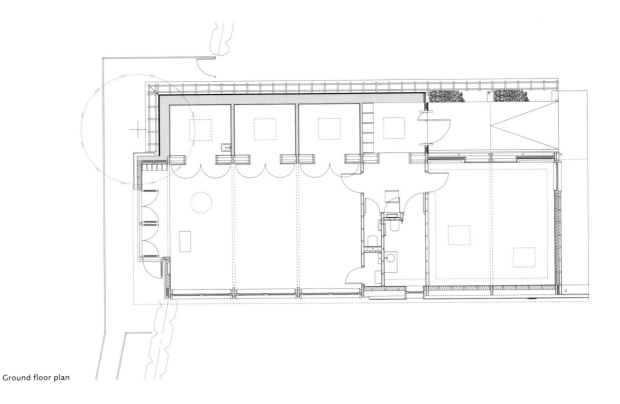

Ground floor plan

ural phenomena under supervised conditions. An underground burrow has even been cast into the ground floor slab, so that foxes or badgers can nest in full view of the children in their classroom above.

The building is clad with a collage of advanced industrial construction materials usually found on smart factory buildings. Corrugated steel, polycarbonate sheeting and oak (which for some odd reason is painted rather than used in its natural state), form a robust exterior envelope. This has practical benefits from a security perspective; however, it is perhaps an ironic nod back to the industrial heritage of Sheffield, a heritage which has mostly disappeared over the past 25 years. As headteacher Maggie Brough explained, the materials and the way they

are used are intended to act as an educational resource in their own right showing the way architecture works. Portal frames made of ply- and softwood support acoustically treated ceilings which provide a generous volume inside the classroom. Child-height windows frame views of the surrounding landscape. As Maggie Brough observed, 'the new building nestles into the landscape rather than standing apart from it...we are all very comfortable about that...' With its restful views of nature and spacious quiet interior, this building has a tranquil, almost spiritual quality; at the end of their lessons, many children do not wish to leave. There is a sobering comparison here between the architectural mediocrity of the existing school buildings and the new classroom. One of the most innovative aspects is the use of virtual and elec-

tronic media to further transform the way in which children see. Collaborating with artist Susan Collins, web cams located in the conservation area and triggered by body heat record animal movement and direct images into the classroom through plasma screens located in the floors and walls. A boat on the pond is fitted with an underwater camera and children are able to remotely control its movement to observe underwater pond life. One of the resource rooms has been made into a Camera Obscura reflecting real-life time images of the exterior directly onto the table top within one of three small group rooms.

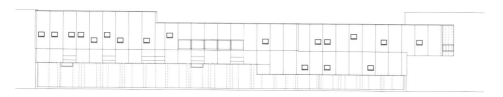

North elevation

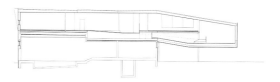

Longitudinal section through daycare centre

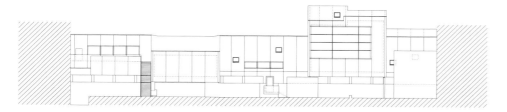

South elevation

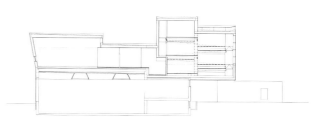

Cross section through sports hall

Taxham School Extension

Taxham, Salzburg, Austria

Architect	Maria Flöckner and Hermann Schnöll, Salzburg
Pupils	150 aged 6-14 years
Building area	1,680 m²
Average classroom	72-122 m²
Parking spaces	7
Build cost	2.47 million EUR
Completion	2000
Year group system	6 age-related groups of 25 children

A lightweight prefabricated structure which is built on top of the existing school sports hall

The extension provides after-school facilities for a secondary school. The architects' proposal works both as a self-contained children's environment and as a fully integrated part of the whole school campus. The original site comprised two teaching blocks from the 1970s, connected in a U shaped plan by a single-storey sports hall and swimming pool. Rather than building the new structure in the existing school yard and losing valuable outside play space, here the architects have used the roof of the school hall and constructed their new building to form a sort of lightweight 'top hat.' The use of a prefabricated skin of laminated birch ply, painted externally, gives both old and new structures a warm welcoming new face. A timber form of construction supplements the insufficient load bearing capacity of the existing structure

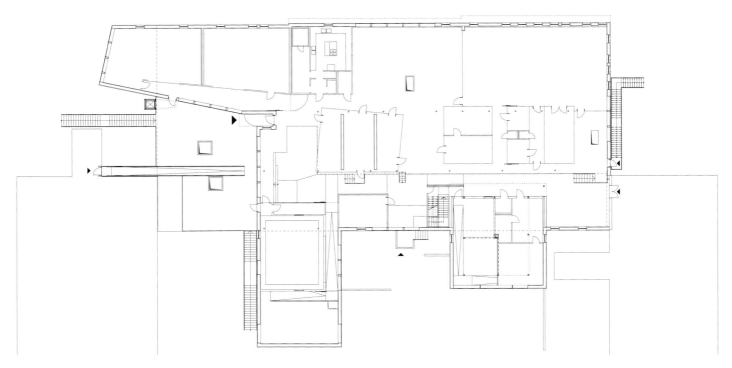

Plan of extension on top of sports hall

View from courtyard showing the indented form with timber cladding to the upper level and concrete connecting elements | Northeast façade to the playing field with the glazed base showing the internal structure with the upper ply cladding panels | The main playroom with small windows and exposed timber cladding panels

underneath. The walls consist of 2 metre wide prefabricated load bearing units, to which the new roof has been rigidly fixed. This forms large lightweight bracing elements which prevent the flexing of the existing structure. This together with a precast concrete supporting slab transmits the loads to the existing columns and walls. The existing concrete sports hall structure only required reinforcement at foundation level. Based on a distinctly environmentally conscious design, the highly insulated new structure helps to limit heat losses from the sports hall. The new building required a carefully controlled ventilation system, since the level of insulation necessitates forced ventilation at certain times to maintain a comfortable environment within. Openable roof and wall windows allow additional control of the environment.

The new structure helps to reinforce the courtyard enclosure as an important focus within the campus. It has been planted with scented flowers and edible fruit which give it an intensity it did not have before. The courtyard elevation is indented and fully connected to the adjacent structures, open at various points on the ground floor which helps it to interlock with the existing complex through a series of access ramps and walkways. At first floor level there are terraces and cantilevered internal volumes creating an interesting spatial variety to the daycare centre's interior. The gently sloping cantilevered volume encloses a cave-like play area for the younger children, with small windows carefully positioned at different heights. Older children in the after-school element occupy a mini tower, a sort of continuous spatial route which spirals up to a

rooftop observation window. The building's spatial experience offers children a choice of different routes and spaces for withdrawing, niches, a mattress storage, the wet area and cloakrooms. The six tranquil and bright playgroup spaces are adapted to suit the children's own age group. Units for the 6-10 year olds are set out like mini apartments. Yet, as glass walls are the only separating internal walls in the main social areas, there is a sense of transparency throughout. Subtle, discreet colours, generally light ochre complementing the natural timber panels with their beechwood surface finish, are used on the internal walls and ceiling. This creates a lightness and warmth making it an ideal place for young children to learn or to simply hang out.

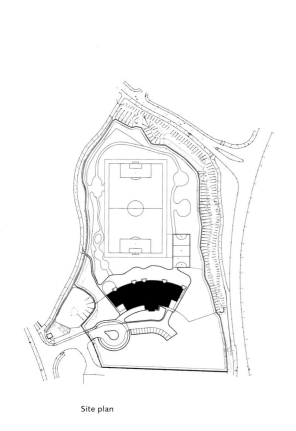

Site plan

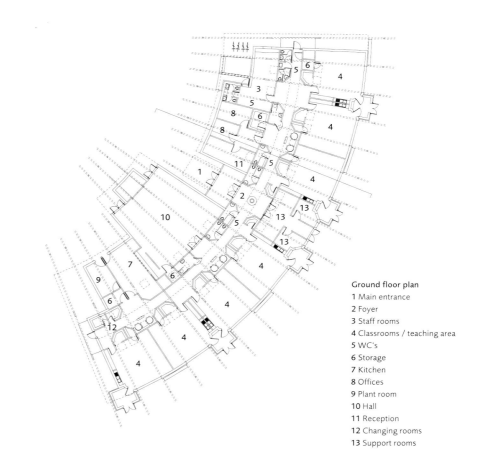

Ground floor plan
1 Main entrance
2 Foyer
3 Staff rooms
4 Classrooms / teaching area
5 WC's
6 Storage
7 Kitchen
8 Offices
9 Plant room
10 Hall
11 Reception
12 Changing rooms
13 Support rooms

Crisp timber detailing on the internal façade illustrates the structural logic | General view from the meadow landscape shows the exterior | Classroom interior as a single open-plan run of connected space | The subtle colour coding creates a cool vibrant yet surprisingly calm atmosphere

Kingsmead Primary School

Northwich, Cheshire, UK

Architect	White Design Associates, Bristol
Pupils	150 aged 5-11 years
Building area	1,230 m²
Average classroom	Open-plan, approx. 60 m² per class
Parking spaces	14
Build cost	1.76 million GBP
Completion	2004
Year group system	Age-related single form entry

Environmentally and sustainably advanced design which feeds into the educational curriculum

The need for new primary school facilities at Kingsmead was a result of new housing developments in the area. The requirement was to create a 150 place, seven classroom school with potential for future expansion. Cheshire County Council promoted the design intention to create a school, which would be an exemplar of sustainable design and construction. The building's orientation on the site, the selection of natural materials, the integration of natural ventilation and numerous other details add to its overall sustainability ethos. For example, by locating the school building close to the existing site entrance, and creating a curved building form, the inside is neatly enclosed to create a clear 'front and back'. This simple planning move reduces the length of the service road

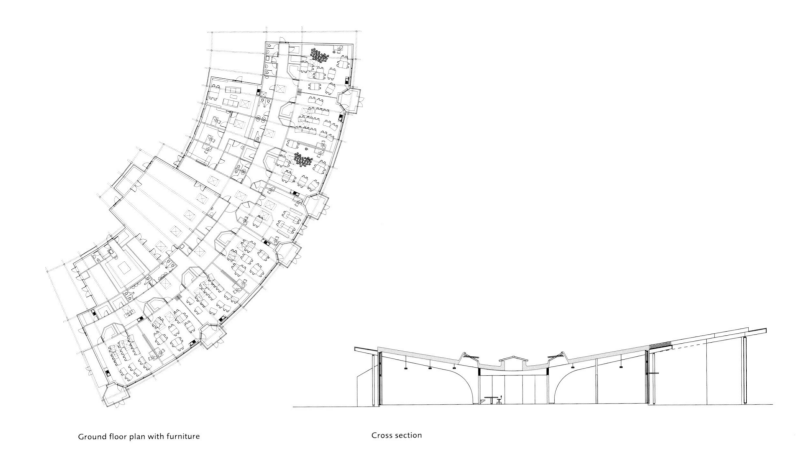

Ground floor plan with furniture

Cross section

leaving the majority of the site to playing fields. The building has a strong, visible timber structure, which adds interest to the internal spaces and allows direct contact with this natural material appropriate on this semi-rural location. The structural 'glulam' frame allows for flexible room forms, so that classrooms can be configured in a number of different ways. The Western Red Cedar cladding provides a soft, warm external appearance. The form of the roof is one of its most distinctive features and not only aids natural ventilation but also allows rainwater to be harvested for flushing toilets and maintaining the landscape in drought conditions. The predominantly north-facing classrooms ensure consistent soft direct lighting. Each classroom has a 'winter garden', which provides an alternative

space to the main teaching zone. In addition there are a number of support spaces and small group rooms for special needs teaching.

Since it opened in July 2004, the staff at Kingsmead School have been working with the aid of the new building on changes and improvements to their teaching methods, specifically integrating environmental awareness into the curriculum. Plans include everything from use of the building's energy-in-use data to support maths teaching, to class gardens for pupils to learn about issues such as 'food miles', while they grow their own food and develop a green 'travel to school' scheme to encourage parents to leave their cars at home. Kingsmead's 'whole school' approach

where educational, design and construction practice is being re-thought, promises to be a wonderful place to learn. Colour is used sparingly yet with real sensitivity to its sensory qualities, so for example cool greens and blues are used in activity spaces such as circulation spaces, whilst warm reds and orange colours are used in classroom areas where students are more static.

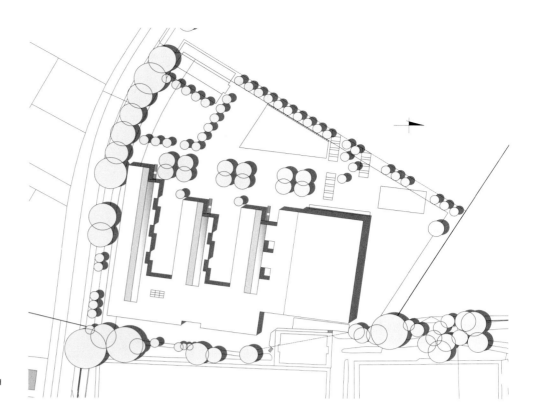

Site plan showing three fingers of accommodation forming two west-facing courtyards. The main entrance is from the south on Goethestraße, with a secondary entrance to the large sports hall complex on the north end

View from Goethestraße | View of the main entrance from Goethestraße | View from the west

Energy-plus Primary School

Hohen Neuendorf, Germany

Architect	IBUS Architects and Engineers – Ingo Lütke-meyer, Hans-Martin Schmid, Gustav Hillmann, Berlin, Bremen
Pupils	540
Building area	7,414 m²
Average classroom	86 m² (including workroom)
Parking spaces	18
Build cost	12.3 million EUR
Completion	2011
Year group system	Age-related groups, 3 form entry
A building which sets the benchmark for environmental design	

How to make a school which reflects two competing ideas, that of traditional cellular classrooms, the proverbial 'machine for learning in,' and a humane place which truly reflects the world of the future, within which its key users, the pupils, will be living decades from now?

Understandably most contemporary architects will look to the knotty issue of sustainability, controlling global warming by minimising the carbon footprint and endeavouring to jangle the child's awareness with bolt-on goodies such as wind turbines and solar panels. Often costs will soar and the project budget will be cut back; that dreaded phrase 'value engineering' will be utilised by the client's quantity surveyor to pol-

Ground floor plan
1 Main classroom space
2 Flexible teaching area
3 Group room
4 Workroom
5 School offices/teachers' room
6 Cloakrooms
7 Store
8 Teaching materials
9 Library
10 Kitchen
11 Auditorium/dining
12 Changing rooms, sports utilities
13 Sports hall
14 After-school club

itely request cost reductions. This process can dilute the architect's original vision to the point where the sustainability agenda is all but lost. This has not been the case here.

The new school at Hohen Neuendorf is for an expanding town 15 km north of Berlin. The brief required a primary school for children aged 6-11 years, with each age group comprising three forms of entry (90 children in each unit), with a total of 540 pupils across 18 classrooms. In addition there was to be an integrated triple field sports hall with community access during evenings and weekends, facilitating all sorts of additional activities for parents, grandparents and other members of the extended family. It has a real commu-

nity dimension, potentially opening education up to everyone for their lifetimes.

Therefore it needed to be robust to resist generations of use and organised in such a way that it retains a sense of small-scale departments within a larger whole. So each age-orientated group of three classrooms takes its place within three clearly defined wings of accommodation on two storeys. Each is orientated with a closed façade to the north and a more open south-facing façade. The designers have adopted well-known typological moves drawn from a rich history of school design, with a linking 'street' of accommodation running south to north (from the main entrance) forming a lively social spine for the new

building. There are in addition staff offices, a dining room with a connected kitchen/multi-purpose hall and a small library.

In consultation with the school teachers and the designer's deeply scientific understanding of sustainability a 'home concept' – as they describe it – has been developed for each group of 30 pupils, a sequence of linked areas comprising a traditional classroom with a smaller workroom directly off it; this is connected by a circulation space which is subsidiary to the main 'street' circulation spine, leading from the classrooms to a children's washroom and cloakroom. The whole creates a logical organisation around which the entire concept for ventilation and lighting can take place.

First floor plan
1 Main classroom space
2 Flexible teaching area
3 Group room
4 Workroom
5 School offices / teachers' room
6 Cloakrooms

Homebase corridor | Corridor with break-out space |
View of interior circulation

These are the age-old problems of school design, where cooling is more critical than heating, and it is where this project gets really clever.

For the head of design, Ingo Lütkemeyer, the unambiguous solution to the overheating problem is firstly thermal mass. Based on the simple concept that a cave is always cool no matter how hot it is outside, whereas a tent gets hot instantly when the external temperature rises, the fabric of the building, predominantly the heat generating roof areas most exposed to the sun, has to be made of a heavy material. This will ameliorate external solar gain, soaking up the sun's energy without stress. Therefore the entire roof is constructed of concrete, in heavy pre-fabricated panels.

Secondly, a so-called hybrid ventilation system, that is a combination of natural and forced mechanical ventilation to the grouped homebases deals with variable occupancy conditions. During break times, when children are outside, air pours into the hot classroom spaces by way of large window sized vent panels. These are motor controlled and full height to completely aerate the space ready for the return of the children who will have been running around and ready to generate their own heat build-up. As they settle back into their lessons and the CO_2 levels begin to rise once more, a mechanical form of ventilation is required to freshen stale air, however only small amounts are required, so traditional full air conditioning is avoided. The supply airflow for the classrooms

correlates to the levels of external exhaust needed for the sanitary units, thus air is sucked out from the classrooms and through the toilets to provide the most efficient use of power.

These two key ideas are the fundamental principles around which the building's sustainability is predicated. Numerous other features add to the overall efficiency, for example thermal comfort during the hot summer periods is achieved by means of passive night cooling using the motor controlled vent windows to air the large areas of thermal storage mass, freshness which is then carried forward to daytime. A sophisticated south-facing façade with automated external blinds and the use of nanogel glazing to diffuse heavy

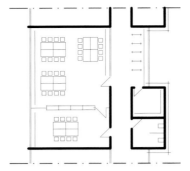
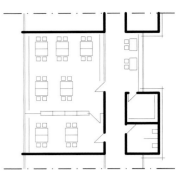

The generous homebase enables flexibility in three different teaching arrangements: the main classroom space can be used as a conventional 30 person classroom, while the project room provides space for more relaxed activities; the tables in classroom and project room can be arranged to accommodate for group work; the external corridor is used for small groups or individual tutoring.

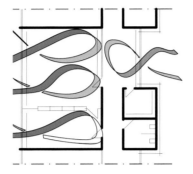
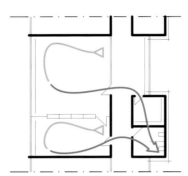
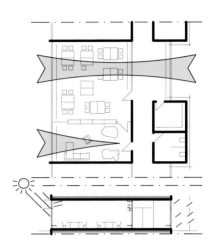

Ventilation and lighting concept for homebase: Air is emitted by large vertical motorised vents which open during break times. This can be complemented by way of the conventional opening window panels. Direct south light to the classrooms is controlled by shading devices while diffused light from the north provides cooler task daylight to the corridor and washroom areas.

solar spray, provides optimum natural light to the deep plan thus minimising the use of electrical lighting. Here the orientation of the building's windows is critical and shapes the internal form. Combined with the use of renewable energy resources such as wood pellets for heating and integrated photovoltaic panels across the entire roof, this building provides 25% life cycle cost savings.

South-facing classroom façade with solar control shading: the integrated ventilation and daylight glazing panels keep the interior cool and emit daylight into the deep plan

Site plan

Lower ground floor plan

1 Nursery playground
2 Early years playground
3 SEN block
4 Nursery

5 Infant playground
6 Crèche
7 Administration/offices
8 Junior playground

9 Staff carpark
10 Junior block
11 Library

Hall with cantilevered roof | Distant view from the south with the main hall and social deck on the left | Main entrance | Nursery entrance | Two-storey classroom block

Jubilee School

Brixton, London, UK

Architect	Allford Hall Monaghan Morris, London
Pupils	420 aged 4-11 years
Building area	3,550 m²
Average classroom	57 m²
Parking spaces	14
Build cost	4.5 million GBP
Completion	2002
Year group system	Traditional 2 form entry classbase system

Tight urban site supports a large institution with a variety of functions on two storeys with a distinctly urban feel

Located in a deprived inner city area in southwest London this community primary school sets out to establish an enclosed and protective children's world using an elegant contemporary architectural style. The scheme is predicated on partial access for community use during evenings and weekends together with a daycare/crèche facility, areas for profoundly deaf children to encourage their integration into mainstream school as well as the statutory infant and junior school classrooms. Here there is both a desire to make a building which is functionally complex to reflect the complexities of the brief, with shared uses interwoven into the planning, and at the same time the need to maintain security and functionality in its everyday school uses.

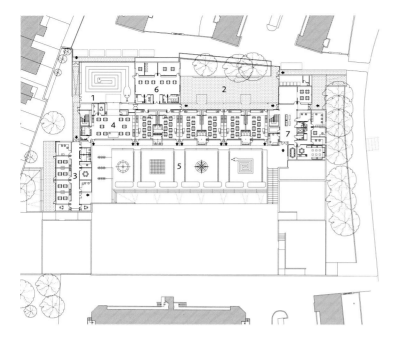

Upper ground floor plan

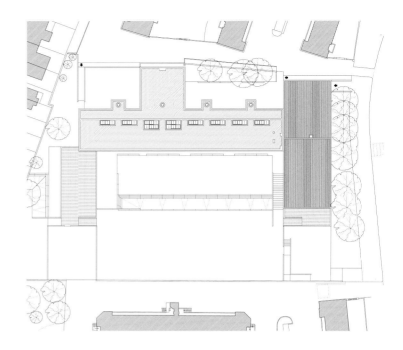

Roof plan

The public face of the building is at first sight austere. From the street it is a box-like high structure, handsomely finished predominantly in white render; this is an architectural language which is not to everyone's taste. 'It looks more like a supermarket than a school' was one comment we heard when visiting, 'It's ugly' was another. Certainly the scale of the entrance block is unlike most other primary schools. It is bulky and uncompromising in its external appearance dominating the streetscape. However, one of the advantages of this approach can be seen inside. On entering through a closely monitored entrance threshold, you are welcomed by a voluminous double-height foyer, an impressive public space that seems to welcome visitors, a statement perhaps of the school's intention to be

right at the heart of the community. This is a two-storey building, which is unusual for a primary. However, it ensures that all required accommodation is incorporated without losing too much outside play space. In addition this creates an imposing statement about the civic dimension of school attendance. The main entrance provides access into all parts of the school. On the lower ground floor there are reception and infant classes with the nursery and crèche (including its own nursery playground and separate early years courtyard) within the main east-west wing of accommodation. Access to the playground is on this lower ground floor for young children and infants. The site slopes significantly up from north to south. The architects have utilised this feature to create an enhanced sense

of enclosure with the main playground dug into the slope and hard landscaping enclosing the south side without over-shadowing the space.

The building itself forms a U shape with functions, which have potential for community use such as the library and main hall (with attached kitchen), on the first, or raised ground floor wing of accommodation, which is at the same level as the natural site level at the southern end of the boundary. A connecting terrace extends the external areas around the hall out along the main road and gives the upper ground floor a sense of space, with a strong inside outside dimension. On sunny days large door/windows can be thrown open, tables and chairs can be taken out onto

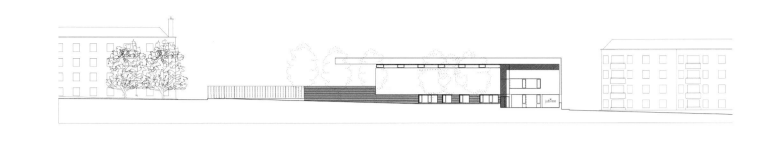

North and south elevations

the terrace giving views into the street below. Enclosing the playground on the west side is, at ground floor, the SEN wing. Above it is a similar terrace feature connecting first floor classrooms to the street and staff car parking on the southern side of the site.

Connecting the two east-west wings is the main junior school block of accommodation with a corridor link, which is broad and generous. It is space which has been 'borrowed' from the lower level circulation areas which are consequently partly external. However, the benefit of this strategy is that the upper level circulation is far more usable. There are cloakrooms and especially useful break-out spaces, which act as small group rooms, complementing classroom functions.

Access to the music, art and food technology rooms complete this tight urban jig-saw, which manages to be both ordered and legible as a plan, yet at the same time endlessly stimulating for the users. Like a mini walled city, children get constantly varying spatial perspectives as they move around the building. The junior school gives a sense of the privileges of age, as pupils are promoted to the upper level classrooms, each with its own south-facing balcony overlooking the playground.

From the outset, there was a wish to invest the new school with a strong and distinctive identity. This has partly been achieved by the use of graphic design to create a corporate image type logo, which is em-

bossed on the entrance wall, on pupil kit bags and on all of the school's stationery. It feels integral to the school itself. With the use of colour to highlight the vertical reveals on either side of the balconies and colourful playground graphics, there is a strong theme running throughout the building. Clearly there has been a careful control exerted between the balance of white render used to express the main structure and applied decorative features. Display boards are integral to the overall design, with children's art being displayed only where it is appropriate to the overall aesthetic. In this respect, the building is something of a statement about the architect's strongly held views on education and the power of architecture to raise aspirations and encourage learning through the care-

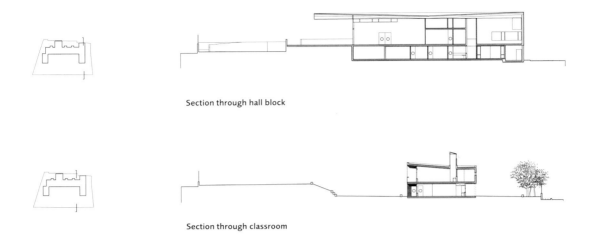

Section through hall block

Section through classroom

Two-storey classroom block with balcony detail and coloured reveals to flank walls | Circulation area | Upper level classroom with wet area worktops made of recycled plastic | Light reflection | Furniture

ful control of the environment. It is slightly doctrinaire at times, yet it must surely give order to the chaotic lives of some families who will use the building.

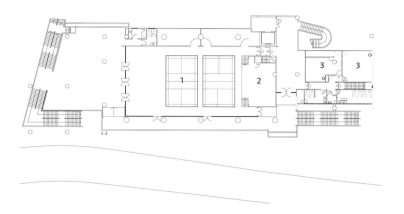
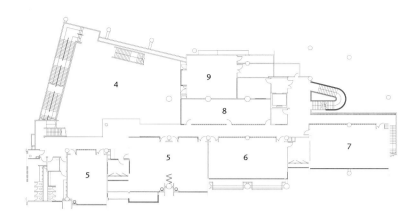

Ground floor plan	1 Assembly hall	6 General studies	11 Language room	Second floor plan
	2 Stage	7 Student activity centre	12 Multi-media room	
	3 Dressing room	8 Remedial teaching	13 Teacher's resource centre	
	4 Landscape area	9 Arts and crafts	14 Music room	
	5 Classroom	10 Library	15 General purpose room	

Jockey Club Primary School

Hong Kong, China

Architect	Aedas + Design Consultants, Hong Kong
Pupils	500 aged 6-12 years
Building area	6,900 m²
Average classroom	67 m²
Parking spaces	15
Build cost	79 million HKD
Completion	2002
Year group system	Age-related 2 form entry

A school which stretches over seven floors utilising a clever structural arrangement to fit the site

The 18 classroom primary school is as a model school, which forms part of a larger conglomeration of education buildings on the Tai Po, Hong Kong Institute of Education campus. The primary school, whilst being a laboratory for educational experimentation, research and innovation in curriculum methods, is also an integral part of the new living and working community. The building straddles the dramatically sloping site which climbs steeply up from the lower road to the upper access road level where the main entrance is located, almost 20 metres above. The architects needed to balance the requirement for outside space with the difficulties of the site and the extensive accommodation schedule. A stepped courtyard arrangement has been developed which provides a range of secure outside areas. They are ingeniously integrated

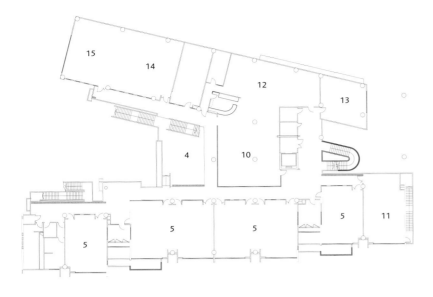

Third floor plan

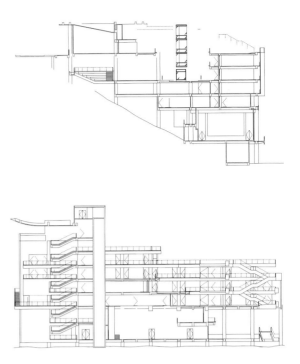

Sections

View of stepped gardens and lift tower with open corridors | View of the upper level elevation with dramatically projecting cantilevered roofs over the multi-purpose hall and the stairway up to staff areas | Sports hall on the upper level | Assembly hall at ground floor level

into the complex sectional arrangement, organised in the form of a monumental concrete structure which appears as a massive six-storey volume at the lower level and a more conventional two-storey building on the upper level. So at the lowest level, the assembly hall has a triple-height external terrace immediately adjacent to provide access and a forecourt during busy times when the hall is in use for community events. The top level has an open basket ball court adjacent to a multi-purpose area which is formed out of the natural extension of the floor plate. Access via a ramp beneath a sculptural canopy at the side of the building takes the visitor gently down towards the main entrance, where he will get a dramatic view of the city and bay below, framed by the open slot between two secondary structures. The route down can then be expe-

rienced by way of a variety of stairways, both open and closed, which lead to the main teaching accommodation below. Here an external space utilises the slope to form an amphitheatre-like terrace of seating for the adjacent performance area and large covered playground. Beneath this space there are a multi-media room, library and other teaching areas. Whilst the linear building spreads itself across the landscape over six levels, the planning is organised around a central axis which embraces the main entrance, stepped gardens and lift core; this provides a clear sense of orientation. The building is most legible when you analyse the section. Its orientation and the relationship between solid and void have been carefully choreographed to maximise the effects of day lighting and cross ventilation. All classrooms are south-facing to

benefit from the summer breeze and to shelter from the cold winter winds from the north. West-facing windows are avoided as the light creates too much glare. The central courtyard helps a great deal in bringing natural light in and promoting cross ventilation. The intention was to create flexible accommodation with an independent structural frame and the use of high performance acoustic moveable wall panels between each of the paired classrooms. With the easy variation of the partitioning between the classrooms, spatial transformations can be achieved with ease to host different group sizes. The open corridor areas outside the classrooms are skilfully offset to create project areas. A small observation area is attached to each classroom to enable future teachers to observe teaching and learning activities.

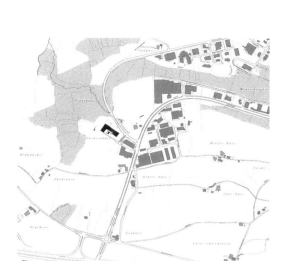

Site plan

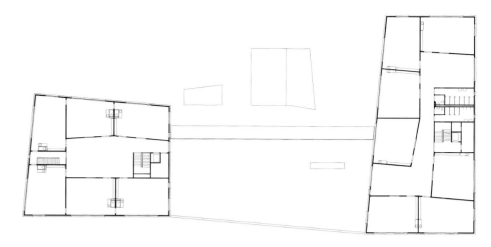

First floor plan

Main elevation facing onto the street | View from main staircase
through the dining area and down into the gymnasium | View from
classroom towards the shared group room | View into gymnasium

Zürich International School

Wadenswil, Switzerland

Architect	Galli & Rudolf, Zürich
Pupils	450 aged 5 -11 years
Building area	6,216 m²
Average classroom	70 m²
Parking spaces	103 and 17 for buses
Build cost	17.9 million CHF
Completion	2002
Year group system	Age-related 3 form entry

A building where staff and students have been closely involved in the
design process to give them a sense of belonging

Two key ideas formed the development of the design, firstly the cosmopolitan and slightly itinerant nature of the student intake. Over 400 boys and girls attending this private English language school come from more than 30 different countries. Most of their parents are employed in international companies and spend two or three years in the Zurich area at most. It was felt that the school had an important social role to play, not just for students, but for parents in helping to establish contact with other parents during their relatively brief stay. Secondly, the location of the site was neither urban nor suburban; rather it occupies a strange interface between an industrial zone and a golf course. The lack of any strong contextual identity was an important issue during the design development. Planning was carried out under tight deadlines and equally tight

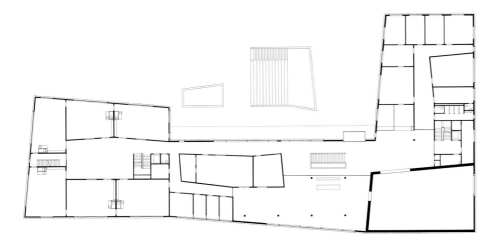

Second floor plan

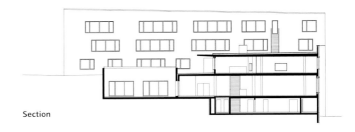

Section

cost constraints. The school users participated by suggesting room arrangements and preferred layouts which were incorporated into the final designs by architects Galli & Rudolf. The school users also came up with other key principles regarding materials, colours, access and transparency, all of which were enthusiastically adopted by the architects. For example they expressed the wish to avoid right angles in the planning. This was achieved by a subtle twisting of the building's grid to achieve functional spaces which are slightly non-orthogonal, thus increasing interest and variation to the classroom spaces without adding to the overall cost. Other principles such as the use of smooth coloured renders rather than brutal fair-faced concrete added to the sense of ownership the users felt with the architectural process.

The need to make a building which was not simply about education, but also about social interaction between parents emerged very quickly as the scheme was discussed. Rather than restricting access to the entrance areas, parents are encouraged to come into the building when collecting or delivering their children. The central part of the school is very open with a double-height multi-functional hall and library which are largely open and part of a promenade route through to the teaching blocks. This encourages a sense of engagement with lots of visual contact between users, staff students and parents. The central hall is full of light and has the main reception desk, a canteen and a parents' association room, to further enhance the sense that this is owned by the parents as well as the students.

The main teaching spaces are grouped in clusters of six classrooms, each has its own small bathroom. Each cluster has a central group space which is used by different age ranges for social and informal study sessions. There are windows between classrooms and this community space, which enhances the sense of an open environment full of light and colour. The primary colour theme is carried out to the external architectural treatment with a light green render and dark red window frames giving the façades a distinctive appearance in this bland setting. The building is a new landmark promoting its own sense of identity to the surroundings to become a beacon for its multi-national users. It is almost childlike in its external form, reflecting the close involvement of the children, and inside it is full of bold primary colours matching the multi-cultural intake.

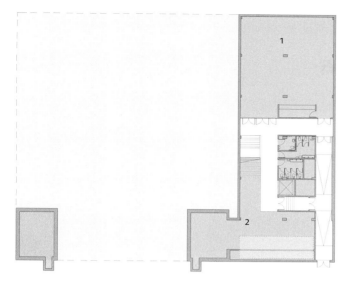

Basement floor plan

Ground floor plan

1 Multi-purpose room
2 Offices and storage
3 Kindergarten
4 First grade classroom
5 Second grade classroom

6 Third grade classroom
7 Fourth grade classroom
8 Fifth grade classroom
9 Sixth grade classroom
10 Music, dance and art spaces

Coloured tiles on the street façade counter the drab post industrial context | Conceptual façade with the suggestion of the use of the dead-end street as a playground during school hours

South Bronx Charter School for The Arts

Hunts Point, New York, USA

Architect	Weisz + Yoes Studio, New York
Pupils	250 aged 5-10 years
Building area	2,100 m²
Average classroom	60 m² (for 24 student class size)
Parking spaces	0
Build cost	2.3 million USD
Completion	2004
Year group system	Traditional single form entry classbase system

Community design and use of existing industrial building to reduce costs and provide more space than usual

The project is unusual in that the process which directed its design and procurement was fully inclusive and local to the point where a new school typology can be discerned; not only is the result a true community building in that it accurately reflects the needs and aspirations of local people who bothered to get involved, it is also comparatively small and orientated towards the needs of people who are not necessarily in education themselves.

Initiated by community activists from the local arts board, the school developed through a series of workshops with board members, school staff and parents, which were organised by the architects. A key concern was how the school might integrate into the wider

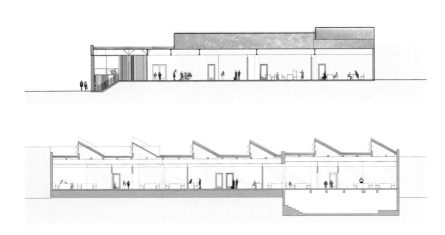

Section through glazed entrance hall

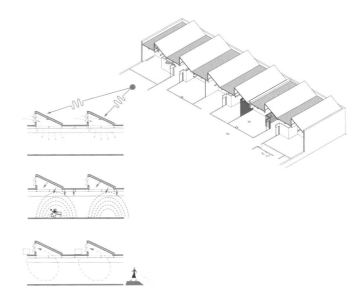

Daylighting concept

View from the reception desk towards the community hall at the heart of the plan | Larger than average classrooms provide for creativity and fluid flexible teaching groups

community; one response to this question was the suggestion that if the school had a gallery, local artists and students might use it. Thus new spaces were being added which aimed at a seamless crossover between school and community. Then several buildings and vacant lots in the South Bronx were visited. Finally, an old sausage factory was selected mainly because of its location, but also because it provided large flexible accommodation with widely spaced columns throughout. One of the main ideas to emerge was the grouping of similar grade classrooms together around shared multi-use spaces, or as one participant described them, 'hot pods'. In addition, all arts-related spaces were positioned in the centre of the scheme and along the main street façade, emphasising their

importance and allowing them to be semi-permeable, by way of moveable partitions, to the surrounding halls and communal spaces, and readily accessible to members of the general public entering from the street.

The limitations of a confined factory building with its deep-plan form meant that there were very few opportunities for conventional windows. The architects designed the building with a regular grid of north-facing openable skylights across the entire roof, which provided for modules of 45 degree south-facing translucent PV panels. The sustainability agenda was addressed with solar electricity generation, the use of recycled building products and certified sustainable wood products.

The end result is a building which is basic architecture on the outside, whereas on the inside there is an unusually spacious feel with high ceilings and larger than average teaching spaces. With exposed service ducts visible within the open ceiling void, up and over moveable wall panels it has funky light industrial feel, more like an advertising agency than a school. The challenge to site a school in an old factory building right at the heart of the community has been very successful. It functions both as a traditional school and a new community learning centre.

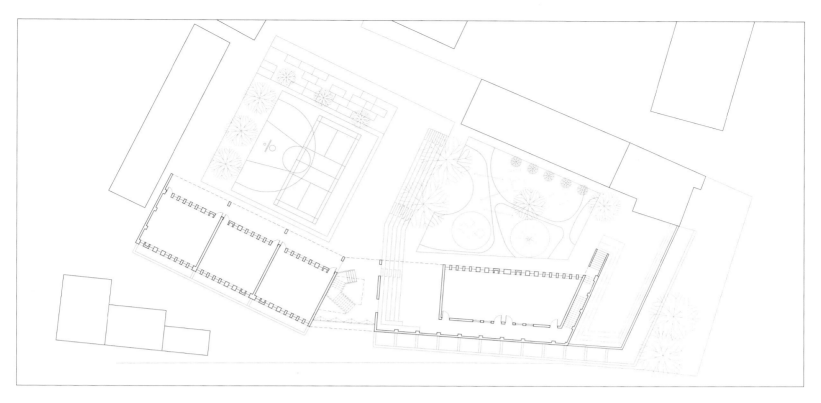

Ground floor plan with three classrooms, an entrance hall, a media room and library with an additional open classroom

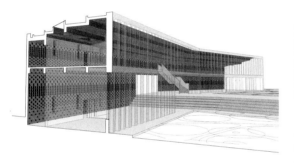

The fenestration on the courtyard side is evenly spread across the length of the façade in form of deeply recessed vertical window finials in heavy recycled brick to provide shading | Perforated thick masonry walls to the south let prevailing winds pass into the colonnade, cooling and de-humidifying air in the classrooms | Internal view of the rear colonnade | Close-ups of columns

Recycled Brick School

Tongjiang, Jianxi, China

Architect	Joshua Bolchover and John Lin, Rural Urban Framework, Hong Kong
Pupils	450 children aged 6-11 years
Building area	1,000 m²
Average classroom	70 m²
Parking spaces	0
Build cost	170,000 USD
Completion	2011
Year group system	Age-related groups in 8 classrooms

A school which uses economical strategies to develop a sustainable and cost effective environment

This project in Shicheng County reflects the nature of its location and combines austerity in its construction processes with a robust and highly architectural form that carries with it the best in passive sustainability practices. With the aim of rationalising down a host of small local schools into larger more efficient institutions, the Chinese government is currently consolidating many primary schools in remote areas. In this case a decrepit old building fit only for demolition made way for a more efficient low cost structure, expanding the school roll from 220 to 450 pupils. The challenge for architects John Lin and Joshua Bolchover, who are part of the University of Hong Kong's not-for-profit design agencies at the Faculty of Architecture, was to make something special within tight budgetary constraints whilst evolving the or-

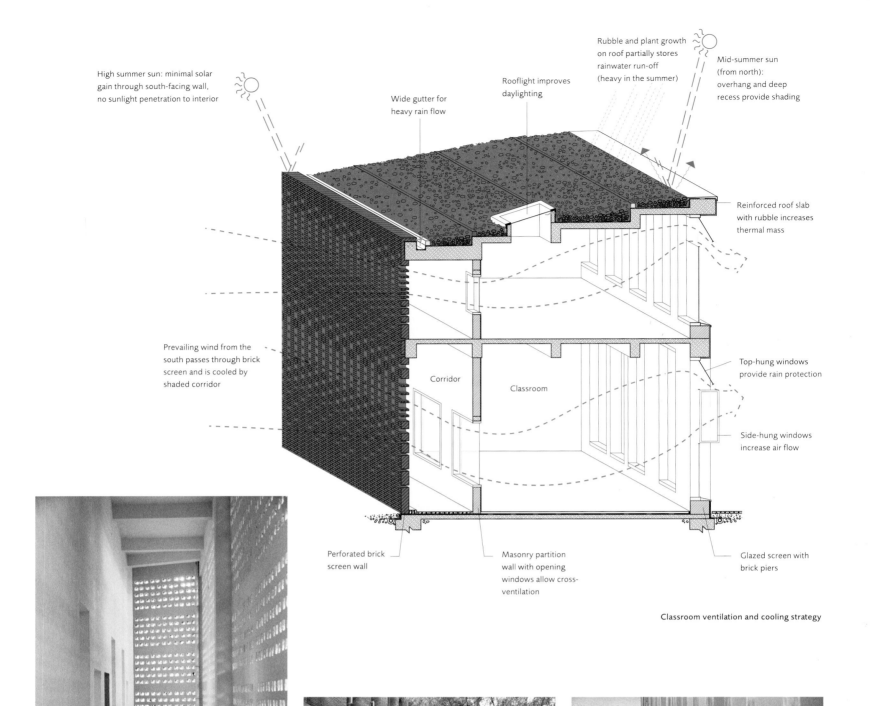

High summer sun: minimal solar gain through south-facing wall, no sunlight penetration to interior

Wide gutter for heavy rain flow

Rooflight improves daylighting

Rubble and plant growth on roof partially stores rainwater run-off (heavy in the summer)

Mid-summer sun (from north): overhang and deep recess provide shading

Reinforced roof slab with rubble increases thermal mass

Prevailing wind from the south passes through brick screen and is cooled by shaded corridor

Top-hung windows provide rain protection

Corridor

Classroom

Side-hung windows increase air flow

Perforated brick screen wall

Masonry partition wall with opening windows allow cross-ventilation

Glazed screen with brick piers

Classroom ventilation and cooling strategy

thodoxies of the traditional Chinese educational system without too much radical change. The hope was that the new form would not only be safer and more hygienic, it would also stimulate learning through wider social interaction.

The site lies in a rural village populated by farmers growing tobacco and lotus seed. Annual incomes are around 260 USD which is near starvation wages. This places a strong emphasis on austerity across the board. For the architects, the idea of recycling felt right from the beginning. Materials from the demolished school were saved and redeployed in the new building. The roof is constructed from reinforced concrete which is strong enough to take a thick layer of recycled brick rub-

ble sourced from the demolished sites. This provides greater thermal mass, creating a substratum for a natural green roof, trapping wind-blown plants and mosses. The roof steps down to meet a brick wall on the street side of the site, which is full of perforations to create natural ventilation transmitting subtle patterns of light into the circulation spine.

The roof and external corridor walls form a thickened protective edge which is a counterpoint to the internal playground façade, which is more open, articulated by concrete fins and vertical strips of glazing. The natural topography of the site is maintained to create a series of external steps that extend into the courtyard. From the stepped roof profile with its mossy growth to the exter-

nal play areas which engage with the surrounding terrain the whole has a coherence that speaks both of nature and new technology, bonding the traditional with the promise of a more comfortable future for its impoverished families. The building itself has an appropriate civic presence and with its simple sustainability it is warm in winter and cool in summer.

Secondary Schools

Many aspects of school design apply equally across all age ranges. For example, the need to define safe secure territories within the overall structure of the institution or the use of colour for wayfinding and legibility. Acoustics are as critical in classrooms for four year olds as they are for 14 year olds. Security is important to keep strangers out and to maintain control of every student within. Maintaining good environmental conditions and providing attractive modern environments which appeal to fashion conscious children are priorities, which apply across the board. However, for a number of reasons, these issues become of critical importance when applied to secondary school building design.

Students are infinitely more mature and independent at the age of 11 or 12 than when they first enter the education system at the age of 3 or 4. Generally, younger children focus more closely onto their immediate surroundings whereas older children will be more outward looking, interested in the wider social and spatial environment particularly as they approach puberty. Secondary schools are almost always larger both in terms of the physical size and the number of pupils accommodated. On average, secondary schools cater for between 780 to 1,200 students, and secondary schools dealing with yet larger numbers are not uncommon. They are much more grown-up environments promoting increasing independence and responsibility as children grow towards adulthood.

Perhaps most importantly, the specialised nature of secondary education generally means that children move around the school campus more frequently to access different curriculum areas. This means that the organisation and grouping of subject areas (often referred to as faculties) is crucial to the efficient functioning of the institution. They can be organised to minimise travel distances, for example art and craft departments should be close to the hall to enable the movement of props and scenery; science and technology faculties should be clustered together for similar logistical reasons. Teachers will feel isolated if they are unable to meet with colleagues in a centrally positioned staff room because travel distances are so long. This is why circulation areas should be interesting and spatially varied; colour used as way-finding is particularly useful.

Schools designed now will be with us for many generations to come. It is the skill of a good architect to plan and organise a complex secondary school brief efficiently, yet at the same time, to challenge educational preconceptions and safe orthodoxies prescribed by governments. This is a skill at which architects excel, making visionary proposals which act as a catalyst to social and educational reform. This may mean the addition of new spaces to a traditional schedule of accommodation. Morphosis, the architects for the Diamond Ranch School (pages 242-243), have added art spaces, a music space and an auditorium. They have also reconfigured the cafeteria so it could operate as a theatre for community events. It is the mark of a great architect to take difficult site conditions and manipulate them to make even more architecture and more space by relating the programme to the site opportunities. This is what makes the Diamond Ranch such as inspiring educational environment. The intention of the whole is to challenge the message sent by a society that routinely communicates its disregard for the young by educating them in cheap institutional 'boxes' surrounded by security fences. Here the environment is an inspiration to all who use it, a turn-on to education for often disinterested students.

Traditionally, school buildings were designed in a conservative way, to reflect a serious and demanding range of competing issues. Usually the need for careful budgetary control cast the architect as the voice of reason within an aspirational client user group who may have been looking for grand architectural statements in their new school buildings. However, the reality with most school projects was that tight budgets meant that 'star' international architects (with a few notable exceptions) did not dirty their hands with a project as mundane as a new secondary school let alone a complicated refurbishment of an existing primary school. They were not viewed as particularly sexy commissions. That attitude is clearly changing with high profile architects recognising that these are important and prestigious buildings, central to the life of the community.

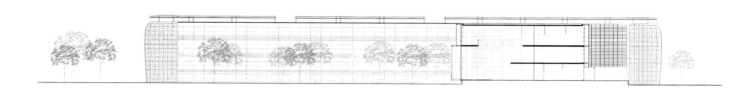

Cross sections

Detail of solar protection panels on west façade | West façade with 'Checkerboard' effect from afar | Views of the side showing three different façade treatments

Collège Nicolas Robert

Vernouillet, Eure-et-Loir, France

Architect	Berthelier Fichet Tribouillet, Chartres
Pupils	700 aged 10-18 years (currently 412)
Building area	6,500 m²
Average classroom	68 m²
Parking spaces	20 (for teachers only)
Build cost	8.8 million EUR
Completion	2004
Year group system	4 form entry age-integrated house groups

The school uses a sophisticated system of solar protection which has unusual and positive effects on the internal spaces

The school comprises two wings of accommodation, which were carefully phased around the existing buildings on the site to avoid closure of the institution during development works. The L shaped plan is on the face of it a simple organisation of lecture rooms on the three upper storeys with communal and social rooms on the ground and lower ground floor (the sloping site immerses one floor beneath ground on the short wing of the 'L'). On the lower ground floor there is the main student entrance, which looks onto the public concourse. This important space is articulated as two broad limestone paths, which intersect at the main entrance; this provides a strong axial emphasis and a formality, which, along with the distinctive curved 'checkerboard' façade, suggests a corporate

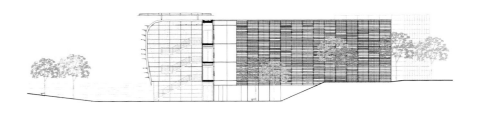

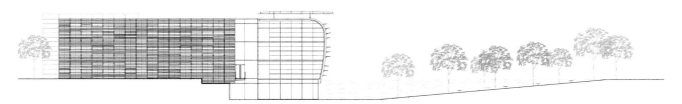

South and north façade

headquarters building rather than a school. On the main (raised) ground floor there is a separate entrance for professors with a wing for administration and the restaurant.

From the outset the architects felt it was going to be difficult to create an interesting education building within a suburban context such as this. However utilising the very lack of a context as the inspiration to do something different, they have created a landmark building which, through the adoption of strikingly modern façade treatment and a positive approach to external (public) spaces, has transformed the setting and the image of education locally. It is first and foremost a technologically advanced building, a machine

for learning, however it manages to be a very humane environment at the same time; it is in scale, flexible and user friendly.

A number of key themes have informed the architecture: firstly the need for a strong architectural expression externally which is achieved by the adoption of a subtly different range of glazing and façade panels all choreographed together in white and crème renders to create an ever changing spatial glow; secondly a highly controllable interior system of fixed and openable windows (on the west façade) which controls views and enables the users to adapt and change the quality of their environment from within. Here they can either be close to the surrounding views and

therefore the life of the neighbourhood, or they can be distant, cocooned within their own academic solitude. The final key theme is the adoption of a sophisticated range of active and passive sustainability devices including solar roof panels and façade shading, to provide a school which is 'green' with its own very contemporary style.

The main wing of accommodation, which runs the entire length of the site (over 100 metres), is orientated towards the west which means that it has direct afternoon sun for most of the year. The sun can be very low in trajectory defeating most conventional attempts to control glare and heat gain. This can be a potentially disastrous scenario in the context of teach-

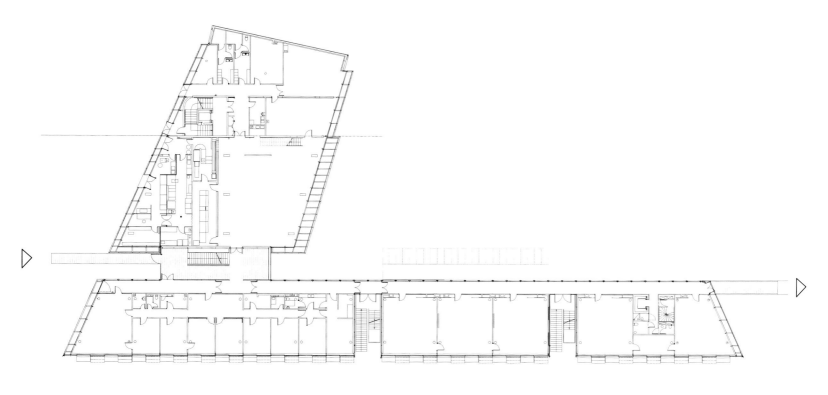

Ground floor plan

ing rooms, particularly in traditional highly glazed secondary school buildings. Here the designers have created a main façade which literally closes up to provide complete solar and glare protection. In the form of a checkerboard layout, alternately fixed and swivelling panels or flaps open or close at the flick of a switch. Not only is this a highly effective environmental device, it also allows for variations in the teaching spaces: they can be light or dark (for ICT or where images are to be projected); views out can be visible or obscured, so that at certain key times the concentration of the entire class can be focussed only onto the subject lesson; no chance for day-dreaming here. But perhaps most significantly, the rooms can benefit from that essential sense of light and shade to create

different moods and an ever changing sense of space. The Italians have a word which they use in the context of painting, 'chiaroscuro', which brings drama and emotion into the image. In a similar way, the designers of the Collège Nicolas Robert at Vernouillet have created a school which is almost unique in its potential for variability and spatial drama, the school classroom becomes like a theatre. As many teachers will admit, effective teaching is often like being on the stage.

However, the west-facing façade is not the end of this story. Structure is in the form of a concrete post-and-beam system which is set within the external envelope so that façades are free of any solid structural elements. The appearance is of a thin skin stretched

across a frame. In addition to the variable checkerboard façade, there is a more conventional treatment on the east-facing façade. It is still in the language of light metallic greys and cream hues, however it comprises horizontal, alternately solid and translucent glazed panels, which light circulation corridors and provide secondary illumination into some teaching rooms where appropriate. A similar translucent glazing system is adopted for the north-facing street, only with a second external screen of plastic Plexiglas plaques which are used as internal screening devices and part of the landscaping. Themes are constantly overlapping both inside and outside in this calm, modern learning environment.

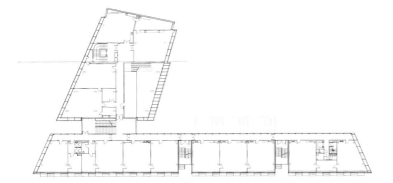

First floor plan

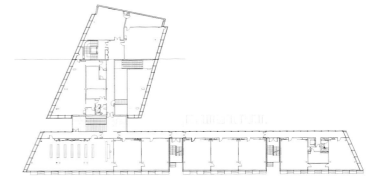

Second floor plan

Entrance from Rue Ch. Péguy for staff and professors | Main entrance path to foyer for student access | View of internal courtyard with canopy and feature benches | Circulation area

At the rear there is an inner courtyard garden which with a large canopy reflecting the internal adjacent chill-out space, a sort of all-purpose student club which opens onto the student garden to provide an appropriate centre for the school community. Right next to this area is the sports complex. The garden itself is a semi-natural meadow with as yet young trees planted in an ordered form around the space. A steep embankment encloses the outside recreation area, which is part of the natural topography of the site. There are five metallic over-scaled benches inside the garden which are made of galvanised aluminium and appear to have dropped off the side of the building. This is an appropriate reflection of the cool interaction which is achieved between the inside and the outside, between formality and informality, and finally between the suburban setting and this important institution, the modern school.

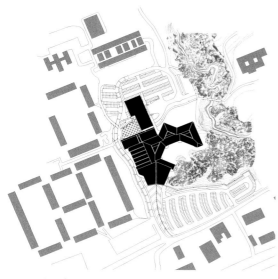

Site plan

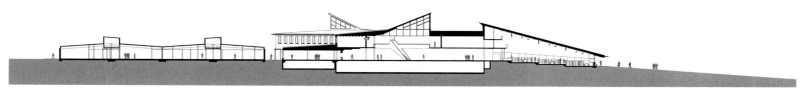

Section

Aerial view | Garden façade | Main entrance is marked by a dramatic
butterfly shaped roof | Library interior near the main entrance |
Atrium with cafeteria

Ale Upper
Secondary School

Nödinge, Sweden

Architect	Wingårdh Arkitektkontor, Göteborg
Pupils	600 aged 15-19 years
Building area	12,300 m²
Average classroom	65 m²
Parking spaces	160
Build cost	132 million SEK
Completion	1995
Year group system	Age-related year groupings

A school with a strong urban and community presence

Back in 1994, architect Gert Wingårdh was commissioned to build a new school in the small town of Nödinge which is roughly 20 kilometers north of Göteborg. The brief was for a new multi-functional secondary school which would also act as a community centre for the town, with a library, theatre, gymnasium and other recreational facilities. In addition, the town wanted a building which was affordable but also architecturally distinctive to help shape the otherwise characterless environment of the town centre. The site strategy entailed the re-location of an existing bus garage which enabled the new school plan to engage with an existing rocky outcrop, an important natural feature within the landscape. This heavily planted area now screens the classrooms from the heavily trafficked area below,

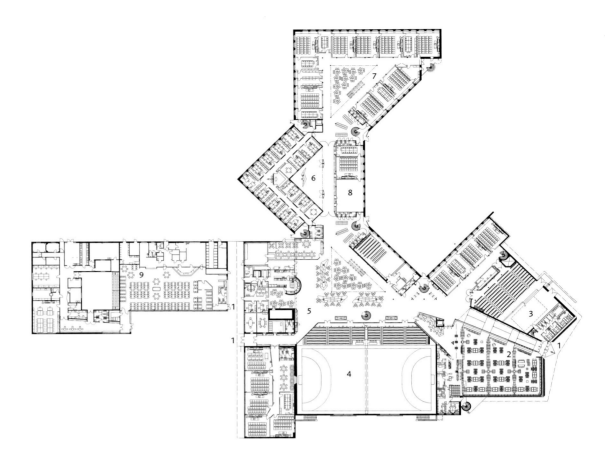

Ground floor plan
1 Entrance
2 Library
3 Theatre
4 Gymnasium
5 Café
6 Information
7 Study centre
8 Classroom
9 Restaurant

as the main classroom wing enfolds the contours of the escarpment. This forms a natural enclosed external play area which is both secure and full of character for students using it, a wilderness garden at the heart of the highly organised school plan. Located on the edge of a medium rise housing project, the mainly two-storey school building features a dramatic butterfly shaped roof over the main entrance block, which breaks the scale of the piece and leads visitors centrally into the rest of the school. The huge duo-pitched roof features a single rainwater drainage pipe which takes water off the roof at the main entrance. The rainwater then runs across the entrance plaza in a blue tiled open channel, which forms a magnificent stream of water on rainy days. The public entrance stair leads into the upper parts of the most

public areas of the school's accommodation, the library and theatre with related meeting rooms and other public facilities. Just beyond is what the architects describe as the Green Square (actually triangular in shape). This is a type of covered agora, with a café and seating area, an interface between the strictly educational areas and the mixed function public spaces. There you might witness a rock band practicing behind sound proof glass, or look down into the gym or back over the entrance and library. The sequence of spaces continues with several more triangular shaped indoor squares surrounded by balconies. These serve as circulation spaces as well as places for socialising or studying, an organisational strategy that derives more from modern office planning than school design. In the planning there is a further quirk,

the teachers' offices are withdrawn from their traditional location, that is on guard over the entrance and circulation areas. Instead they are in a more discreet position deep within the building and away from the activities so that teachers themselves have the chance to study and reflect in a calm and privileged position. Instead of treating teachers as policemen on constant patrol, the scheme relies on openness itself to establish the sense of security a school needs: there are no dark corners where bullies can misbehave. Enclosure and visual monitoring by teachers are limited to the classrooms, which are not connected to the common areas except for a carefully sound-insulated opening for ventilation purposes. The view is that these are places for concentration and distractions should therefore be minimal.

Elevation to communal block

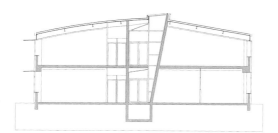

Sections through a typical teaching block

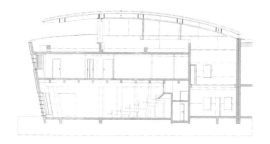

Section through the library

A bridge link across the courtyard gardens connects the teaching blocks | The main communal building with learning resources and social areas projecting out into the landscape | The entrance lobby with mezzanine bridge link | Typical internal corridor within the teaching blocks

Lycée Camille Corot

Morestel, France

Architect	Hérault Arnod Architectes, Grenoble
Pupils	850 aged 10-18 years
Building area	11,250 m²
Average classroom	approx. 60 m²
Parking spaces	86
Build cost	9.5 million EUR
Completion	1995
Year group system	Age-related year groupings

The architecture is a collage of individual buildings under one roof

The plan of this new high school is very formal with six articulated blocks of teaching accommodation laid out in a clearly delineated grid pattern. On the north end of the grid a powerful main block of accommodation is skewed at a 45 degree angle to the main grid. The designers have taken what for them is a familiar theme, the school as a city in miniature. Adopting a strong linear organisation, it could be imagined that the school would fit easily into a city centre context. However, this is not an urban school. In fact the school is located in cultivated farmland with a grid pattern of fields and hedgerows, which is a key influence. The hedgerow pattern follows a predominantly north-south orientation, which helps to generate the powerful asymmetrical plan. The six teaching blocks within the grid suggest the idea of order and con-

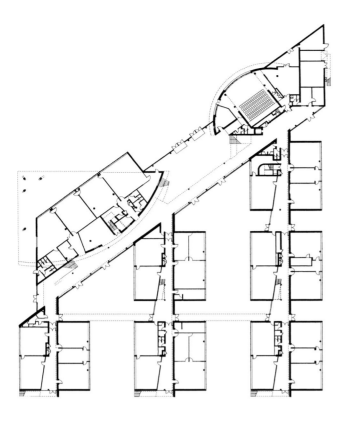

Ground floor plan

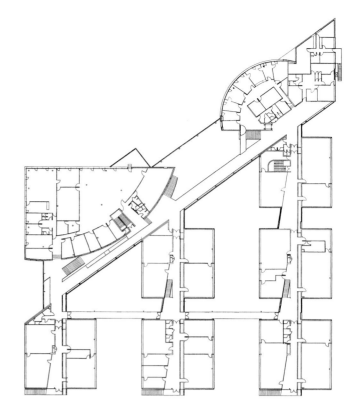

First floor plan

trol. They are each dedicated to a particular subject area such as arts, humanities and science, the idea being that students move around for their lessons between clearly defined 'mini-schools'. The blocks are positioned in such close proximity to each other that students are only ever five or six minutes away from each faculty area. Internal corridors run north to south and a first floor bridge link connects each row of buildings together east to west providing a continuous network.

The benefit of having space between the blocks is that the users are never confined by built form; they always have views either looking out towards the surrounding countryside or inwards to the enclosed courtyard gardens between the blocks. In addition, the buildings are

readily identifiable as buildings in their own right, which helps to break down the institutional feel of this large complex. These mini landscaped streets are laid out with wavy sculptural paths, which meander across the lawns between the teaching blocks. The communal or service building provides the geometrical logic to the twist in the plan. This block contains the administration wing, the main assembly hall (which doubles as a community hub for whole school events and evening activities) and the learning resources center. The main circulation is at first floor or mezzanine level. The wide gallery over the hall links into the faculty passageways. Each element of the accommodation within this dominant block is articulated as powerful sculptural forms in light coloured stone or white render. Each of the disparate elements is unified

beneath a vast curved roof clad in copper, which runs across the entire length of the block. The architects describe this communal block as a 'nave', the centre of the scheme in terms of its social programme. The metaphor can be carried through to interpretations of this unusual school as a medieval cathedral, dominating the near countryside and surrounded by subsidiary elements, the cloister, the baptistery and the monk's quarters all essential components of the whole, yet retaining their own identity as buildings in their own right. Each part is carefully choreographed to ensure that students are never overwhelmed by the sheer size of the whole building. As you walk round its perimeter it is like an ever changing landscape of architectural events, coherent yet fragmented.

Sections

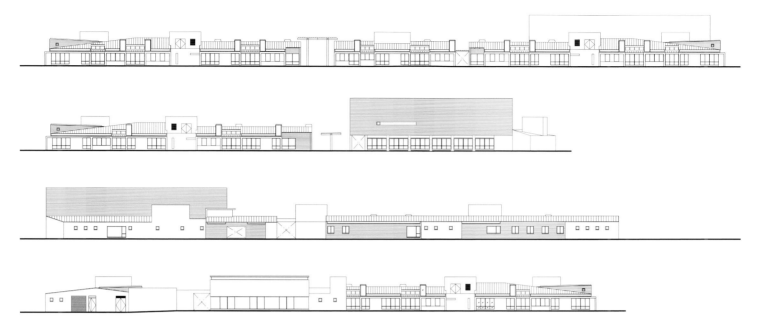

South, east, north, west elevations

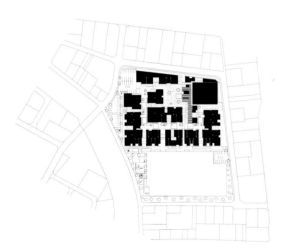

Site with roof plan | View down courtyard street | Circulation space |
Typical open classroom with English class underway

Gunma Kokusai Academy

Ohta City, Gunma, Japan

Architect	Kojima, Uno, Akamatsu; Yanagisawa
Pupils	972 aged 6-15 years
Building area	8,510 m²
Average classroom	49 m² each (closed classrooms)
Parking spaces	60
Build cost	16.7 billion JPY
Completion	2005
Year group system	Age-related groups of approx. 36 students

Nine year groups are divided into three 'neighbourhoods'; within each, 300 students are divided into three linked houses to create a city of childcare

This single-storey building covers the entire site and is striking in its prescribed functionality. Each part is linked to a larger part to create a dense web of closely connected 'schools within schools' which relate precisely to the educational and social curriculum. Every corner of the plan has a precise function, from three different types of classroom, to quiet rooms, counselling rooms and even designated water stations. There is a rigorous consistency about each of the teaching houses which is based on a grid system comprising of five different grid widths. The planning has been developed in this distinctive form as part of a national pilot project within a recognised special educational district. Here the educational authorities working with experts from Chiba University have collaborated closely with

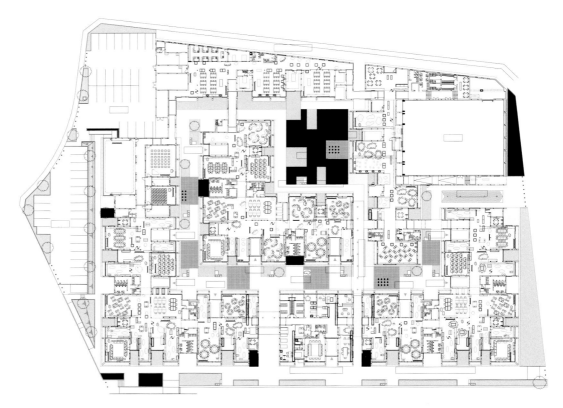

Ground floor plan

the existing school community to come up with this unique arrangement. Whereas most schools are fairly standard, comprising rows of closed classrooms identical in size, the Gunma Kokusai Academy recognises the different spatial needs of the new educational curriculum and the educational value of good social interaction between students. They are divided into three large groups, described as 'neighbourhoods' which are first to third grades, fourth to sixth grades and seventh to ninth grades. Within each neighbourhood, there are three school 'houses'. Each has its own dedicated zone for the 100 or so pupils, however each of the three is connected and semi-open to the other two houses in the group, to encourage interaction between other age grades. Although pupils study all of the core subjects,

including mathematics, science, music, physical education, art, home science and social science, the distinctive aspect is that both Japanese and English are taught by two teachers working side by side; one is a native English speaker and the other a Japanese speaker. The plan is organised so that teaching can take place in large single groups or in smaller groups. This radical bilingual approach is seen as an essential element of future economic success, English being viewed as the world language of commerce. Students are encouraged to choose their own favoured learning space, particularly in the post eleven age range, depending on the subject grouping offered within the curriculum framework. Within each house, there are various kinds of teaching space. There are different types of classroom,

closed, semi-closed and open. The closed classrooms tend to be used for Japanese language work and social science classes because it is felt that the Japanese environment should be clearly distinguished from the English speaking areas. The open classroom can be used for house assemblies, there is a dedicated art and science area with its own wet corner and a teachers' space which is completely open to the general student areas. There is a quiet room for counselling or small group learning and dedicated staff and student bathrooms. Each house has its own clearly defined entrance, accessed from formal outdoor courtyards.

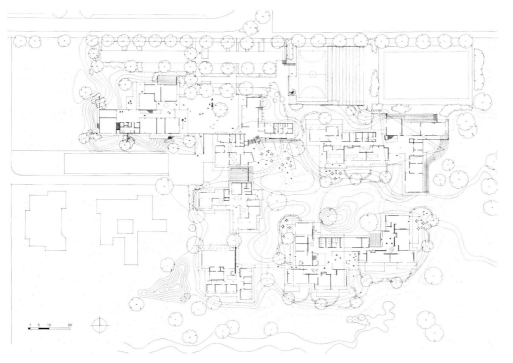

Ground floor plan
1 Community centre: management, kitchen, seminar room
2 Secondary school: 11 classrooms
3 Primary school: 13 classrooms
4 Kindergarten
5 Therapy rooms

Site plan

Primary forms such as triangle and circle are organising devices for the school complex | Exterior space | Circulation zone

Montessori School

Ingolstadt, Germany

Architect	Behnisch & Partner, Stuttgart
Pupils	450 aged 3-16 years
Building area	5,300 m²
Average classroom	60 m²
Parking spaces	38
Build cost	14.5 million DM
Completion	1996
Year group system	Age-related single form entry classbase system

Developed on a green field site, the individual parts are articulated as distinctive buildings, thus creating a campus school type

Schools are by their very nature institutional. Here the architects for this Montessori school in Ingolstadt-Hollerstauden have deliberately set out to break down the institutional feel. They have achieved this by articulating the various parts of the school with different architectural forms, creating a campus of smaller buildings each with its own character. The architects took as their inspiration the work of Dutch architect Herman Hertzberger with study trips arranged to look at a number of his projects. They were particularly interested in the form of the class rooms with a less authoritarian non-directional arrangement, and in the way in which the fluid relationship between the inside and the outside spaces was promoted. Thus the green external areas can become learning and teaching spaces in their own right, functioning as exten-

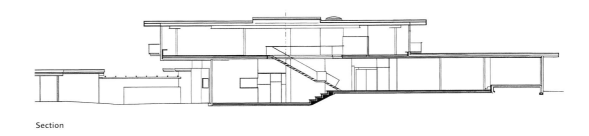

Section

Section

sions to the somewhat confined classroom areas. The location for the new school was a edge of town green field site with ample space to spread the building across its attractive setting. Rather than one large building, the school is broken down into five smaller two-storey buildings each with its own functional logic. Thus there is the secondary school for 240 pupils, the primary school for 180 children, the kindergarten for 30 children, a special needs building with therapy and small group rooms and a community centre with management offices, seminar rooms, a kitchen and canteen.

The individual buildings are organised to create a central communal green area. With classrooms and other areas such as the library and canteen opening onto it, the courtyard is full of life and activities, an environment which encourages social interaction between different age groups. Here the detail design is particularly important with level thresholds between the inside and the outside, pupil planting and cultivation areas and a special tree relating to each one of the classrooms to provide shade and to enhance the distinct symbolic identity of each year group. Although the central area is predominantly communal in atmosphere, each classroom has its own wooden deck surrounded by hedges and high shrubs to provide a degree of enclosure and privacy for teaching sessions to run without too much visual distraction. Although the architecture generally shares some common features, such as window types, roof projections, and wall paneling, the interior treatment of each building varies. Staircases are constructed in slightly different ways, there is a subtle variation in lighting quality between each building, and most particularly, each has a very particular geometrical form, which becomes apparent at first floor level in the shape of the communal hall. The primary forms, the circle, the square and the triangle are used as major organising devices within the community centre, the secondary school and the primary school respectively. This provides legibility for easy way finding, without sacrificing the inherent spatial complexity of this fascinating architectural collage. An inspiring and unusual approach to architecture for education so often dictated by the prosaic principles of order, control and discipline.

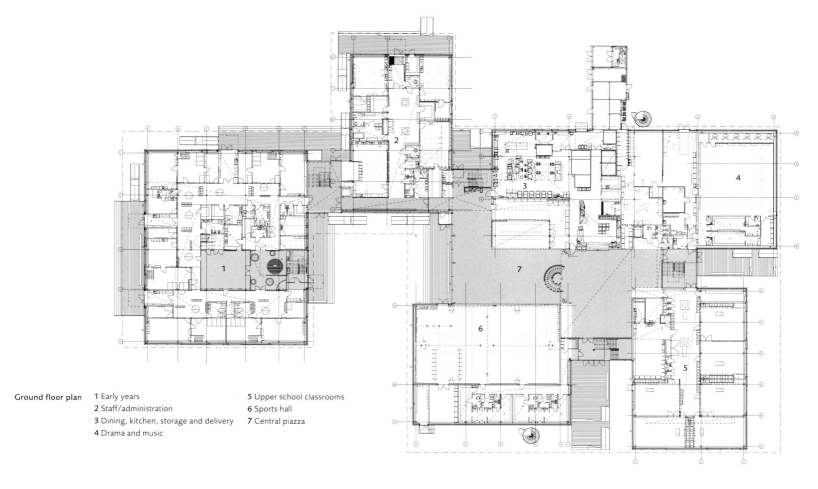

Ground floor plan
1 Early years
2 Staff/administration
3 Dining, kitchen, storage and delivery
4 Drama and music
5 Upper school classrooms
6 Sports hall
7 Central piazza

View towards entrance area and access to main piazza space | Computer room with curvy desks are a welcome contrast to the generally rectilinear form | One of the break-out spaces in the upper school with views into the classrooms | View of mediatheque with distinctive curved soft furniture

Kuoppanummi School Centre

Nummela, Finland

Architect	Perko Architects, Vantaa; Meskanen & Pursiainen, Helsinki
Pupils	650 aged 7-15 years
Building area	12,100 m²
Average classroom	60 m²
Parking spaces	20
Build cost	17 million EUR
Completion	2004
Year group system	Age-related 3 form entry, 22-30 per class

Unusual grouping of age ranges in a single educational institution

Located at the edge of a residential area close to the town centre of Nummela, the school is broken down into a number of smaller school units each of which is connected to the whole. A large overhanging roof slopes gently down from the three-storey upper school buildings to the lower two-storey daycare building creating a subtle spatial dynamic, a dramatic contrast between the verticality of the heavy red-brick and glass walls and the horizontality of the lightly tilting roof plane. This roof is a unifying element which asserts the integrity of a single building, albeit one which has separate and distinctive parts.

Overhanging the perimeter walls all the way round, the roof has a functional as well as a symbolic effect, acting as a shelter for those entering the building from a number

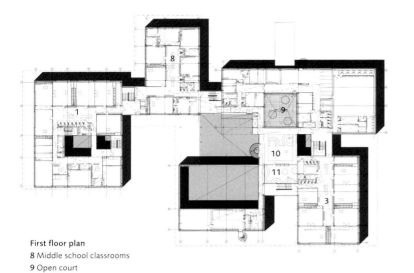

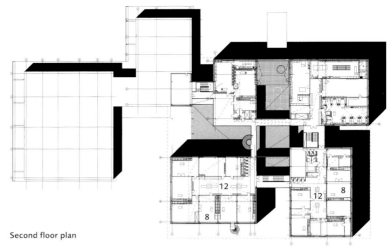

First floor plan

8 Middle school classrooms
9 Open court
10 Mediatheque
11 Computer room
12 Communal work and social areas

Second floor plan

Sections

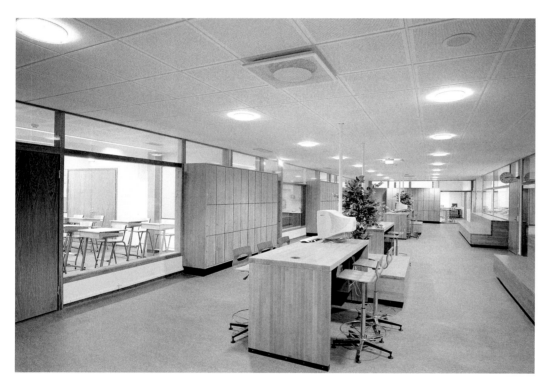

of different directions (there is no single main entrance, rather each part has its own entrance for differently aged children). All entrances are treated as terraces, each with its own wooden deck, roof canopy and entrance porch, a transitional space between the inside and the outside. Children's areas each have their own communal work/hanging out area. Classrooms cluster around these courtyards with generous glazed vision panels enabling teachers to monitor children working in the group setting from adjacent classrooms. Each communal area is fitted with computers, attractive storage and side benches for informal group interaction. There are eating zones and refreshment areas integrated into the study zones. Most circulation takes place within these social spaces, their very spaciousness helping to keep students calm and engaged

with the learning ethos, dissolving the usual segmentation of the school day into strict functional time periods. Common spaces bring children aged 7-15 together at various points of the day. At its very heart lies the three-storey-high covered piazza, a sort of grand village square for the whole community to meet and dine. There is an adjacent kitchen and sports hall with sliding folding wall panels which can be drawn back on occasion to create a single whole school meeting place or a theatre for community events. Slung one level above the piazza is the glazed 'mediatheque', a central information point. Right next door is the quiet computer work area, each of these three spaces visually linked by glazed panels which create a sense of relaxed transparency, a spatial quality common throughout the building, providing a natural form of supervision.

The central feature in the media centre and library is the distinctive curvy blue seating. It can be used in a variety of ways for group gatherings or simply for hanging out as well as for computer work, reading and studying. Tables for computers can be inserted in the middle, power being drawn up through the floor. Within the computer suite, curvy tables are used to line the walls which bring a sense of fun to the spaces. In many ways this is a very adult form of design, one might almost describe it as 'corporate' in its spirit, reminiscent of a high tech headquarters office building rather than a school. Yet fundamentally this is the central idea, that even the youngest people should be treated as citizens, with an uncluttered relaxed form of architecture which does not set out to patronise.

Map of Tenerife island

Location plan

Long elevation looking towards the sea | Aerial shot shows the edge
of town location | Internal courtyard lit up by night | Dramatic open
access staircase projects towards the sea

Instituto Rafael Arozarena

La Orotava, Tenerife, Spain

Architect	AMP arquitectos, Tenerife
Pupils	690 aged 12-18 years
Building area	7,496 m²
Average classroom	50 m² (standard), 60 m² (special)
Parking spaces	25
Build cost	3.27 million EUR
Completion	2004
Year group system	Age-related groups; 40 students per class

A challenging hillside site which is used to dramatic architectural effect

One of the recurring questions within this case study section is how one can create an environment which is humane and user friendly when the pupil intake is so huge. Many contemporary secondary school architects grapple with the problem of scale especially when the new building is due to be located on a single, edge of town site, which may be replacing a number of smaller buildings previously situated on separate lots in the town centre. As many new secondary schools are completed to tight budgets, the scale problem is often handled with limited success. In the case of Rafael Arozarena High School, the constraints of the site and the careful consideration of the historical context have created a building, which is both contextual and user friendly whilst clearly ex-

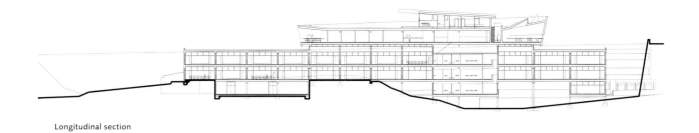

Longitudinal section

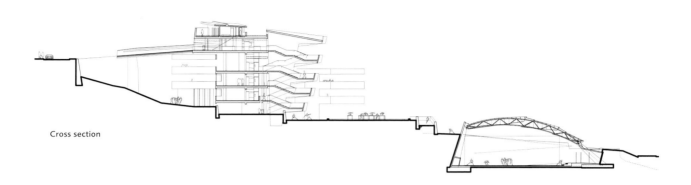

Cross section

pressing its important institutional presence within the community. The architects have worked with the existing urban framework, the historic town of La Orotava, on a number of important levels. Firstly, the existing site is characterised by former wine growing terraced slopes with attractive stone retaining walls and stone paths crisscrossing the entire site. The new building in reinforced concrete and large spans of structural steel appears to rest lightly on top of these walls; they are an important memory of what was there before according to the architects, so rather than obliterating these obsolete structures, they are retained and restored. The new building appears to rest on them at some points and passes over them at others, allowing the land to flow under the building,

enclosing external spaces where necessary into the fabric of the new, integrating the old with the new. The concrete structure is colour washed in various shades to both blend in and communicate important functional messages about the various zones of the new building to the student body.

Furthermore the entrance has been placed on an axis with the important edifice of Calle Colegio and with the historic church and medieval buildings of Calle S. Francisco. There is only one reasonably accessible road from the existing network of streets connecting the school to the old town. This road is the main collection point for the largest number of students arriving in the mornings; therefore its termination

marks the main entrance to the school. One arrives by ascending a ramp up to the school's main hall where the entrance lobby, porter's office, administration offices and library are positioned. The library is adjacent to the main entrance and placed strategically so that the inhabitants of La Oratava cannot just see it but can also access it outside of school hours. The new library has become an important community facility and is in almost constant use.

Because of the site, which slopes down from this entrance point, most of the school's teaching spaces are located on the two floors immediately below the entrance level. On the first lower level of accommodation, there are general teaching classrooms facing

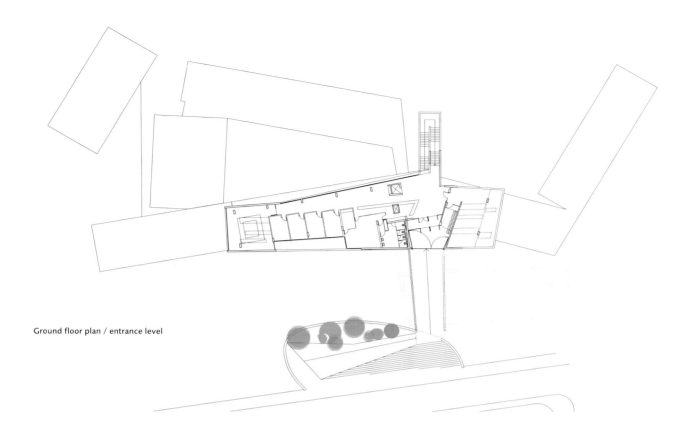

Ground floor plan / entrance level

Entrance bridge from street | The exposed concrete lends drama to this interior space | The windows of the circulation areas frame views to the outside | Semi-submerged ymnasium

southeast (back towards the town), with special classrooms facing out in the opposite direction towards the open countryside beyond. On the second lower floor there are science laboratories and the sixth form computer room with spaces for vocational training, student social areas and workshops, which have direct access to the outside areas. There is a large gymnasium which is positioned at the northern end of the plan (and at an even lower level). In order to disguise its bulk and so as not to obscure views towards the sea from the upper terraces, it is half buried in the slope of the hillside to create a building which utilises the marvellous orientation to best effect. This is not a cheap building, the extent of engineering ground works has seen to that, and the end result is a stylish,

often spectacular agglomeration of dramatic forms and colliding geometries which step down the hillside to diminish its scale and general impact on the landscape without compromising the overall architectural drama of the composition. This is particularly the case when seen from the town side. The building emerges gradually on approaching the site, with the entrance level seemingly balanced across the lower supporting structure, which is hidden from view. The entrance is linked by a tapering access bridge. Here the symbolism is clear, students are leaving a world of heavy traditional architecture (of the old town) for something altogether lighter and more futuristic, an island of educational experience.

When the entire building is visible from the bottom of the slope, subtle earth coloured washes (both outside and inside) render different parts of the building with a particular spatial quality to effectively break the scale down further and assist students in finding their way around. Everywhere there are distant views of the landscape beyond, framed by openable windows or from airy stair and roof terraces, which provide students with break-out areas, fresh air and a constant experience of the dramatic surrounding landscape. Everything works in a complementary way, with calm cool interiors which function as internalised boxes for concentrated learning when required, and conversely, with engaging communal areas which act as informal meeting points for the school community. On many

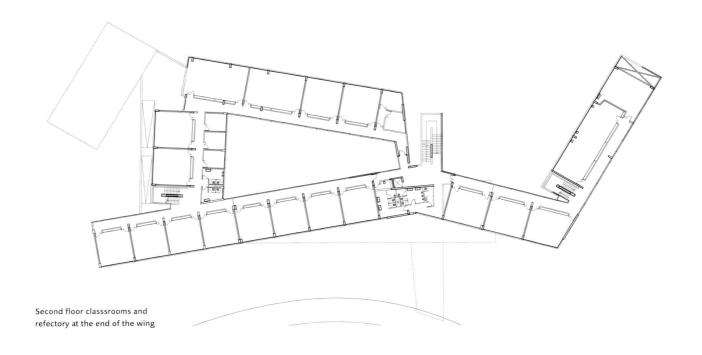

Second floor classsrooms and
refectory at the end of the wing

levels, the Rafael Arozarena High School is an exemplary case of contemporary school design.

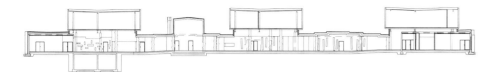

Cross section through courtyards and main entrance hall

Elevation of main south-facing façade

Kvernhuset Junior High School

Fredrikstad, Norway

Architect	PIR II Arkitektkontor, Duncan Lewis
Pupils	540 aged 11-16 years
Building area	9,956 m² (incl. sports hall)
Average classroom	73 m²
Parking spaces	60
Build cost	23.2 million NOK, total cost incl. fit out
Completion	2002
Year group system	Flexible class groups, 8 -10th year

Ecological agenda with natural ventilation, heat pump, natural sewage system throughout and enhanced use of daylight

In the design of Kvernhuset Junior High School sustainability is viewed as being a crucial aspect of the pedagogy. As a consequence, the building adopts a range of active and passive features which optimise on key aspects of energy and lighting usage. The building is set in a rocky, lightly forested valley. The three main wings of teaching accommodation and the gymnasium located slightly further down the hill are cut dramatically into the granite hillside, half buried by the cut-and-fill landscaping, half floating above it. Accommodation is organised on two levels with servicing spaces on the ground floor. These include administration, the main common room, music and drama, home economics, teacher's offices and arts and crafts. At first floor level the main teaching areas are organised in year 'homebase' groups, each wing hav-

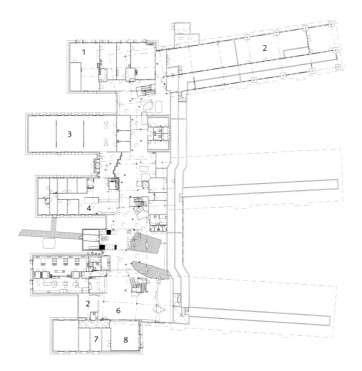

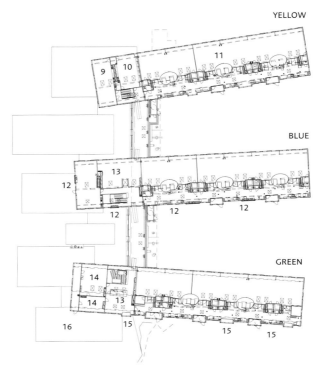

YELLOW

BLUE

GREEN

1 Arts and crafts
2 Storage
3 Teachers' workroom
4 Administration
5 Home economics
6 Student cafeteria
7 Music rooms
8 Stage
9 Art studio
10 Chemistry
11 Home bases
12 Aquarium space
13 Library
14 Biology
15 Greenhouse
16 Roof garden

Ground floor plan with much of the building cut into the landscape

Main teaching level, first floor plan

West façade showing contrasting lower and upper level architecture |
View of main stair rising up from hall with the use of tree sections and
roughly hewn rocks to evoke the natural context | View of classroom

ing its own common room. Students enter the building directly into their own classbases with three separate entrances in each wing. The three wings of accommodation, which relate to the three year groups at first floor level, are colour coded with a subtle strain of yellow, green or blue. These colour themes help to articulate a site-related architectural narrative; the yellow wing containing classrooms focuses on energy, primarily on the active and passive use of solar energy. Solar cells capture energy which is in turn monitored by pupils as part of their energy studies. The green wing has an ecological focus with the evident use of recycled materials. The presence of planting both inside and in the courtyards outside further emphasises this idea. The blue wing of accommodation focuses on water, harvesting it from the roof, and

grey water recycling in toilets and washbasins. Teachers asked for standard classrooms which could be divided down for use by smaller groups and opened up to effect open-plan arrangements when appropriate. This flexibility is achieved through the use of sliding folding wall panels alongside fixed solid partitions surrounding toilets, offices and small group rooms. Although there are some concerns regarding acoustic separation between classrooms, overall this arrangement enables a variety of group sizes which keeps teaching sessions fresh and stimulating. One of the key school spaces outside the classroom is a library. Situated at the centre of the building, it also acts as a circulation route for the entire school. The common area is for 'hanging out' between lessons and as a lunchtime restaurant space. Adjacent is the music room; with

its sliding wall it can be used as a stage for concerts and to further enlarge the area for community activities. The pleasure of this school lies especially in its harmonious relationship to its natural setting. The varied furniture layouts in the home base learning wings are reminiscent of leaves on the forest floor, simultaneously orderly yet random. Approaching the building one crosses a bridge which straddles a wildlife pond. Holes drilled directly into the rock provide geo-thermal energy. The bark from trees cut down to clear the site has been utilised as facings for columns in the main hall. These trees are used in a rough unfinished form in the main façades, a counterfoil to the concrete framework, an appropriate combination of the natural and the man-made.

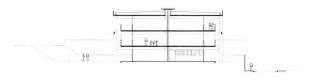

Cross section

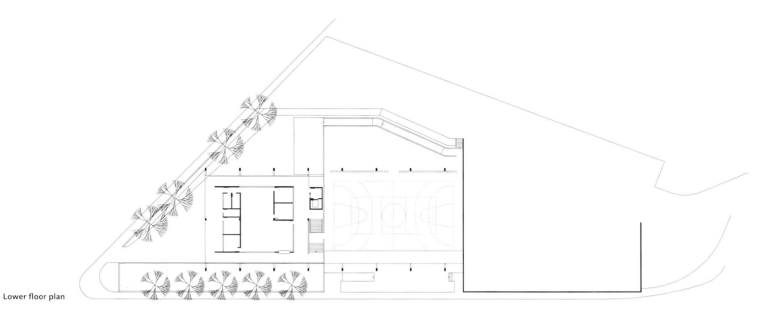

Lower floor plan

Night view | The school looms over its urban surroundings |
Playground space with murals by artist Speto | Typical classroom |
Circulation areas open to the elements

Public School Jardim Ataliba Leonel

São Paolo, Brazil

Architect	Angelo Bucci, Alvaro Puntoni, São Paolo
Pupils	653 aged 15-17 years
Building area	4,210 m²
Average classroom	50 m²
Parking spaces	10
Build cost	4.76 million BRL
Completion	2006
Year group system	15 classrooms, age-related classes

Innovative school as 'warehouse' concept

The architects describe their work as 'an intervention approach', which emphasises the extent to which the new school is expected to provide dramatic possibilities for local children. Located on the sprawling periphery of São Paolo city, the area is characterised by low cost self-build houses with few building regulations applied. As a result, it is a shanty town in all but name. There are no local parks or public open spaces in this low rise high-density environment. It is a degraded and depressing place to grow up in. The FDE (Foundation for the Development of Education, the governmental organisation responsible) has promoted the development of a group of projects which are innovative educationally in recognition of the problems children and their families face. There is a secondary agenda which is the use of prefab-

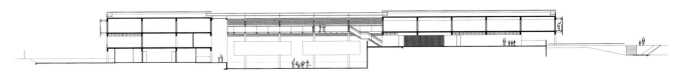

Longitudinal section

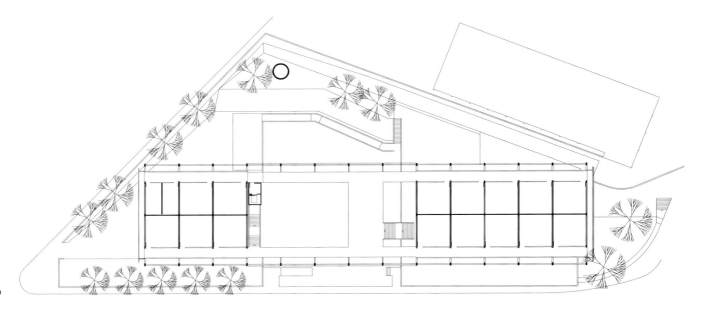

Upper floor plan

ricated structural systems anticipating the need for the mass production of numerous new schools over the next 25 years. The government recognises that education is the only long term solution to the huge social and economic problems of its urbanised poor. The form of the building is reminiscent of a large factory or warehouse building rather than a school. It looms over its surroundings like a medieval cathedral dominating its low scale context. Whereas even the most urban schools usually feel slightly detached from their immediate surroundings, set back from the street and surrounded by high fences and playing fields, the Jardim Ataliba is so close it almost assaults its neighbourhood with its powerful 'in your face' architecture. This is partly a function of the confined site which has very little space to fit such a

large building let alone provide outside play spaces, but it is also an attempt to create a strong and positive image of education to local people. However, where are the playground and external areas for physical recreation? The answer to the question is that they are contained around and under the building. Rather than the building having a self-contained envelope with walls which define inside and outside, here the building bridges over the entire play area, creating a covered yet semi-porous space, a playground at the base of the building itself. A system of huge steel box beams creates a wide span structure which forms a vast open space. It is available in the evenings for games, indeed, it is shown on the plan as a marked out multi-function games pitch which can also be utilised for many different school events ranging

from whole school assemblies to concerts and theatrical performances by the community. It is a most unusual space being robust and vandal resistant, yet at the same time, colourful and stylish with two huge abstract murals by Brazilian artist Speto. A dining space and toilets are located on the upper mezzanine level, whilst 15 back-to-back classrooms and an office are on the top floor. At a time when the value of education is undermined by an intrusive global media presence, this project sets a precedent. It is a three-storey ocean liner of a building, dominating the surrounding streets, straddling three layers of undulating terrain, and evening it out with dramatic full-length galleries on both sides of the classroom block; as such it states unequivocally the importance of education.

Cross section

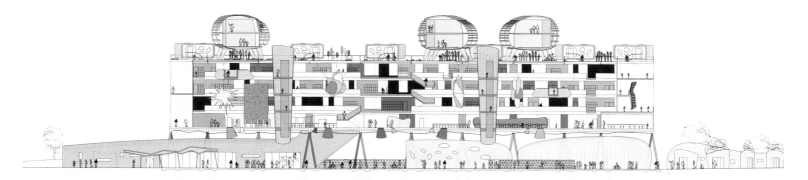

Campus section

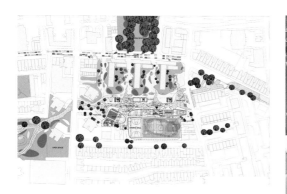

Site plan | View from sports pitch | Internal perspective | Exploded axonometric view showing the elemental breakdown

Exemplar School

Lambeth, London, UK

Architect	Alsop Architects, London
Pupils	1,200 aged 11-18 years
Building area	12,000 m²
Average classroom	60 m²
Parking spaces	5
Build cost	18.2 million GBP
Completion	2003
Year group system	Age-related 5 form entry with tutor groups

Research orientated unbuilt design exploring the issues and potential benefits of a multi-storey school

Over the coming decade virtually every existing school within the UK will be significantly up-graded or completely re-built. Profound debates have taken place over recent years as to the best way to design the coming generation of school buildings. This debate has focused on the need to build in new ways which are appropriate to the 21st century. Many believe that the traditional school solution is an obsolete model and needs to be radically up-dated. Good innovative architecture, they would argue, has the power to transform the way in which young people view education and will make them see it in a more positive light. This was the scenario for a government sponsored competition to design a number of new schools speculatively. The designs were real in all except the fact that they would not actually be built on

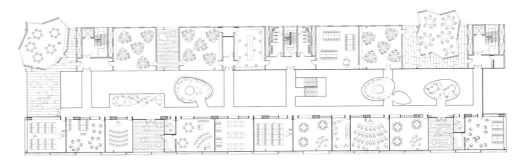

Level 4 plan

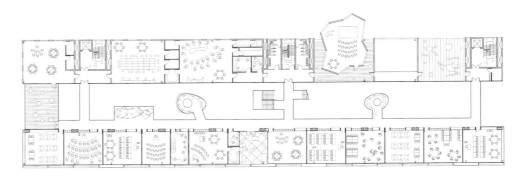

Level 2 plan

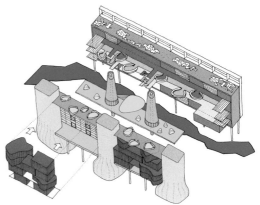

the designated sites. Instead they were to be explorations of new ideas by architectural practices with a high reputation. This was intended to inspire and guide future school designers and promote cutting-edge thinking.

One of the most interesting schemes to emerge was this multi-storey proposal for an inner city site in south London. Based on the principle that different teaching modes would encourage new ways of learning, the proposal comprises four floors of school accommodation, elevated above the ground on stilts. Thus ground floor areas are part of the surrounding sports and recreation areas. The cross section illustrates the breakdown of accommodation with fairly conventional classrooms on the sunny south side with more practical accommo-

dation such as art and science labs on the north side. In the middle there is a four-storey high atrium with break-out areas at each level slung between the circulation decks. These are articulated as freeform organic shapes which lend the area a strange space age feel, unlike any conventional school building. The school's heating and cooling systems are deliberately emphasised within the framework of the overall design with two big cooling stacks at the centre of the atrium.

Throughout the scheme there is a sense of a building communicating with its users and the surrounding environment in many different ways. On one elevation, façades are brightly coloured with moveable sun shades along the perimeter which enable the staff and

students to have a degree of control over heating and cooling. Having this sense of control of their environment develops spatial awareness and helps students to relate to their building. Even the plant room is centrally located with glazed walls so that students can see and begin to decipher the systems which support and control their environment. Strange rock-like shapes appear at different places on the roof or protrude from the façades on the north side. It is possible to read the different forms of accommodation as they are strongly emphasised. The building is like a cryptic puzzle, constantly unfolding and sending out overt and subtle messages to students who have a natural interest in their environment.

Sectional elevation looking east-west from games court

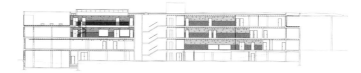

Section through southeast accommodation block and entrance canopy

Southwest entrance elevation

Main southeast elevation showing level changes

Aerial view | Games court with classrooms cantilevered above |
First floor courtyard with the mature oak tree | An internal corridor
with coloured light filtering through perimeter windows

Lycée
François Magendie

Bordeaux, France

Architect	Brojet Lajus Pueyo, Bordeaux
Pupils	1,200 aged 10 - 18 years
Building area	8,950 m²
Average classroom	n/a
Parking spaces	n/a
Build cost	60 million FRF
Completion	1998
Year group system	Age-related classes

Retains and integrates existing mature trees to provide attractive
courtyard architecture

This handsome Lycée in Bordeaux is the last work of
architect Michel Sadirac (who died in 1999). Designed
in association with Olivier Brochet, Emmanuel Lajus and
Christine Pueyo (BLP), the scheme reflects Sadirac's
previous work in its synthesis of modern rationalism and
contemporary lightness and dynamism. This can be ap-
preciated in the precisely engineered façade treatment,
which meets the tight urban site in a sensitive contextual
form without ever resorting to pastiche. This is a strong
robust architecture, which clearly states its modernist
lineage whilst weaving its external spaces around the existing site edges with their three-storey houses and back
gardens. In particular, the retention of most of the existing mature trees on site exemplifies the way in which
the tight modern lines of the new provide a resonant

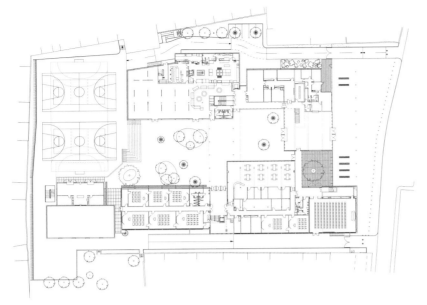

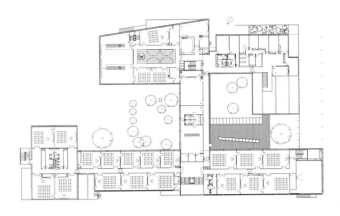

Ground floor showing entrance and external courtyards running
down to the games court

First floor plan

contrast to the rustic forms of nature. For example, the
framing of a large oak tree in the southwest courtyard
enables the tree to take on the quality of sculpture when
framed by this type of architecture. Here the context is
everything, and the architect's undoubted skill in marry-
ing landscape and architecture is a key design statement.
The Magendie Lycée replaces the original five-storey
pre-fabricated buildings designed by Courtois-Sallie-
Sadirac in the late 1960s, and due to its spread across
the large rectangular site, the new building never rises
above four storeys in height. A large single span concrete canopy marks the school's main entrance from the
street. Cast in-situ and supported on slim, concrete filled
metal pillars, the canopy superbly establishes the public
presence of the building, occupying the entire south-

western street frontage. Between the canopy and the
building, light filters through an aluminium sun-break,
providing an attractive shaded area on sunny days which
is furnished with timber benches. This sets the tone for
the rest of the building, and the spaces unfold as an alternating sequence of solid and void spaces, which the
architects variously describe as courtyards, cloisters and
patios. The rhythm for the building is established by the
use of a 4.8 metre grid, which works well for the layout
of study rooms as well as the façade system itself. The
50 centimetre horizontal service zone created by the
structural depth of the slab flooring is rigorously maintained around the perimeter of the building and provides
a discrete and efficient zone for ventilation and service
ducting. In order to counter the limited architectural

palette of materials used here, the depth of the window reveals on each elevation varies in relation to the
façade's orientation. For example, the main southeast
façades have the deepest set glazing to provide maximum solar shading. Thus the concept of 'variation within
sameness' enables a subtle environmental experience to
emerge during the course of each day, hot or cold, wet
or dry. The entire composition creates a play of light and
shadow, which is carried through to enliven the interior
passageways. Light filters through slatted shutters and is
then diffused through screen-printed glass (designed by
a graphic arts student at the lycée), which is then further
modified as it enters the space through glass bricks set
into the concrete walls of the corridors and circulation
spaces.

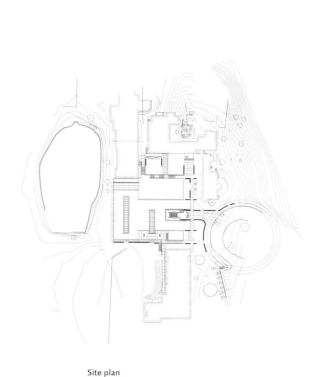

Site plan

Ground floor plan

1 Light chambers
2 Math/science classroom
3 Science courtyard
4 Arts classrooms
5 Humanities classrooms
6 Library
7 Library courtyard
8 Middle school library
9 Student commons room
10 Administration
11 Information technologies lab
12 Sports terrace

View of library courtyard, the axial view deliberately frames the historic buildings | Aerial view shows grass roof and the new building bridging between the existing buildings on site

Greenwich Academy

Greenwich, Connecticut, USA

Architect	SOM 'Education Lab', New York
Pupils	240 aged 13-17 years
Building area	3,900 m²
Average classroom	79 m²
Parking spaces	60
Build cost	12 million USD
Completion	2002
Year group system	4 form entry, 22 students per class

Departmental areas organised around 'light chamber' communal spaces designed in collaboration with light artist James Turrell

Greenwich Academy is a private school for girls with a long tradition of educational excellence. Founded in 1827, the school currently occupies a 16 hectare campus in suburban Greenwich. Despite this, the scope of the project was constrained both in terms of the available site which could be built upon and also in terms of funding available. The new buildings would have to be sandwiched between topographical grades and existing buildings and built at an economical cost of 1,830 USD per square metre. The school's requirement to create a new upper school which would somehow unify the disparate parts of the existing campus, provided an opportunity for alternative thinking about how architectural design could support learning.

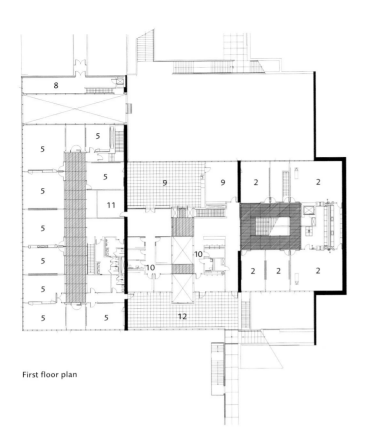

First floor plan

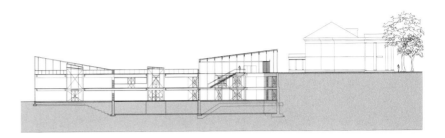

East-west section

Gentle steps up to the roof extend the concept of space and light |
Blinds drawn and seen from a far, the building becomes volumetric

The theory that student attendance and academic performance are higher the greater their daily exposure to natural light, was adopted as one of the main driving forces behind the design. New classrooms are clustered around circulation areas which are described as 'Light Chambers'. The new library, maths/science, arts and humanities classrooms which comprise the main elements of the accommodation are organised around these light filled covered courtyards; they act as circulation and communal areas, one for each of the faculty departments. Transparent glass façades and glazed rooflights maximise daylight penetration throughout the structure. Sharon Dietzel, head of the upper school, told *Architectural Record*, 'All the light has a physical and psychological affect on people; it relaxes them.' Grassed roof terraces further integrate the building into its wooded setting and provide a subtle visual extension of the grassed areas around the new building. Strategic orientation and massing integrate the new building into the landscape, opening up views to the surrounding forest and hills. Unification of the campus was achieved through selective preservation of existing buildings.

Planted with sod and flowers, the roof also contributes to this synthesis of nature and architecture. Glazed light chambers perforate the plane of the roof, creating a dynamic sculptural environment. Students and visitors are drawn to the roof by its lush planting, its views onto the adjacent playing fields, and by its luminous light chambers, whose glass reflects the verdant horizontal rooftop plane into the interiors below. SOM have developed a clever strategy for unifying the campus and providing the school with the new facilities it required. The green roof enhances energy efficiency and promotes environmental sustainability. It also provides effective insulation which lowers overall cooling and heating costs for the building. Altogether, the combination of thin semi-transparent glazing throughout with the heavy roof makes this a visually stunning building, giving upper school students the privilege of a distinctive and advanced form of school architecture.

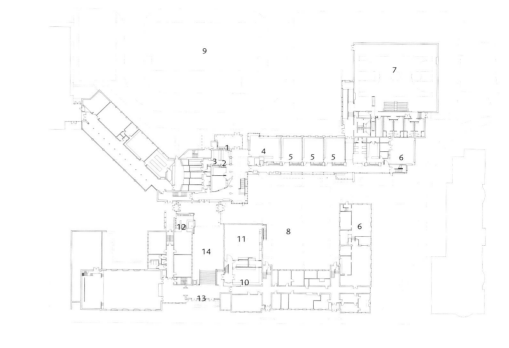

Ground floor plan
1 Entry of new middle school
2 Corridor
3 Administration
4 Resource room

5 Classrooms
6 Multi-purpose room
7 Gymnasium
8 Outdoor amphitheatre
9 Parking court

10 Great hall/court (renovation)
11 Art facility (renovation)
12 Retail
13 Original entrance
14 Exhibition space

Site plan

Staircase detail and view into cultivation courtyard illustrates the transparency between inside and outside | New entrance showing the range of natural materials | View of new art/exhibition area | Typical new laboratory with timber cladding and viewing screens

St. Andrew's College

Aurora, Ontario, Canada

Architect	Kuwabara Payne McKenna Blumberg, Toronto
Pupils	640 aged 11-16 years
Building area	4,975 m² (art area 734 m², gallery 924 m²)
Average classroom	90 m²
Parking spaces	278 (visitors), 76 (staff), 49 (students).
Build cost	11.9 million CAD
Completion	2003
Year group system	Age-related 3 form entry, grades 6-12

Sensitive extensions to existing campus result in a modern school retaining the traditional setting of this private boys school

St. Andrew's College is set within a generous 45 hectare campus along the rolling river valley of Oak Ridges Moraine. This pastoral landscape of mature trees, numerous playing fields and the distinctive character of its red brick Georgian Revival buildings has considerable merits both as a place to grow up and as a memorable heritage setting in its own right. The facilities were, however, becoming outdated and constrained. Many of the original buildings date back to 1926, when the school was relocated to this edge-of-city site. The design recognised the need to bring facilities up to modern standards without losing this historical quality. The master plan established key strategic requirements such as the need for a new arrivals court on the north side of the campus to alleviate traffic congestion. One issue was to improve the sense of

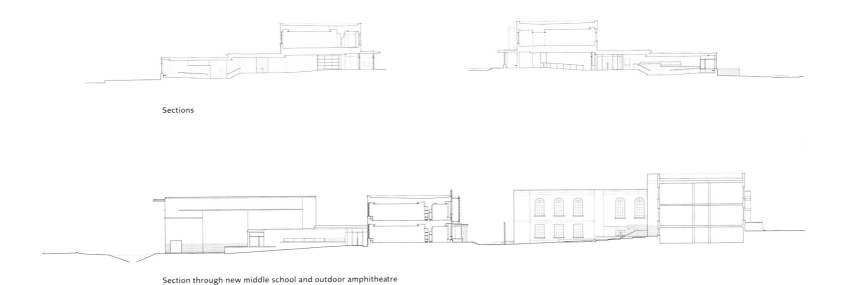

Sections

Section through new middle school and outdoor amphitheatre

community by developing new gathering spaces indoors and outdoors. This was an important catalyst prompting the architects' first move; by enclosing and redefining a left-over area of space between two existing buildings, the school has gained a large communal area and a new heart. Complete with its elegant timber roof and clearstory glazing this area connects the original campus buildings of the 1920s to the postwar buildings located on the north side of the campus. It also provides a public exhibition area for student art work produced in the adjacent art studios. A suite of new classrooms in the middle school is furnished with specially designed timber fittings and integrated wireless Internet access. There is seating for up to 20 students in each. Special consideration has been given to classroom acoustics in recognition of the

need for quiet concentrated study, which was sometimes a problem in the earlier classrooms. Student lockers are located immediately outside each classroom, integrated into the spatial architecture of the generous light filled circulation areas. The enhanced sense of arrival and improved circulation areas became a positive by-product of the major new build programme, which has provided generous laboratories and libraries, a new gym plus the aforementioned classrooms. This has in turn enabled the adaptive re-use of spaces in the existing buildings; for example the original gym, which was too small, was converted into a state-of-the-art music and art facility. The overall design emphasises transparency to encourage a sense of community and to take advantage of the views to the surrounding countryside. An enfilade of glazed

openings is cut into both end façades of the new middle school to provide extended views through the length of the classrooms on each floor. The materiality of the additions is harmonised with the existing structures by the adoption of a common palette of materials comprising red brick, Manitoba Tyndall stone and copper. The massing of the gymnasium is scaled down to that of the historic buildings and adjacent trees. The use of rustic Wiarton stone paving and ipewood screens to the façades provide a suitable contextual reference. This attention to detail both in practical terms and in the aesthetic use of materials in their correct place, the strategic opening up of views and vistas has created a school fit for the 21st century, yet one which retains its historic character.

Site plan

Ground floor plan

Nærum
Amtsgymnasium

Nærum, Copenhagen, Denmark

Architect	Arkitekter Dall & Lindhardtsen, Helsingør
Pupils	900 aged 15-19 years
Building area	12,400 m²
Average classroom	68 m², 8 laboratories 100 m²
Parking spaces	200
Build cost	202 million DKK
Completion	2004
Year group system	Age-related 10 form entry

Corporate image with highly glazed open-plan feel to the teaching areas

The challenge here was to create a compact building which nevertheless incorporated all the key elements of a traditional campus school minus the long corridors which traditionally cause significant problems in terms of pupil safety and security. The solution was to adopt a contemporary office plan form which organises classrooms around a large covered atrium. This zone, which unfolds over four storeys as a series of generous gallery/deck areas above the main ground floor area, provides breakout spaces relating directly to formal teaching rooms. The general layout provides all the formal teaching spaces required, however, by far the largest space is the social mixing area, i.e. the public square utilising the atrium's entire volume and containing public facilities like the school's restaurant, the library and the auditorium.

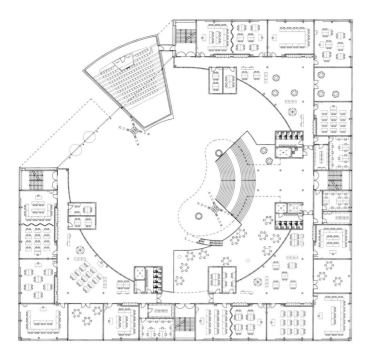

First floor plan

Sections

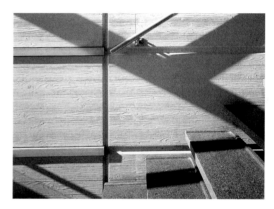

Main façade, part pinewood part full-height glazing | View of library pod from entrance | Interior view of atrium with patterned floor | Staircase from first floor balcony to second floor library deck | Detail of stairway with fair-faced concrete finish

The plan then comprises a square block of teaching accommodation approximately 7 metres deep which wraps around the circular central zone. All the teaching spaces flow off this high and almost monumental circulation zone which features a glazed kidney shaped library slung above a grand access stair. Like most of the teaching spaces within this dramatic environment, it is almost completely glazed, again giving the idea of the ubiquitous early 21st century open-plan office building. However, because of its sloping sides and strange organic shape, it is the room which receives the most immediate attention, and inevitably attracts student learners like flies to a honey pot. The entrance is orientated towards the main road, to the northeast, and cuts one corner of the square main block diagonally. This diagonal glazed wall also has

a wedge shaped assembly hall to the left of the entrance. Its raked stalls, accessible from the ground floor rising up to the second floor projection room, provide seating for over 130 students. Compositionally it is, like the library, another space expressed as an object, with its heavy solid form crashing through the glazed external screen slightly at odds with the formality of the rest of the building. Inside, it stares blankly back at the library across the urban square. The position of the school in relation to the terrain, which slopes down from east to west, is incorporated into the building's sectional form. The descending hill is used inside the building, forming an amphitheatre visible beneath the library on the eastern corner of the square. The great roof slopes down complementing the natural topography. The sports facilities are placed in a separate

building. Main external façades are clad in heat-treated timber paneling, giving the building a warm brown colour, which balances the colder more engineered glazing system, a palette of cold and warm, soft and hard. The planning concept incorporates a natural way of dividing the building into distinct zones of public, semi-public and enclosed private groups ranging in size from 35 to one on one. Communal teaching areas which service each zone of classrooms are connected to the main square by three sets of stairs. Study areas are close at hand, in various bays and smaller teaching zones which relate to classroom areas. The distinctive hierarchy enables a subtle understanding of territories. As a result the layout is all very legible yet somehow anti-institutional.

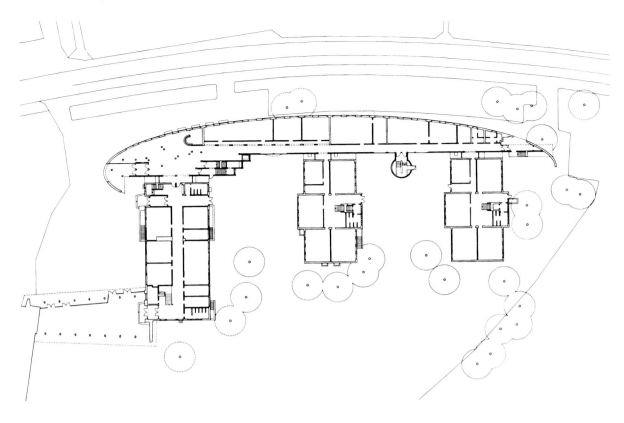

Ground floor plan

Site plan | The curved wall, a strong architectural symbol of unification | The entrance foyer with durable 'street' finishes; exposed fair-faced concrete and brickwork for ceilings, walls and floors | The escape staircase penetrates the wall at its eastern end

Albert Einstein Oberschule

Berlin, Germany

Architect	Stefan Scholz Architekten, Berlin
Pupils	1,000 aged 12-19 years
Building area	5,400 m²
Average classroom	74 m²
Parking spaces	20
Build cost	12.1 million DM
Completion	1999
Year group system	5 form entry, age- and subject-related groups

The extension of an existing school by a new three-storey 'wall' of teaching spaces

The existing school buildings comprised three separate 1950s blocks standing within an attractive 3 hectare semi-suburban site in Berlin-Neukölln on what was formerly an edge of a city zone, being located close to the old Berlin wall which separated the east from the west for almost three decades. The architects' project was to provide additional teaching and administrative accommodation with a new multi-purpose sports and meeting hall. One of the most important requirements was for a new entrance to ensure a less porous and more coherent sense of place, connecting the existing free-standing blocks of teaching accommodation. From a distance it is apparent that the attractive campus site with mature trees and an open accessible feel required the imposition of a clearly defined site edge to the street, the

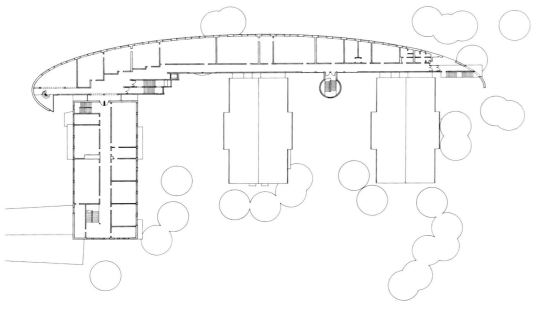

Second floor plan

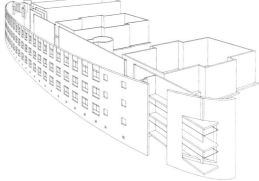

Conceptual perspective showing the new wall with existing teaching blocks behind

point where most of the users arrive. This was important not simply because previously the reception area was poorly defined thus creating security problems, but also because the client felt a communal space such as an entrance was potentially a critical area for social interaction between the various age ranges. The issues have been cleverly resolved by way of a new block which runs along the street edge, gently curving with the curve of the street and on the interior of the block, linking the three separate classroom buildings by a new corridor which runs across on three levels. At one end of the new addition there is a major new entrance, at the other a feature escape stair which penetrates the 'wall' before disappearing into the rear of the block. The sports hall stands alone to the rear part of the site. Within the new

extension there are four physics rooms, four rooms for arts and crafts, a photographic laboratory, a crafts room for heavy construction (such as vehicle maintenance), four rooms for music and a library. New staircases and a lift provide much-needed access to the existing accommodation which is on three levels as well as new accommodation, so that rather than being separate disparate schools, the whole is integrated and made coherent with functional access routes which are generous and social. This is important particularly in a secondary school setting where there tends to be much more movement between different teaching areas. The connections between old and new parts are subtle; materials flow one into the other, the 1950s blocks seamlessly attaching themselves to the new classroom wing.

The palette of materials is limited, yet it creates a warm atmosphere. With granite floors, in-situ concrete stairwells and light timber doors it is also robust; having been in use for several years now, the building remains largely undamaged, an important aspect in any new school and a factor which perhaps distinguishes this building from most others. Schools must be built to last. Inside the classrooms, walls are white rendered; however, the rhythm of the structural grid is clearly stated with exposed concrete beams spanning the space from the rear corridor grid to the curved external wall. It all adds up to a highly successful balance between old and new, security and openness, open social spaces and more traditional closed teaching spaces.

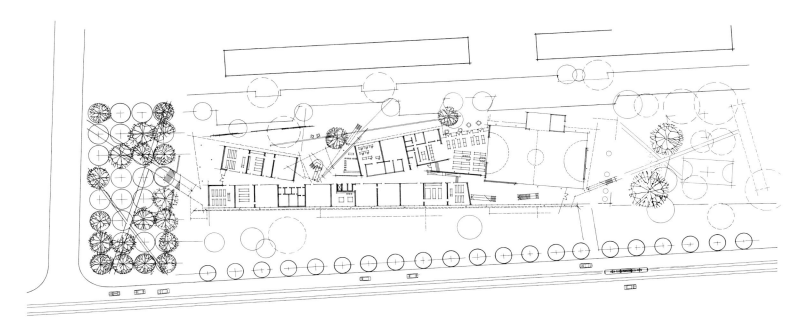

Ground floor plan

East façade, showing the more closed aspect presented to the street |
West façade with multi-purpose hall in foreground | One of the main
student staircases cutting through the heart of the plan | View down
into main recreation hall

Sankt Benno
Gymnasium

Dresden, Germany

Architect	Behnisch, Behnisch & Partner, Stuttgart
Pupils	720 aged 11-18 years
Building area	10,000 m²
Average classroom	54 m²
Parking spaces	10
Build cost	49.5 million DM
Completion	1996
Year group system	25 classrooms arranged in faculty blocks of 4

This church secondary school is articulated as a series of solidly constructed
blocks to the road

The urban site for this new school is close to the city centre at the intersection of two busy roads. The site comprises a long thin strip of land between two four-storey residential blocks. Classrooms turn their backs on the heavy traffic streets opening up to the predominantly residential west side. This is part of the architects' concept which they describe as a building where the rooms are positioned logically, 'where they ought to be'. However, the overall effect is much greater than this modest statement suggests. The entrance is on the south side, set back from the road. It comprises a grand flight of stairs which takes you up to the raised ground floor, forming a sort of 'piano nobile' where the main communal spaces, such as group rooms, cafés and offices are located. From here you can either go down via

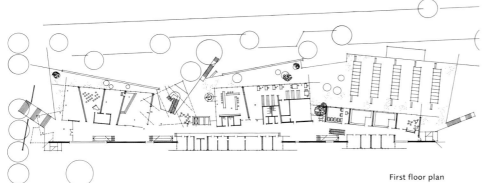

First floor plan

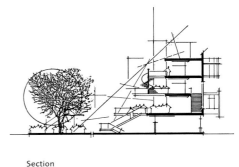

Section

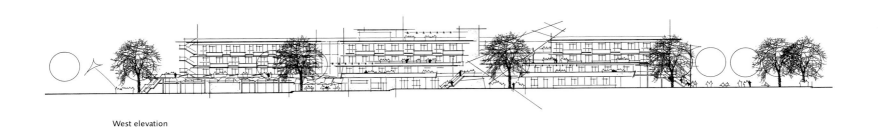

West elevation

a range of open staircases, to the ground or basement levels, containing a sports hall, music and drama rooms and the library; or up to conventional suites of classrooms and the rooftop art studio complete with viewing gallery providing vistas across the city. This is a building which celebrates the circulation areas as promenades where people are likely to meet each other and hang out. Entering into and through the building, a passageway carries the visitor all the way along its entire 150 metre length. One is enclosed in an atmosphere of varying modulated light, a route which naturally leads you up towards a glazed three-storey high roof above a large communal space. Roughly at the centre of the plan is this enclosed winter garden, with angled fenestration, staircases and galleries which are pitched and skewed

to create a dynamic space full of warm light. This has become an important social focus for the building, either for children to use during the day, or as an evening forum for concerts and other performances, connecting the school into the patterns of the local community. In order to reduce the impression of length, the architects have introduced angles into the planning of the solid classroom blocks. The anti-orthogonal organisation deliberately subverts the ordered linearity of the housing blocks on the opposite side of Pestalozzistraße, creating a more humane, almost organic architectural form which fits its context in scale terms, yet shouts out how special it is in architectural terms. Here is an architecture of schools which sets out to show how special it can feel to be in education. Every vista within this internalised cir-

culation world provides a context for social interaction, whereas classrooms are largely conventional enclosed spaces for formal learning.

The building unfolds like an exotic plant, enclosed in thick ochre-rendered walls towards the east, opening up to the west with explosions of dynamic form, individual components merging together into a coherent architectural composition. At ground, first and second floor level, decks and staircases project out like fingers exploring the cultured formal landscape around the edges of the site, an interface between public and private life. The architectural response to its context enhances the life and institutions of this urban landscape.

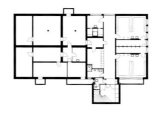

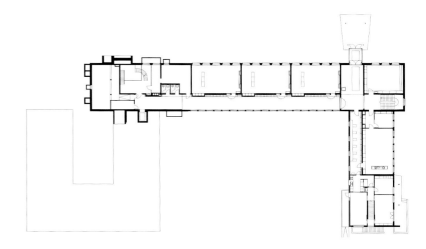

Ground floor plan

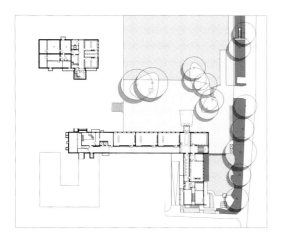

Site plan

Terrace with new extension connected elegantly onto the existing building | View from northeast | Renovated classroom with coordinated furniture and timber wall paneling | Old building with new corridor façade with integrated storage and pupil lockers

Lachenzelg
School Extension

Zürich, Switzerland

Architect	ADP, Beat Jordi, Caspar Angst, Zürich
Pupils	420 aged 12-16 years
Building area	1,175 m² (extension only)
Average classroom	55 m² each with its own group room of 27 m²
Parking spaces	approx. 30
Build cost	4.7 million CHF (extension)
Completion	2004
Year group system	Traditional 5 form entry age-related classbase system, 24 students per class

Extension and renovation to existing historically significant school buildings

The original school designed by Roland Rohn in 1953 was influenced by the landmark Zürich exhibition 'The New School' which took place in the same year. Taking its cue from the modular construction of the post war schools construction boom, Rohn designed two very different buildings, one a solid traditional structure with low pitched roofs with a long run of undersized classrooms serviced by a single access corridor on each of its two levels, similar in style to the surrounding residential buildings. The other was an altogether more interesting building; a split level modernist concrete frame construction organised around a glazed quadrangle. The two styles achieve a spatial intimacy without losing the essential principles of an undisturbed, calm teaching environment full of light and

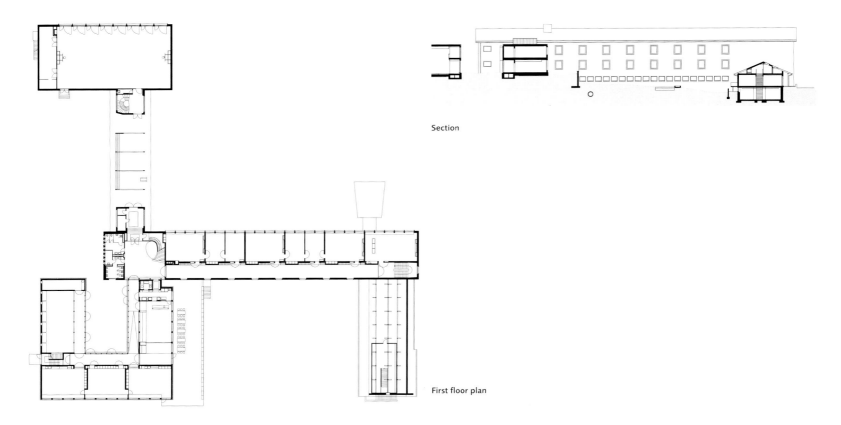

Section

First floor plan

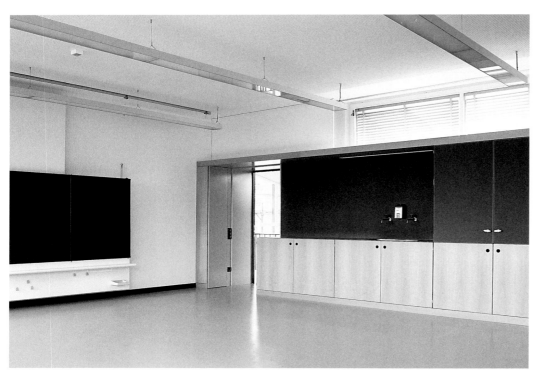

fresh air. This historical background was an important starting point for the architects. New additions which comprise a main building for communal activities including a school hall, a library and a canteen respect the materiality of the original using robust sympathetic finishes such as ceramic floor tiles and exposed concrete walls where appropriate, whilst also introducing contemporary touches such as the wood clad window reveals to soften the existing situation. It is a contextually appropriate series of modifications and additions.

One of the primary tasks for the project designers was to enlarge the existing classrooms which at around 55 square metres were simply too small to accommodate new ICT learning strategies. The enlargement

has been achieved by dividing existing classrooms in two to create group rooms of 27 m², one for each classroom. This works particularly well at secondary level, giving seminar type spaces to each class group which can be used for smaller ICT based self-teaching sessions.

Additional classrooms have been provided in the new block along with the aforementioned hall, library and canteen which can also be used by local residents outside school hours. The new two-storey extension adjacent to the main entrance refers architecturally to the original modernist building with its stern rectilinear façade form. The corridor bordering the quandrangle links three unequal wings: the two-storey hall in the

north, the canteen and library in the south and special classrooms for crafts and the natural sciences in the west. A large wood paneled garden terrace unites users to the whole plan, creating a harmonious and satisfying new school.

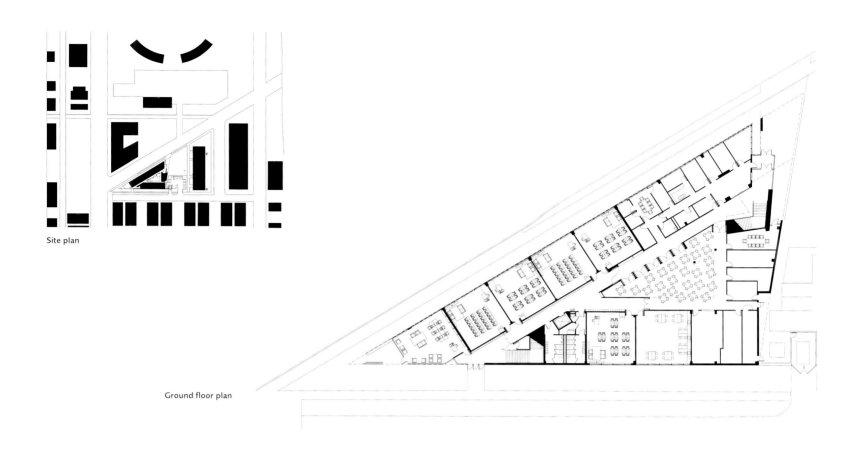

Site plan

Ground floor plan

The new school in its urban context, the forms giving expression to the horizontality of the railway tracks and the verticality of the sky-scrapers | Dramatic elevation to the school square where most students enter beneath the canopy | Break-out spaces at the end of the prow, with graphics articulating the educational and spiritual ethos

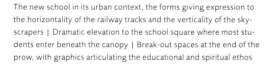

Perspectives Charter School

Chicago, Illinois, USA

Architect	Perkins+Will, Chicago
Pupils	350 aged 11-17 years
Building area	3,030 m²
Average classroom	60 m²
Parking spaces	20
Build cost	4.5 million USD
Completion	2004
Year group system	Age-related classes with special needs groups

Signature architecture to emphasise the importance of education on a city wide basis

This new education facility takes the form of the given site being triangular in plan. The urban location ensues in a restricted site; however, the triangular form is also intended to make it stand out in this transitional area on the edge of the city. The classrooms wrap around the inner open core, an exciting multi-height space which is called the 'Family Room'. The room's two-storey high walls graphically display the school's educational philosophy, 'A Disciplined Life', in both English and Spanish. This core philosophy encourages students, teachers and outside visitors to reflect on the ethical commitments of all members of the school community. It is a central organising principle of the school's belief system, its curriculum and its planning. The architecture is intended to support this ethos and

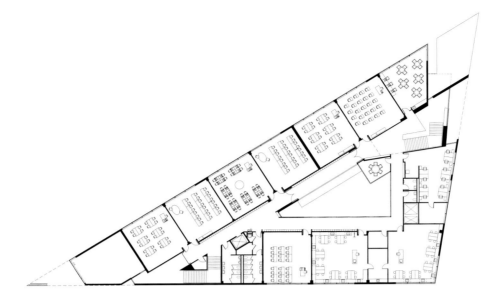

First floor plan

be a physical expression of the Charter School mission, that is to provide working class students with a rigorous education to prepare them for life in a changing and competitive world.

However, the new building is also exciting, an expression of something more optimistic than the inscriptions suggest. Although the building uses what may be considered to be industrial materials, metal cladding panels with an exposed steel frame on the inside, its expression is more high tech than industrial. Windows are either long and horizontal for classrooms or vertical with dramatically angled reveals around the main entrances, staircases and multi-height internal spaces. Its signature design signals to the community

at large that learning is a paramount civic priority. The architects describe it as 'participating in an architectural conversation with Chicago's commercial and cultural landmarks,' and the illustration of the school in its wider context shows clearly how the new facility emphasises the role of education in the civic landscape, standing out as another architectural landmark in this most architecturally minded of cities.

The initial planning process took place in a workshop format with a series of presentations to the local community to illuminate current trends in education. Integral to these workshops were many formal and informal discussions with the community regarding a disciplined life, the culture of the school and how the

building should be a physical embodiment of these important concepts. The result is a new building full of light and space, which reflects the unique culture and philosophy of the new school. Constructed on a limited budget, this is a civic building which stands in contrast to much 20th century school planning locating schools on green field sites distant from the residential areas. Here the intention was to create a school right at the heart of its community, a focus for future generations.

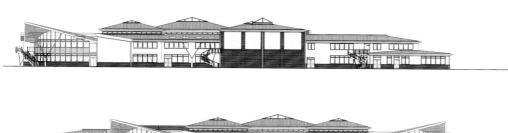

Elevations

Bishops Park College

Clacton, Essex, UK

Architect	Architects Co-Partnership (ACP), Northaw
Pupils	960 aged 11-16 years
Building area	9,274 m²
Average classroom	50 m²
Parking spaces	146
Build cost	17.5 million GBP
Completion	2005
Year group system	Age-related 5 form entry

Schools within a school format comprising three schools each with a cohort of 300 pupils

In the first line of their own description, the architects of this extensive new school structure raise the issue of its funding and procurement approach, the private finance initiative (PFI). This is perhaps an understandably defensive stance since the much criticised PFI process is often explained as an expediency which places the priority on the main contractor's profits ahead of good design. Certainly many of the initial schools designed, built and maintained in this way are poor. However, this is not the case here, partly as a result of the complex and inclusive planning process required to incorporate a range of different uses into a single building, including a community library, a nursery and a centre for the over-60s.

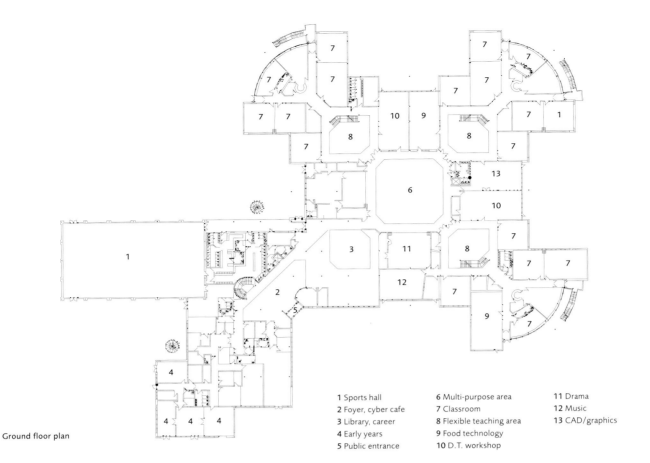

Ground floor plan

1 Sports hall	6 Multi-purpose area	11 Drama
2 Foyer, cyber cafe	7 Classroom	12 Music
3 Library, career	8 Flexible teaching area	13 CAD/graphics
4 Early years	9 Food technology	
5 Public entrance	10 D.T. workshop	

Over-sailing roof has a nautical feel | Main entrance | Aerial view showing the communal hall at the heart of the plan | Community library | First floor gallery with library below

The head teacher, Mike Davies, had a clear vision of what he wanted from his school. The brief was to organise the structure into three relatively self-contained units, schools within schools, all assembled under one roof; the intention was that this would be a compact two-storey plan, since a second priority was to minimise travel distances thus avoiding long internal corridors. The head teacher wanted good 'policing' of all the communal areas to help improve social interaction; as a result, circulation zones are broad and punctuated by social spaces and informed by elements of the brief which are open to circulation, making everything seem spacious and fluid. Students have glimpses of the library from first floor galleries, top-lit atria are positioned in close proximity to classrooms, to provide social 'house' areas acting as student common rooms.

Aspects of the architecture take inspiration from the coastal location. This has influenced the design in a number of ways, from the coloured panels on the elevations, reminiscent of the brightly coloured beach huts, to the sail-like projecting roof canopies over each classroom wing. Externally, seating areas are incorporated informally as well as formally by way of a number of subsidiary structures, including low timber walls styled on sea defence groynes, large rocks and wide bollards. A timber deck has been installed as an outdoor performance area and each of the three 'sub-schools' has been themed in tidal, heath and beach landscapes. Thus a 'fresh air and sea breeze' character is intended to symbolise an optimistic and bright future for the new school. At a time when many communities seek smaller, more localised school buildings, particularly at secondary school level, Bishops Park College illustrates the scope for large structures to provide good community facilities with which the users can relate well. The skill of the designers within the framework of the PFI funding regime shows how an inclusive process of consultation linked to good planning can create a sense of belonging to the individual parts of the whole. Add on a significant investment in art and landscaping, and the end result is an economical structure with all the benefits of the best contemporary public architecture.

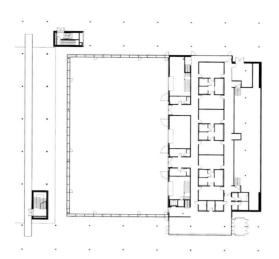
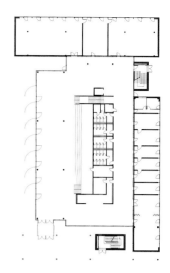

Ground floor plan

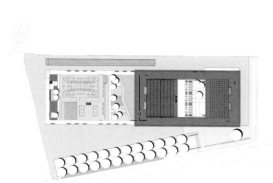

Site plan

View towards the main entrance | Elevation from the riverbank |
View to internal courtyard with broad steps running up to first floor
teaching areas | View of typical classroom, with the use of simple ma-
terials and even controlled colour coding

Gymnasium
Markt Indersdorf

Markt Indersdorf, Germany

Architect	Allmann Sattler Wappner Architekten, München
Pupils	1,200 aged 10-18 years
Building area	19,112 m² (not incl. sports hall)
Average classroom	60 m²
Parking spaces	130
Build cost	27 million EUR
Completion	2002
Year group system	Age-related 5 form entry

A strong architectural form using robust natural materials and underpinned
by a sophisticated sustainability ethos in harmony with its setting

The school lies at the edge of Markt Indersdorf, surrounded by an idyllic meadow landscape stretching to
the banks of the nearby River Glonn. The meadows are
frequently drenched with water; ground water occasion-
ally rises to the surface. The aim was to design a building
that respects and brings out the poetry of this place, con-
serving and protecting its natural beauty. The architectural idea was to raise the entire building above ground
level, to create a floating effect. The building is a harmonious and complementary partner to its surroundings,
a structure fully engaged with the modern world like
Le Corbusier's iconic masterpiece, Villa Savoye. Only
the sports hall and multi-purpose hall are on the ground.
The result is a clear compact building that leaves most
of the site for the sports facilities and the school garden.

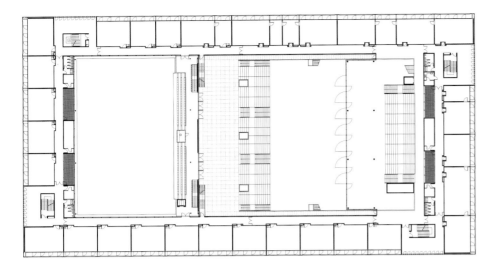

Second floor plan

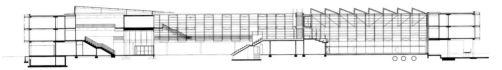

Longitudinal section

Cross section

The commission was won as a competition entry in 1998. The architects stressed their view of the school community as a mixture of different age groups from varying backgrounds all with their particular experiences. The aim of the educative process was therefore to nurture the individuality of each and every child within the framework of a disciplined environment. The essence of the architecture is this combination of order and clarity and a strong sense of identity. The elevated rectangle appears as an appropriate symbol for this ideal. Therefore the internal organisation is equally simple. On the west side of the two-storey accommodation block are the classrooms, while the eastern part contains course rooms and specialist classes. Teachers' rooms, administration and the gymnasium take up the ground floor. Facing the main

entrance courtyard are a pair of broad staircases, partly in the open and partly within the leisure hall, encouraging movement between the ground and upper levels. The geometric centre of the site is the tree-shaded courtyard. The formality of the building grid contrasts with asymmetrically positioned deciduous trees, which when mature will dominate the courtyard and integrate the building further into the natural landscape. The layered planning creates a clear social hierarchy starting with the relative intimacy of the classrooms, a place for individual and small group learning. The naturally lit corridors provide views out to the landscape and a place for accidental meetings.

Another key principle informing the architecture is the sustainable agenda. A sophisticated lighting arrangement

allows an optimum level of natural daylight to penetrate the building. The heavy internal construction reduces maximum temperatures and creates a stable, comfortable environment. The integrated gymnasium and main hall at ground level enable the use of alternative natural ventilation systems, thus reducing energy use. Exploiting the energy within the ground, an earth duct system cools the inflowing air, which then flows out again through wide vents over the roof. The massive floor construction, which is well insulated from the ground, is a composite of load bearing ferrous concrete and seamless industrial flooring. This has a thermal storage effect. High insulation windows and efficient ventilation provide heat protection in summer. Many other energy saving elements contribute to this thoughtful, mature school building.

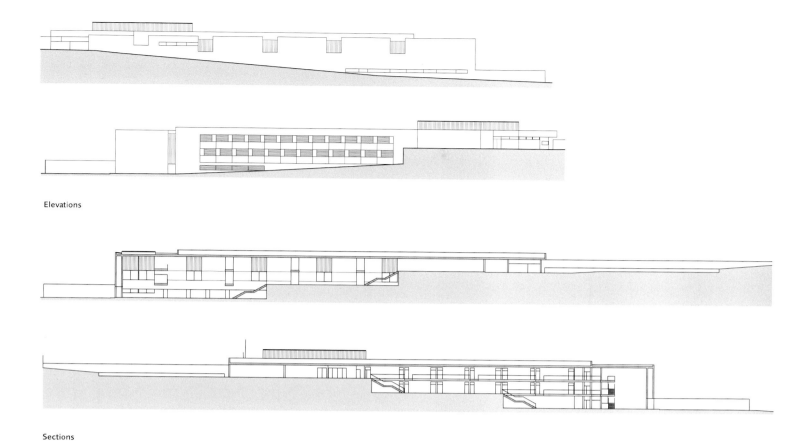

Elevations

Sections

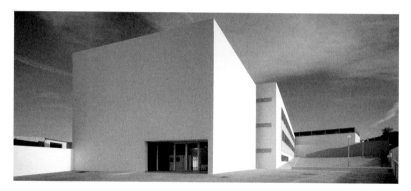

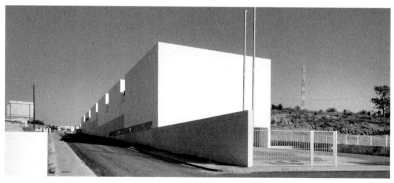

Instituto Villanueva del Rio y Minas

Seville, Spain

Architect	J. Terrados Cepeda + F. Suárez Corchete
Pupils	240 aged 12-16 years
Building area	2,832 m² (not incl. sports hall)
Average classroom	55 m²
Parking spaces	15
Build cost	1.6 million EUR
Completion	2002
Year group system	Age-related 2 form entry, 60 students per year

Strong and restrained architecture with carefully controlled fenestration elements and a solid concrete structure

The design sets out to create a strong statement about boundaries and walls, a fitting metaphor for this end-of-town site. Indeed the scheme comprises a sort of inhabited wall in the form of a long linear block of accommodation finished in sleek white render. The accommodation block breaks down into three connected elements, all of which are closely linked (and part of the wall metaphor) but at the same time articulated architecturally as separate buildings. It is a subtle balance between a strong coherent linearity and a more fragmented expression of three different functional zones, classrooms, sports hall and library media centre. An additional factor which informs the architecture is a steeply sloping site running from the southwestern edge down to the northeastern edge, a level change of

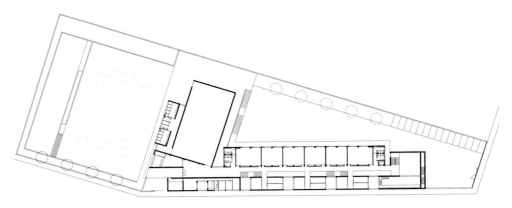

Second floor plan showing gymnasium and upper parts of classrooms

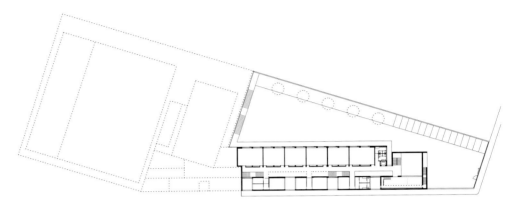

First intermediate floor plan showing upper parts of entrance atrium and library

The low discreet entrance prior to three-storey atrium volume inside |
Street façade | Classroom façade and external ramp up to gymnasium |
View from corridor into classroom from upper mezzanine | View of
gymnasium

approximately 7 metres. This topographical feature is
accommodated within the long section of the building.

The main circulation spine along the street side starts
at the top of the slope with a single-storey space; this
in turn opens up to a two-storey space which finally de-
scends into a three-storey volume, the entrance atrium.
Two grand staircases function as staging points along
this route, providing glimpses in one direction into the
classrooms or out into the surrounding landscape. Thus
the overall form of the building does not drop down
with the change in levels, rather a constant roof line is
maintained across the slope, with the landscape stepping down against the white walls of the street façade.
This creates an impression of solidity, the building has

an almost monumental quality within the barren landscape.

The regular façade rhythm is reinforced by a very limited palette of materials and colours, with two shades
of white and the grey and yellow of the sloping external
ground floor plain creating a crisply detailed modernist composition. The organisation of this building has a
rational dimension which is characterised by the use of
light and orientation; for example, to the southeast, the
block which contains the main teaching spaces, with
classrooms (and WCs) opening up beyond the site with
distinctive horizontal window openings on the main
façade each with an external solar control device. To
the northwest, the spaces for administration, teachers'

offices, seminar rooms, meeting rooms, storage and
technical rooms all have limited views with small windows onto mini landscaped patios. At the lower end of
the site where the head of the building is located, there
are no windows with direct views out, rather a limited
rooflight arrangement spreads a white even light down
to the three-storey volume beneath. The library is positioned on the street side almost within the atrium; it
borrows its light from the atrium by way of a translucent glazed curtain wall. Internally the architecture is
less successful, with a slightly over-bearing clinical feel
emphasised by the bland even lighting which makes
it too cold and impersonal at times. Nevertheless the
finishes are consistent and robust; consequently, one
suspects this building will stand the test of time.

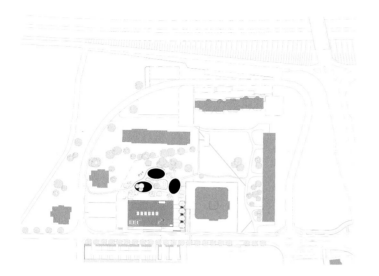

Site plan

Cross section through sports hall and atrium

Cantilever with entrance beneath | View of entrance and street elevation | Views of the building from the northeast

Collège des Tuillières

Gland, Switzerland

Architect	Graeme Mann & Patricia Capua Mann, Lausanne
Pupils	450 aged 12-16 years
Building area	7,995 m²
Average classroom	80 m²
Parking spaces	30
Build cost	25 million CHF
Completion	2005
Year group system	Age-related grades 7-9

An efficient block arrangement, which optimises heating and ventilation

The new Collège des Tuillières is located in the heart of the 'Cité Ouest' residential neighbourhood. The dominant planning strategy of the quartier is the old-fashioned Corbusian notion of high-rise buildings within a park-like setting. Despite their poor architectural quality, the compactness of the existing blocks is a theme the architects of this new school have followed, concentrating all of the new accommodation into a single, four-storey rectangular block (with subterranean basement) set in a spacious green setting. The impression is one of bulk rather than height, with solid regular fenestration, which is rectangular and squat in appearance; the new school is reminiscent of an Italian palazzo, wider and longer than it is tall, despite the fact that it dominates its site.

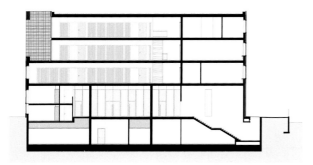

Cross section

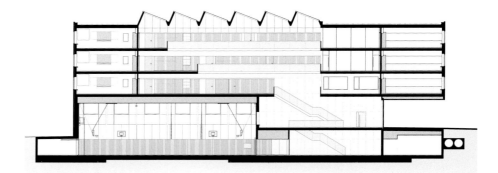

Section through central atrium

A somewhat extraordinary design feature is visible at the short southeast end, in the form of a huge cantilevered section of building three storeys high. The unsupported end is 9 metres deep and 35 metres across. This eccentric structural gesture takes up the entire length of the short end of the building. From certain angles it makes the edifice appear to be toppling over. However, it is a design motif which makes sense when you begin to explore the interior, which is full of cantilevered balconies and staircase details. Despite this, there is a sense of solidity about its architectural expression, with a limited palette of robust natural materials used throughout; this is very much an institutional building made to last. Beneath the cantilever at ground floor level is the main entrance. Once in-

side the recessed glazed entrance screen, the foyer is a broad wood lined hallway with the main staircase on the left side and the office/reception to the right. Beyond the entrance hall, views open up across and down to the large semi-submerged sports hall. Moving through towards the centre of the building, the dominant internal feature appears in view, which is a four-storey galleried atrium with large north-light roof windows at the top. The effect is impressive, students entering the building are at once aware of a new internal world, a monumental space which allows physical and visual connections throughout the building, an intermediate world between the privacy of the classroom and the street. Indeed the scale of this space is very much akin to a street, with activity and move-

ment enhancing the overall sense of community; only this is a street which runs vertically up through the building, terminating on the third floor. It gives the school a unique sense of its own combined public and private identity, with stairways and galleries encouraging movement around this stylish volume. However, the route or promenade does not simply permit internal views. At each level (above ground floor), there is a classroom wide void and two large staircase windows, which give users direct views out to the surrounding area. It strikes a subtle spatial balance between the intimacy of a single internalised shared space, the atrium, and the openness and excitement of space and scale, vista and distant views of the surrounding townscape.

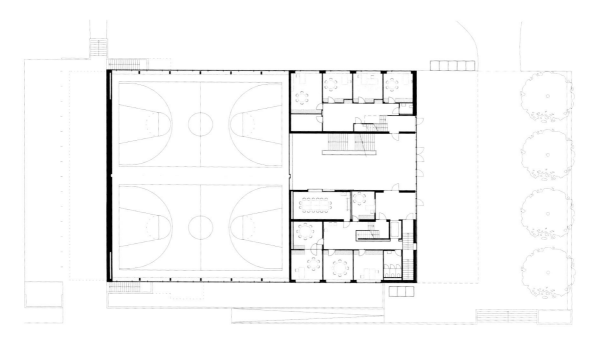

Ground floor plan

The building is laid out in a predictable way with classrooms stacked within the three upper storeys, around the atrium light well. At ground floor level, on either side of the main entrance is the staff and administration area with offices and meeting rooms, which effectively police the comings and goings of students in and out of the main entrance area. Beneath ground floor level the sports hall and associated changing rooms together with plant rooms form a solid base. The double basketball courts benefit from natural side-lit windows with views of the sky and natural cross ventilation. The careful orientation enhances the overall transparency of the entire building which connects the interior to the outside play spaces and, as explained previously, the classroom accommodation

to the administration and leisure facilities. The sports hall has its own entrance, which provides access to the local community during evenings and weekends.

The materials used on this concrete frame structure are spare and somewhat austere creating an almost colourless environment. Inside the building, exposed concrete forms a framework for polished timber cladding in light beech, used on classroom walls, balustrades and classroom floors. The balustrade timber provides a colour/texture routing system through the building, as generous open staircases take visitors on a promenade walk up through the building. It is a gentle and spacious environment, a place for calm reflection. Externally, rich blue-green ceramic tiles are the

chosen cladding material, used as a decorative skin, which gives a subtly changing reflective hue as the sun moves around the building. The building has developed an iconic imagery for the modern school building, a little institutional for some tastes, but for most, a reassuring presence within the community.

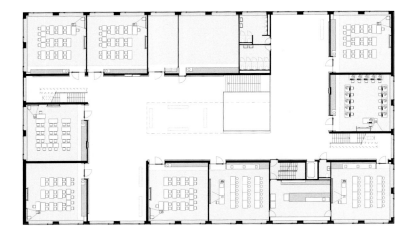

First floor plan

Third floor plan

First floor atrium with views down to sports hall | Second floor deck with rooflights above | Typical classroom with full-width paired windows | Outside-inside transition

Elevation/section classroom block

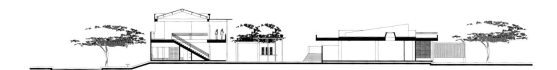

Cross section

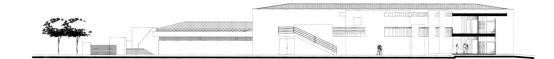

Elevation/section of main communal block

The colonnade provides shade for the classrooms | Entrance corner with stair tower for cooling and ventilation | Views of internal courtyard showing restrained use of colour

Colegio Secundaria Industrial

Santiago de Cali, Colombia

Architect	Luis Fernando Zúñiga Gáez, Cali
Pupils	600 aged 11-18 years
Building area	3,546 m²
Average classroom	50 m²
Parking spaces	n/a
Build cost	2,352 million COP
Completion	1999
Year group system	Age-related year groupings

A collage composition which establishes an urban heart to the community

This school aspires to become a symbolic centre for its community in terms of its architectural expression and its open plan forms. From its sun-shaded internal colonnades to its iconic entrance tower building on the outside, it is a mini city complete with its own medical centre and restaurant. In short it is far more than a school. Commissioned by the education department for the Municipality Number 17, the site is in the south of Santiago de Cali in the green belt which forms an environmental lung between high rise social housing blocks and dense inner city industrial areas. The plan comprises two main linear blocks which are hinged on their eastern corner and rotated at 45 degrees to each other creating a triangular inner courtyard which has buildings on two sides and a semi-open, partly landscaped third side. The hinge

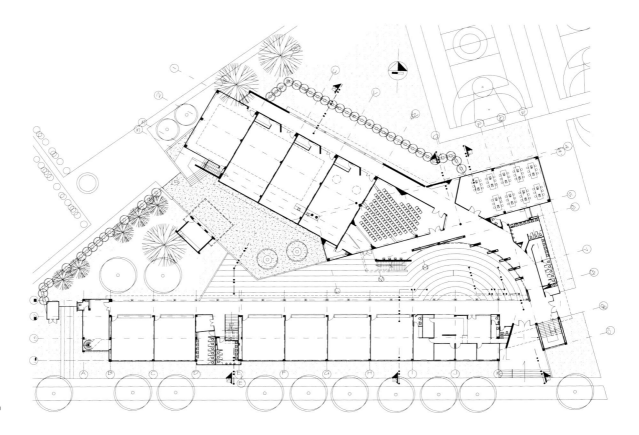

Ground floor plan

and its two wings of built form create a hard geometrical outside edge to the surrounding streets. The complex architectural geometries of the whole resolve themselves at the corner. The hinge is also the main entrance from the street corner, however it is a semi-permeable edge with clear thresholds and deliberate breaks in the built form. They create welcoming entrances, views and vistas into the courtyard beyond. On entering inside from the street corner the composition unfolds as a colonnade of two-storey standard size classrooms to the left and a more free form range of communal spaces including a 300 seat theatre on the left, with design workshops and other flexible spaces. The third side of the colonnade opens up to the landscape beyond with views towards children's play spaces and sports fields. The solid south

and east façades with the single open edge towards the west creates a cool shaded space. The organisation is a direct response to the climatic conditions, high humidity and extreme solar radiation. The built form with its solid concrete and masonry construction and enhanced natural cross ventilation works extremely well in this respect.

The architecture not only provides a strong environmental theme in this hot climate, but also refers to the idea of monastic cells and cloisters. The architects have deliberately drawn on this metaphor which they describe as a 'continuity – discontinuity' spatial ideal. The architecture establishes a clear distinction between the classroom, which is essentially a non-social space and generally an internalised world for personal reflection and individual

study, and the colonnade, an altogether more social interactive school space. The clarity of this view may be slightly uncompromising, however it is a very effective way of organising the architecture.

This is a stylish building but also one which is practical; for example there is a robustness about the architecture with the use of durable hard wearing materials which are standing the test of time. Its scales are resonant with the scales of its users, with large and smaller scale architectural moments throughout. Perhaps most important is the overall spirit it transmits to the users, a sense of playfulness and austerity at the same time. There is in effect a time and a place for both moods within this pleasing composition. This is an example of best practice.

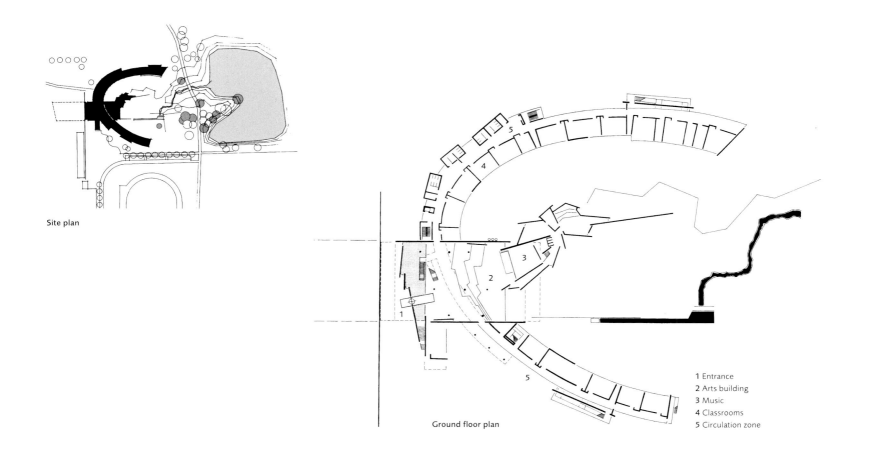

Site plan

Ground floor plan

1 Entrance
2 Arts building
3 Music
4 Classrooms
5 Circulation zone

Oskar Maria Graf Gymnasium

Neufahrn, Germany

Architect	Hein Goldstein Architekten, München
Pupils	1,000 aged 10-18 years
Building area	38,000 m²
Average classroom	66 m²
Parking spaces	340
Build cost	41.07 million DM
Completion	1996
Year group system	Traditional age-related 3 form entry

The 'wall' form is a direct response to the site conditions forming an acoustic baffle between the noisy side and the quiet inner court

Neufahrn is a growing town with a large residential community which required a new secondary school. The architectural approach has evolved from a careful analysis of the site conditions combined with the stylistic influences of the wider town context, with its eclectic range of architectural styles. The land selected for the development was an edge-of-town site with a noisy motorway ring road on one side, a railway line and a sports ground along the other two sides. On the only quiet side, to the east, there is a former gravel pit which has been flooded to form an attractive bathing lake. The new structure is in the form of a three- and four-storey inhabited wall which separates the noisy functions from the potentially calm sanctuary of the lakeside setting; the wall is a vast horseshoe shape which is 100 metres across. It not only provides for the bulk of the

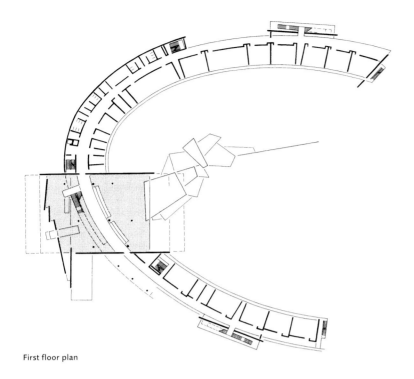

First floor plan

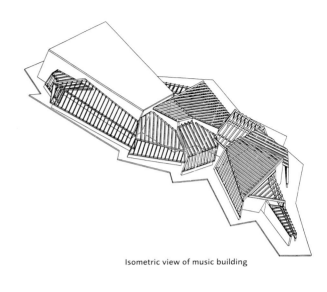

Isometric view of music building

View from a distance illustrating the defensive form | Dramatically cantilevered main staircase with typical wall and roof cladding system on the external curve | Internal façade detail with projecting solar shading | Foyer and circulation area

school's accommodation, but also encloses the open space in front of the lake.

This strong response to the site, with the new building curving away from the noise and embracing the lake, is a gesture which is carried through into the detail design. The 'hard' outer side is where all the school's noisy functions occur; circulation corridors and stairs, storage and washrooms help to form a protective wrapping around the inner core of classrooms which are all orientated towards the 'softer' lake side. Thus the classroom façades are highly glazed well-ventilated rooms, with views onto the inner court. By contrast, the outer walls are less open, with a mixture of aluminium cladding panels, rendered blockwork, horizontal metal sun shades and meshes panels,

which shade and secure the façades. From a distance the curving wall with its reflective metallic surfaces shimmers in the afternoon sun, welcoming and protecting at the same time. On the inside, the façade treatment is less interesting, consisting of almost continuous horizontal bands of curtain walling. Here the building expresses its functional role as a straightforward 'machine for learning', with one architectural aberration: there is a dramatically fragmented music building, which has detached itself from the wall and 'landed' in the courtyard garden. It is a deliberate compositional gesture, mediating between the formality of the wall idea and the semi-natural landscape beyond. It is built of heavy-duty fair-faced concrete, the fragmented internal shape providing good acoustics for music and recording purposes. However, the logic of its shape is as a counter-

point in this rich architectural composition, an expression of the idea that individual creativity, within the framework of disciplined orthodoxy (as seen within the main school block) is the key component of the whole school vision.

The result is a building which is not just practical, providing state-of-the-art accommodation in an economical form, but is also highly faceted and inspirational. Whilst the drawbacks of the site were self-evident from the outset, the new building helps to create a new sense of place. Even if some of the travel distances between classrooms may be rather long, the layout is legible and the generously proportioned circulation areas, with subtle side and top lighting, promote the social dimension for staff and students moving around.

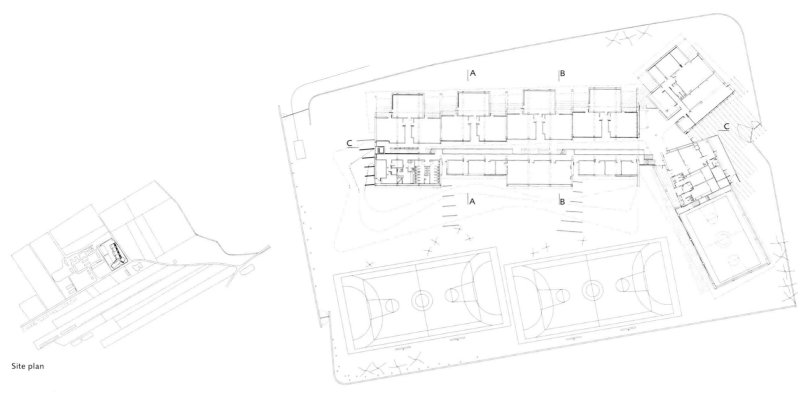

Site plan

Ground floor plan

Instituto La Serra

Mollerussa, Lleida, Spain

Architect	Carme Pinós Desplat, Barcelona
Pupils	480 aged 12-18 years
Building area	4,300 m²
Average classroom	50 m²
Parking spaces	5
Build cost	2.35 million EUR
Completion	2001
Year group system	Age-related 3 form entry, 30 students per class

Complex baroque form-making to provide an exciting school environment

The starting point and inspiration for this project was the site, a flat lowland agricultural area with a patchwork of orchards and related sheds and small outbuildings providing a distinctive landscape within which the new school is located. Despite the fact that this is a large building comprising over 4,000 square metres of accommodation, the designers were determined to create a broken, fragmented form, which they believed was an important architectural motif to lighten its presence within the rustic setting. The result is a large building, which is surprisingly compact and low key especially when viewed from a distance. The compact appearance is partly a result of the tripartite twisted plan organisation adopted by the designers; it is a Y shaped plan which works well in conjunction with three distinct function-

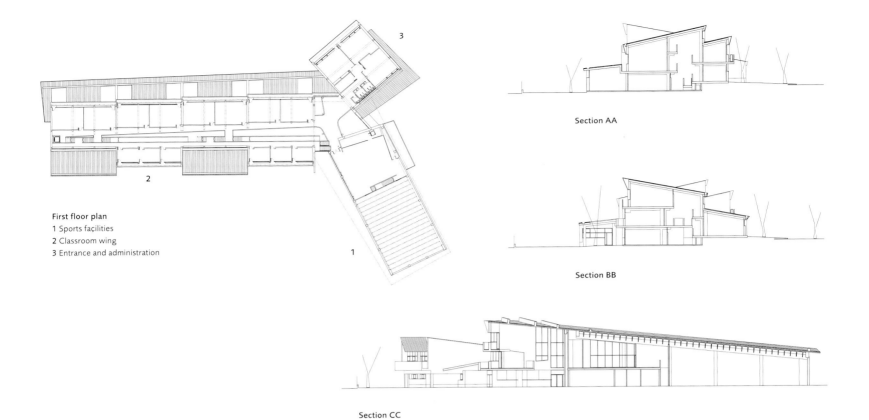

First floor plan
1 Sports facilities
2 Classroom wing
3 Entrance and administration

Section AA

Section BB

Section CC

Classroom façade | View from the street – a game of roofs | Typical classroom with heavy structural ceiling | Communal circulation spaces with curved galleries

al zones identified by the client, one being for sports activities, one for classrooms and academic activities and finally a wing for the entrance and administration. The car park grid corresponds to the building grid, in some ways a progressive philosophy, when so many large secondary schools of this type are surrounded by a sea of parked cars. The designers have deliberately set out to contain them within the fabric of the architecture, and to good effect.

Within this overall strategy, three classrooms are grouped around an open courtyard, each contained by the tight structural form within the long arm of the Y. The courtyards provide a communal space for students to mingle within each year group, allowing light and air to filter

into the deep, tightly organised plan and creating important intermediary spaces between the inside and the outside. All classrooms are orientated towards the east, only the service areas and administration offices get direct afternoon sun. A broad triple-height central spine, which is top-lit and highly ventilated, connects the whole teaching wing together. The recurring theme of the 'internal street' within large linear secondary school buildings works particularly well here with curved upper galleries providing a plastic spatial form which is full of drama and movement. Because of its complex geometry the building, highly modulated by the designers' subtle manipulation of natural light from both the side and the top, offers an engaging social landscape.

In some senses it is surprising to find such a large development in this isolated setting. The architectural treatment is careful to create an environment, which is legible to its users yet full of intriguing spaces, dramatic collisions of geometry and form both inside and outside. The architects explain the building as 'a game of roofs', which is a neat way to explain the initial inspiration and its adoption as a generator of form. However, it is much more than this, the result being a most unusual and successful building. In an age where so many school buildings promote the sense of institutional control, this is a building full of poetic moments and inspiring architectural details which promotes a sense of natural relaxed informality, an anti-institutional school.

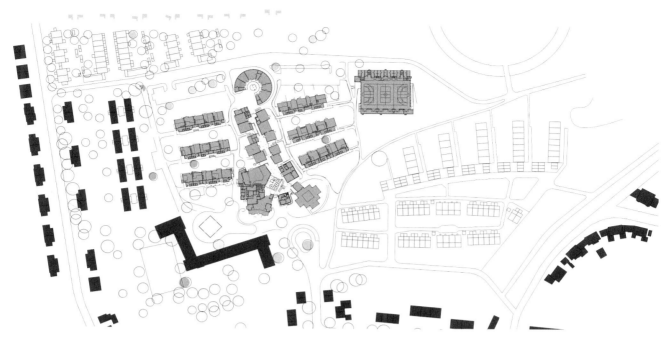

Site plan

Linked classroom pavilions looking onto the meadow gardens |
Classroom blocks combine to a rich variegated architecture which
looks nothing like a conventional school | Exterior views

Protestant Comprehensive School

Gelsenkirchen, Germany

Architect	Plus+ Bauplanung, Neckartenzlingen
Pupils	900 (planned to be 1,100) aged 11-19 years
Building area	13,650 m²
Average classroom	60 m²
Parking spaces	20
Build cost	18.13 million EUR
Completion	2004
Year group system	Age-related classes with special needs groups

A school designed as a small town with subject areas described and planned as stand alone townscape elements ranged around streets, squares and gardens

The church client for this comprehensive community integrated school chose their architect carefully. Considering Plus+ Bauplanung Peter Hübner's reputation as designer of a distinctive organic form of architecture which incorporates community participation throughout the process, even utilising parents to 'build it themselves' when budgets run low, their choice was not without risk. Although self-build approaches were not required here, the radical concept, which supports this design, has created something which hardly resembles a school in the conventional way we might understand it. No slick corporate architectural statements here or high security CCTV cameras and metal fences to keep people away. Instead we have what appears to be a series of linked pavilions,

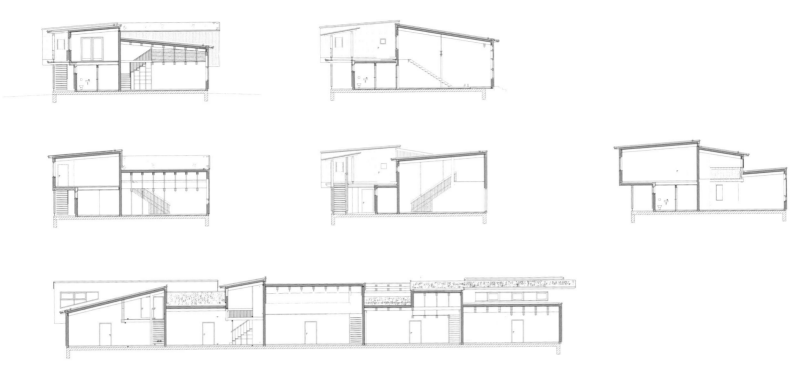

Sections

mainly two storeys in height, clad in timber and surrounded by well-manicured gardens. Walking around the disparate fragmented classrooms and departmental areas, this resembles a very well-conceived suburban housing quarter, with neat courtyard gardens, streets and squares which are knit seamlessly into the surrounding residential quarters. Stylistically it sets out to be deliberately anti-institutional, a school which does not try to be intimidating, rather it is friendly and accessible, a sort of 'home from home.'

The school is one part of an extensive residential quarter planned by the town of Gelsenkirchen-Bismarck. Through its green areas and low-scale forms the school is fully integrated into the new urban residential envi-

ronment and forms part of the social heart of the town itself. An approach called 'Familien-, Erziehungs-, Lebens- und Stadtteilschule' (literally translated as 'school for the family, education, life and the neighbourhood') informs the concept; education is matched closely to the real experiences of the children within that community. The school is the community, and in some ways the community is the school. Education is not seen as something which stops and starts when students pass over the school's threshold, rather education happens everywhere, conceived as a process which is inextricably woven into the fabric of the community; there is a particular emphasis on nature and awareness of the individual's place within a fragile world. The architecture, whilst elegant and modern, reflects this world view. It

is an architecture which is in harmony with the educational philosophy.

From its inception, the architects recognised the importance of involving future users in the planning. They engaged teachers, parents and above all pupils in the design process using a number of participatory techniques, but in particular presenting ideas and concepts in the form of 1:10 scale models over a two-month consultation period. The relatively long planning period and the readily understood and humane architectural language adopted from the outset allowed community participants to concentrate on organisation, size and detail. As individuals, they could imagine where they might sit in their schoolroom, the

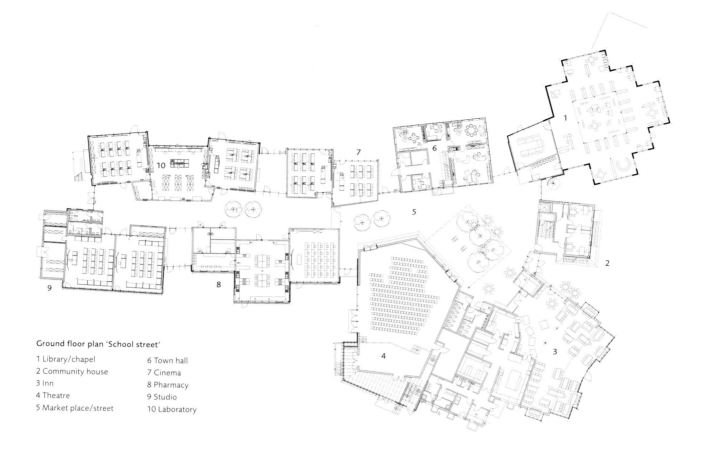

Ground floor plan 'School street'

1 Library/chapel	6 Town hall
2 Community house	7 Cinema
3 Inn	8 Pharmacy
4 Theatre	9 Studio
5 Market place/street	10 Laboratory

view they would get from the window, or the special garden seat they might use to meet with a teacher to discuss their assignment. Current school performance (after the main buildings have been in operation since September 2004) suggests that this approach has resulted in significant improvements; involving the school's immediate neighbours has developed a sense of community ownership, which can be evidenced by the lack of graffiti and vandalism.

In order to integrate academic, practical and social learning more effectively, the architects developed the scheme as a series of low scale buildings organised along streets, with linked classroom pavilions ranged along secondary avenues off the main street,

like branches off the trunk of a tree; the main street terminates at one end with a mini town square surrounded by the school offices (like the town hall), the school hall (like the theatre) and the library. Thus the experience of passing from one subject area to another is essentially social, conducted along pleasant traffic free streets, rather than along enclosed corridors. This reflects the school's conceptual model as that of a miniature self-managed town. What makes this such an engaging metaphor is that the streets are actually like streets you might find in any interesting historical townscape, with architectural variety and no little drama in the way the various elements come together. It is an extremely attractive alternative to most conventional school buildings.

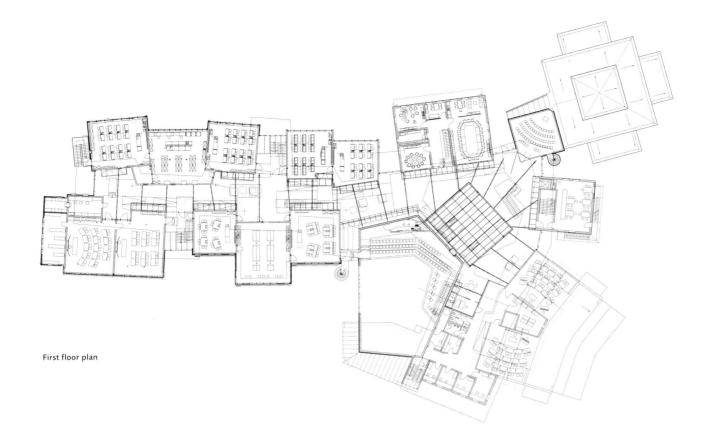

First floor plan

Reading space | Chapel | Typical classroom in use, relaxed and informal with timber staircase access to first floor 'think pod' | Interior view of dining areas with decorative water feature | Sports hall

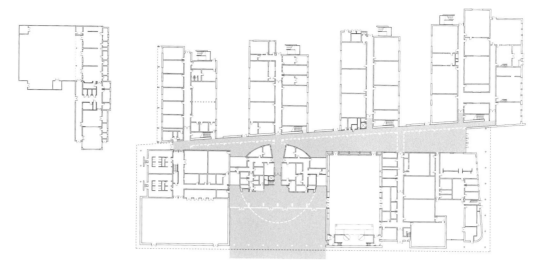

Ground floor plan

Main entrance elevation

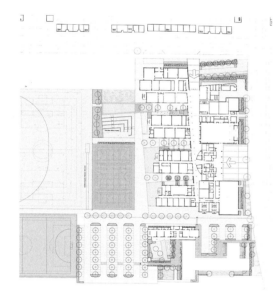

Site plan | Main entrance and façade illuminated at night, a very public building | View down 'street' towards curved yellow entrance drum | Secondary entrance

Jo Richardson Community School

Dagenham, London, UK

Architect	Architecture PLB, London
Pupils	1,500 aged 11-18 years
Building area	16,004 m² (not incl. sports hall)
Average classroom	75 m²
Parking spaces	180
Build cost	29 million GBP
Completion	2005
Year group system	Age-related 5 form entry

'Extended school' providing a comprehensive range of activities and services for use during and beyond the traditional school day

The Jo Richardson Community School is a new 1,500 place secondary school at Castle Green in Dagenham, one of the most deprived communities in greater London. The new facilities are one of the first authentic 'full service extended schools' in the UK. The brief includes a public library, a sports centre, a performing arts suite, ICT and adult education facilities. There is also the provision of vocational courses within the new school including engineering, plumbing, electrical installation, painting, decorating and catering. As part of the early development work, the local education authority commissioned an 'exemplar' scheme to be worked up prior to the formal appointment of the architect. This entailed a great deal of user participation and resulted in a clear vision of what the community wanted. A close relation-

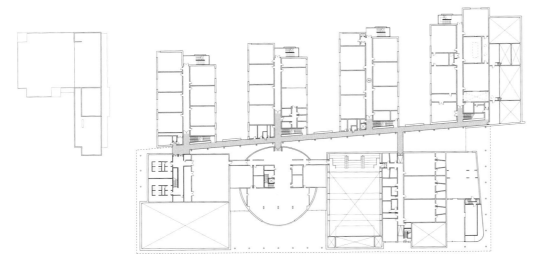

Second floor plan

Section/elevation of main entrance and main hall showing upper level teaching and triple-height street

ship was forged between users and client. The design that ensued succeeds in balancing the need for security and discipline with an environment which feels relaxed and open incorporating a rich mixture of education and community spaces which are equally inclusive. One of the key priorities which emerged early on was the need for clear organisation of the different parts of the scheme, to break down the scale of the development. Centred around a triple-height 'internal street' which gives easy access to all areas, secondary circulation corridors bisect the street service into four wings of accommodation which are almost self-contained, like schools within schools. The four wings contain DT, vocational and food technology, science and art, PBSC (positive behaviour support), staff, geography and history, Eng-

lish, ICT and business studies. There is a grand entrance lobby leading onto the internal street. On either side of the entrance there are more community orientated areas such as music, drama and sports together with the main assembly hall and dining. These spaces can be open when the rest of the school is closed. The classrooms are of particular educational interest in that they have been specially designed to meet the requirements of Dagenham's innovative pedagogical model. İt involves interactive whole-class teaching for which a single 'horseshoe' arrangement of desks is required, allowing all students to see the teacher and each other during lessons. This has resulted in larger than average classrooms which also offer flexible arrangements for group work. Long term flexibility is provided not by way of moveable wall panels

but by clear planning hierarchies (allowing future expansion), generous space standards and most importantly, robust construction to resist the attention of present and future generations of young people.

This is an approach which has delivered on a vision of extended use. Why should school sites close their doors to the users at 4.30 on a Friday afternoon? Here the school is open until 10 pm every night of the school week and until 8 pm at weekends. The huge investment at Jo Richardson not only provides an efficient learning environment for school students, it extends the use of those valuable facilities towards the wider community, providing a new learning campus of which all members of the community who use it can be proud.

Academies and Vocational Schools

As a distinctive and relatively new school form, academies and vocational schools are an attempt to bring progressive change to the secondary school traditions within the state sector. The Academy School programme, which is particular to the UK, takes elements of the semi-privately run Charter School movement in the USA and mixes them with a more vocational curriculum form, which is relatively common in Europe. In this category secondary schools in mainland Europe, which illustrate a progressive or radically different approach to the traditional comprehensive educational umbrella, are also included; to the extent that they are specialist schools, however the terminology should not be confused with special schools for students with more extreme educational difficulties. Definitions are not strictly consistent across national boundaries, however we have grouped those institutions together, which reflect a culture of change within this final category.

The secondary school sector is notoriously conservative and resistant to change even where it is seen to be failing. What is clear about this section of case studies is the extent to which architecture is used to make grand statements about the significance of a specialist educational institution, largely state funded, yet outside the mainstream secondary school academic tradition. Progressive thinking acts as a catalyst to new and innovative practice, with the emphasis on architecture as well as education to promote new ways of thinking in the secondary school sector.

In the UK the Academies programme aims to challenge the culture of educational under attainment and to deliver real improvements in standards. Most academies are located in areas of deprivation with high levels of family unemployment and poverty. They either replace one or more existing schools facing challenging circumstances or are established where there is a need for additional school places. Perhaps the most contentious aspect is the semi-private ownership of essentially state funded schools, which is described as 'sponsorship'. The context for this is that a faith group, a commercial organisation or even a local authority can submit £2 million in sponsorship in return for a degree of control of the institution. The key idea is that private management strategies will help to bring efficiencies into the system and connect education more readily with the needs of the commercial world. Huge investment has been underway over the past five years, however the success in academic terms is open to question. The jury is out, as they say.

For example, the Bexley Business Academy is sponsored by City of London institutions to provide special support for children in this traditionally deprived part of southeast London (pages 234-235). Designed by Foster and Partners, it uses the architectural language of the contemporary office building to illustrate its specialist qualities and appeal to its often disaffected pupil intake.

The Charter School movement in the USA is an attempt to free publicly funded elementary or secondary schools from some of the bureaucracy that applies to normal public schools. This is in exchange for some sort of accountability for producing certain results, such as an educational experience which is qualitatively different from what is available in traditional public schools, hence, the term 'charter'. The idea here is that new and creative teaching methods can be replicated in traditional public schools for the benefit of all children. In 2006-2007 the number of charter schools was up by 11% with schools in 40 states educating more than 1.15 million children. Often a progressive form of environment signals the schools agenda of change. For example the Perspectives Charter School (pages 200-201) in Chicago eschews the traditional modesty of low-key secondary school architecture. Instead it states its support by the city fathers for lower-income students with a landmark building which has a city wide profile in this most architectural of cities.

Dutch education is characterised by a system in which both public and private education facilities enjoy equal governmental funding while being subject to some national regulation. For several decades the Netherlands has implemented policies aimed explicitly to address the needs of children with educational disadvantages. Traditionally these were geared towards disadvantaged Dutch pupils. However, due to large increases in migrant groups from the 1960s, they have become the main focal point for change strategies, with an increasing emphasis on a vocationally orientated curriculum. The Montessori College Oost in Amsterdam (pages 236-237) offers practical job training, with workshops, kitchens and a small sports hall to provide vocational training for the students who come from 50 different countries. Many of them are from unstable family backgrounds, and the less academic, more practically based curriculum options enable skills to be learned for a highly competitive workplace. However, the most important features of the building are proving to be incidental elements such as generous circulation spaces outside the classroom, which like village streets, with exciting balconies and staircases traversing the open atrium spaces below, make chance encounters between students and staff part of the enriched social experience.

In Germany the tradition of a vocational stream from the secondary school level is well established. It is system to which the British and US systems aspire. One of the most distinctive new specialist schools is the Marie Curie Gymnasium in the suburbs of Berlin (pages 240-241). Its architecture is very much of the moment, modernistic and utilising cutting edge sustainability technology. However, it is not a specialist building for deprived students; rather it is for those students who are gifted academically in science subjects, with an intake from throughout the state. Here the response has been to address the needs of gifted children, those who may find mainstream secondary education too slow to cater for their educational requirements. Again the architecture is more contemporary high tech office building than what we are used to seeing in normal run of the mill secondaries.

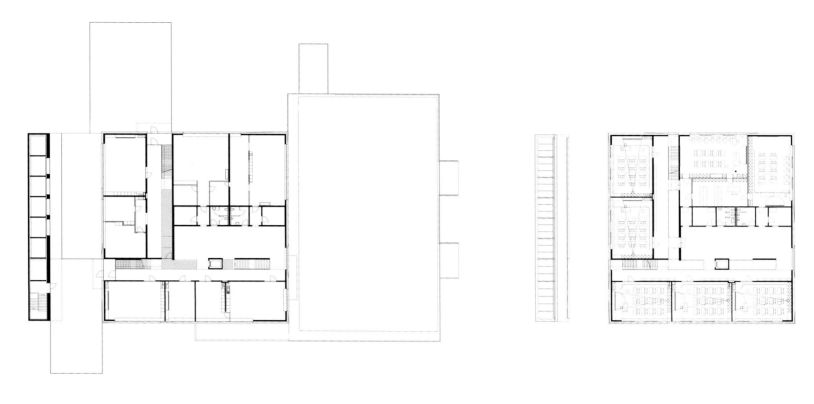

Ground floor plan

First floor plan with furniture

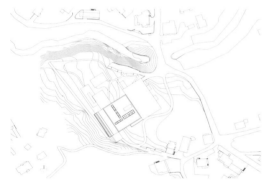

Site plan | Elevation to the south | Third floor view along corridor with bridge link connecting across to teaching spaces | View into gymnasium, the interface between the lower and upper schools

Flims
Comprehensive
School

Flims, Switzerland

Architect	Werknetz Architektur, Zürich
Pupils	320 aged 6 - 16 years
Building area	3,580 m²
Average classroom	75 m²
Parking spaces	approx. 30
Build cost	15.5 million CHF
Completion	2003
Year group system	Traditional 2 form entry classbase system

A community school combining primary and secondary school students in one compact and economical multi-storey block

The Flims Comprehensive School is a five-storey block building located in a semi-rural mountainous area. For cost and construction reasons the architects have rejected the usual fragmented departmental approach to school design instead combining the lower and upper school into a single unified form. On each of the main teaching levels there are seven classrooms with WCs and a common room space with an open community room. The circulation space is articulated as an L shaped 'cut' with a lift and two staircases which run through the entire five-storey block to provide a clear and legible organising device. Stairs are positioned at right angles to the external walls providing dramatic views to the landscape beyond. Natural light filters down by way of rooftop skylights; the lower levels of

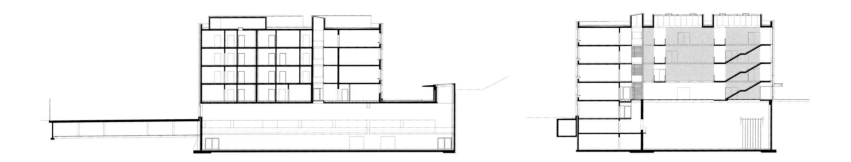

Longitudinal section   Cross section

accommodation are ventilated by way of gallery cuts in each floor plate.

This unusual and modern school structure combines the lower and upper schools in one compact block. Rather like a contemporary office structure, it makes little use of traditional school iconography or scale references to the widely varying age of children using it; rather a sense of belonging comes through the subtle play of structural grids and the use of modern cladding materials on the highly reflective façades, both internally and externally. This is a grown-up piece of architecture which bestows on the children a sense of their own significance within the adult world. Ultimately its users, a close knit village community,

have three buildings in one: a lower school, an upper school and a gymnasium, each of which is connected internally, and each with its own entrance. The sense of community is enhanced without losing the intimacy of the individual teaching spaces by way of this 'magic cube'.

On the outside it appears like a solid shimmering block floating on the hilly landscape, inside it is all lightness and space with dramatic views up and down. This allows the users a real sense of what is going on in other areas as they move around the building from the inside to the outside. As the bell sounds at the end of each lesson period the atmosphere transforms dramatically, as students from all parts of the building

circulate. Movement and colour is suddenly reflected via the matt black and grey façade glazing on the inside. Visual and physical contact between different year groups is encouraged in this social mixing pot.

The mix is enhanced by the way in which the younger and older students share classbases on each floor. Thus from floors 1 to 3, there are classes for both 13-16 year olds and for 7-12 year olds. With a common room dedicated to integrated age activities on each floor, the developers have managed an interesting mixed age range system, which maintains order but subtly breaks the convention of only permitting similar age students to come together in a school setting. It is a lesson in its own right.

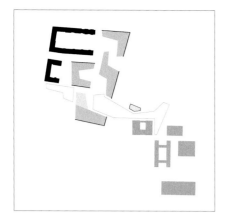

Site plan

The sophisticated vehicular controls create spatial continuity between the buildings | Entrance court or 'Ankerplatz' | The architecture creates comfortable public spaces in the form of east- and west-facing court-yards with rooftop walkways and terraces

Education Centre 'Tor zur Welt'

Hamburg, Germany

Architect	BOF Architekten (Bucking Ostrop Flemming)
Pupils	945 in new building, 670 in existing building
Building area	10,800 m² new building, 20,169 m² combined
Average classroom	85 m² (incl. 10 m² wardrobe, 15 m² workroom)
Parking spaces	76
Build cost	29.1 million EUR
Completion	2013
Year group system	Partially age-related and age-integrated groups (grades 1 + 2 and 3 + 4), up to 5 form entry in primary school

A building with a radical approach to community engagement

In the early part of the new millennium, the City of Hamburg hatched its ambitious plans for an Internationale Bauausstellung IBA (International Building Exhibition), held in 2007-2013. The focus of this programme was the residential quarter of Wilhelmsburg, an underdeveloped 35 km² area which was already home to 50,000 people, located on the west side of the Elbe, between the northern and southern branches of the river. What the existing community lacked was a coherent infrastructure of routes and key public buildings, such as schools and adult education centres, which would connect its people to wider city communities and to Hamburg's cultural richness.

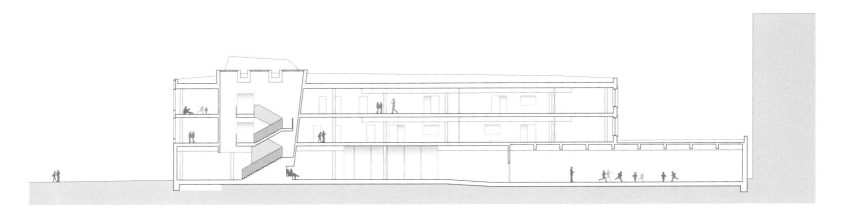

Section

The so-called 'Metrozones', one of the key concepts of IBA, offer space for intelligent growth on the edges whilst trying to avoid the dreary, disconnected sub-urbanisation characteristic of much late 20th century US and UK urban design. Central to IBA is the idea of raising awareness about the environment through its architecture. This was an attempt to show and to teach people about the environment by creating de-centralised renewable energy plants which were there on the doorstep for locals to see and comprehend. Like a prominent wind turbine on the horizon, only much more sophisticated in its diversity of power gen-eration, this was to be highly visible, promoting the rhetoric of sustainability awareness, in order for its lessons to cascade down the generations.

The main public buildings within this plan for a 'Bil-dungszentrum' (Education Centre) are a secondary school (age 11-12) with a business centre, a primary school (age 5-10) and an environmental science centre. The secondary schools for pupils aged 13-18 years remained in the existing building. The science centre is to enable an understanding of environmental issues from the very outset of the pupil's education with primary and nursery school children being given the formative opportunity to experience topics such as the fundamental nature of water, energy and air with 'hands-on' demonstrations not just by teachers but also by experts from industry. This facility extends and enhances the science curriculum opportunities up into the secondary school, with the addition of various

high-tech laboratories feeding off the visual transpar-ency of its integrated power plant (it has glass walls).

The centre of this learning architecture, is the 'Torhaus' which acts as the metaphorical gatehouse to knowledge, and the entrance to the new educa-tion centre, where the 'Tor zur Welt' (Gateway to the World) welcomes the entire community to use its generous facilities. This is much more than a second-ary school, which is traditionally a building typolo-gy closed off to all but its dedicated school students, thus making for a rather synthetic view of the world, as if mixing with younger or older people is only per-mitted when they are at home or travelling in the city. Rather it sets out to establish an openness to all the

1 Entrance court, 'Ankerplatz'   10 Workshop
2 Foyer 'Torhaus'   11 Science room
3 Parents' café   12 Therapy and movement space
4 Cafeteria   for speech impediment school
5 Auditorium
6 Backstage work room
7 Main break area
8 Sports hall
9 Art room

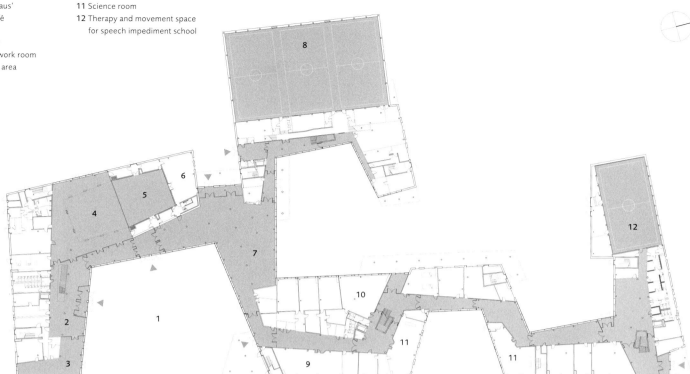

Ground floor plan

View of playground in courtyard | Street facade | The energy centre
with its glazed walls, twin chimneys of the main wood pellet fired boiler
and integrated solar panels in the façade

people it serves, engaging with a richly mixed community of all age ranges; ultimately this reflects the realities of the modern world, where learning can and should take place anywhere.

In order for this open-access approach to work safely and efficiently, the school has a number of different zones or departments within the framework of its singular character. The main entrance on school days is via the courtyard or 'Ankerplatz' whose enclosing wings of accommodation on either side present three different entrance thresholds. The Foyer or 'Torhaus' comprises the restaurant and auditorium, a type of community theatre which is used for a broad range of events throughout the year; there is an entrance

to the school's academic wing, which is in turn stratified into various departmental zones such as art, music and science faculties, and finally there is the main school entrance itself with a large foyer and information point which is full of public events, exhibitions and a busy café. This in turn gives onto the sports hall, again a self-contained faculty which is particularly popular with older residents during the evenings and weekends. There is a duality about this institution: it is one institution, however, it is also a number of separate entities depending on the time of day.

This attitude is clearly expressed in the building's architecture, which is efficient but loose, with skewed angles in plan almost everywhere and a building form

which appears to wrap itself seductively around the existing residential blocks that surround the site. The disparate angles of the various levels of accommodation laid whimsically one on top of the other snake inside and out, to create enclosed courtyards and rooftop terraces of great spatial quality. Almost every interior space is also informed by this unusual geometry (except for the sports halls which must for obvious reasons be conventionally formed of rectangular spaces). Thus corridors and classrooms take advantage of the slightly disconcerting effects of the skewed grid. It is systematic yet willfully eccentric at the same time, a quixotic mix.

1 Classroom
2 Learning centre
3 Administration
4 Teachers' room
5 Meeting space teachers
6 Seminar room for community use
7 Self-study centre
8 Staff café
9 Roof terrace
10 Changing rooms

First floor plan

The business centre also extends the radical dimensions of the curriculum to provide career orientation and pupil preparation for vocational training courses, developing university and work-related educational methodologies. School children will be able to set up their own companies, develop products and services ready for the market with the help of real business partners. Regular work placements with local companies and similar study times at Hamburg's various universities and technical colleges will promote the idea of learning for a tangible future. In every sense this is Wilhelmburg's gateway to the future, a gift which is rich in opportunities for all members of the community.

Second floor plan

1 Classroom
2 Work space
3 Administration
4 Conference room

5 Teachers' room
6 Music room
7 Art room
8 Seminar room for community use

Seating area in after-school club, grades 4-6

Table units designed specifically for this building | Views of classroom |
Custom-made furniture | Reading area in learning centre

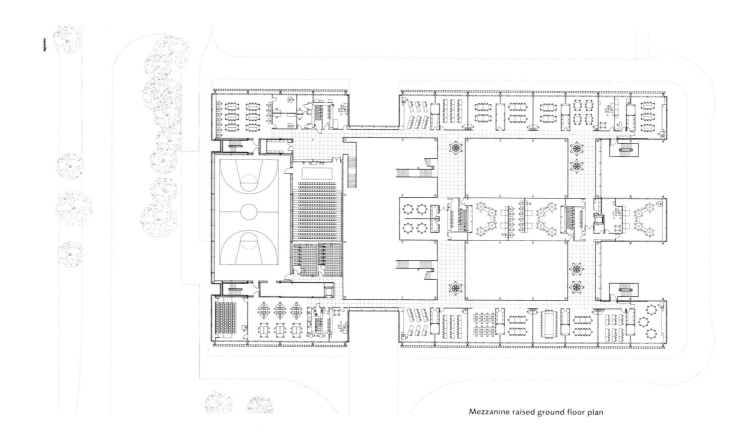

Mezzanine raised ground floor plan

View of teaching spaces from across the art courtyard | Main entrance | Interior view of technology courtyard | View of business courtyard with restaurant beneath mural showing all new pupils | A lesson takes place in the courtyard

Bexley Business Academy

Bexley, London, UK

Architect	Foster and Partners, London
Pupils	1,350 aged 11-17 years
Building area	11,800 m²
Average classroom	70.6 m²
Parking spaces	n/a
Build cost	n/a
Completion	2003
Year group system	Age-related groups

Corporate image with highly glazed teaching areas and the use of open-plan teaching areas

The Bexley Business Academy in southeast London is one of the prototypes for the new generation of secondary schools in the UK. The idea is to bring a touch of market driven commercialism to the world of education. Where this vision manifests itself most obviously is in the design of the building. Walk through the doors of Bexley, and the interior immediately feels more like a corporate headquarters than a school. From the entrance and reception desk, visitors have views into a large top-lit atrium space and beyond to the restaurants, meeting rooms and classes, some of which take place in open-plan areas. To make the banking idea more explicit, the entrance atrium even has a raised stage area to mimic the dealing floors to be found in the City of London.

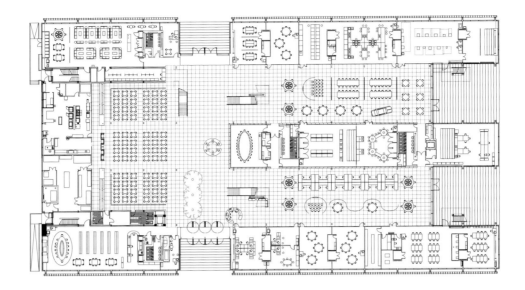

Ground floor plan with main entrance into business courtyard

Even traditional closed classrooms are mostly glazed to make the activities transparent. The use of a structural steel frame gives plenty of scope for future changes to the form of individual rooms. At present the basic layout follows a traditional programme with four class bases of 60 square metres for each year group. Each classroom has flat screen Apple Macs with teachers standing at interactive white boards.

The scheme is organised around three glazed courtyards, each with a different functional theme; there is the entrance or business court, a technology court and an art court. When we visited there was a still life art class taking place with the group clustered around easels in the art court. Users are made constantly aware of the whole school community simply because they can generally see what everyone else is doing.

According to lead architect, Spencer de Grey, the scheme's sponsors took some lessons from the architects' own office layout in Battersea, which consists of open-plan working areas with discrete bays off the main spaces to provide for quieter and more contemplative activities. 'The main emphasis is on transparency to create a different slant on the normal educational experience', he says. There is a radical agenda here which raises real questions about how far change in architectural typologies can successfully mediate between the traditional pillars of education and the government's desire for more work-savvy school-leavers.

Perhaps inevitably, the flaws in this approach can be seen in the somewhat closed-off nature of the building. It largely ignores its surrounding site and tends to function as an internalised world where students can, if they choose, remain indoors throughout the day; and many do. With its single entry point and constant surveillance which the layout enables, this is an inherently secure environment which feels somewhat institutional. Time will tell if it wears well at the hands of subsequent generations of school students. However, in its pristine new condition, it is very much a place to be seen by both staff and students alike. It is a building which makes education sexy.

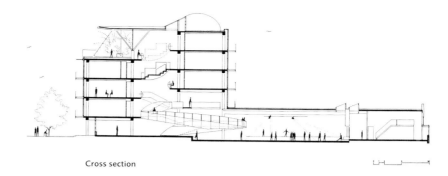

Cross section

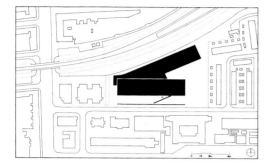

Site plan

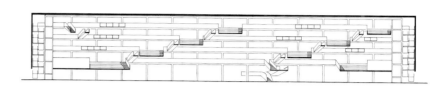

Longitudinal section

End bookstop elevation | Main street elevation makes the building out like an ocean liner, sleek and modish | Connecting staircases and social chill out spaces bridge the void at first floor level | A student works on his laptop in one of the pod study areas between the void | View up towards the void taken from the main assembly hall: A symphony of materials collaged to create a stylish layered space ideal for teenagers' sensibilities |

Montessori College Oost

Amsterdam, The Netherlands

Architect	Herman Hertzberger, Amsterdam
Pupils	1,600 aged 11-16 years
Building area	17,016 m²
Average classroom	65 m²
Parking spaces	32
Build cost	15 million EUR
Completion	2000
Year group system	Traditional 2 form entry classbase system

Montessori Vocational School with enhanced communal and circulation spaces to emphasise the social and interactive side of education

The architects believe that teenage children prefer to hang out together rather than with adults. However, there is little dedicated space for teenagers to do this in the modern city, so they have developed the school as a place not just for formal learning but also one with lots of areas beyond the classroom, zones which are ideal for chance encounters. The architecture of the building also has a peculiarly 'cool' style, which feels unusual, a sort of refined street architecture, yet internalised and made secure for students to enjoy and for staff to keep a discreet eye on the diverse range of students attending Montessori College Oost. Diversity is one of the key aspects of the brief which the designers had to address. Oriented towards the needs of the refugee population in this area of Amsterdam, this is a school with a critical role to play in

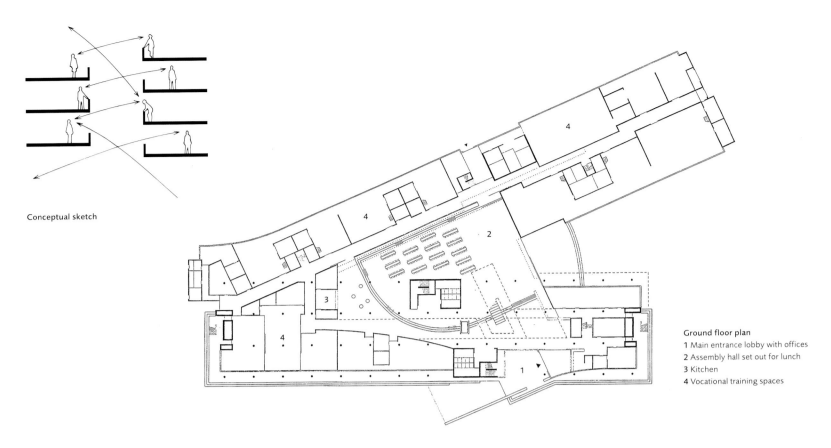

Conceptual sketch

supporting vulnerable children and helping their families to integrate into the community. Students of more than 56 different nationalities attend. Most speak little or no Dutch. For that reason alone, the architects believed that the environment needed to play a vital role in reassuring students, primarily through a sort of architectural legibility within the space-making, it being complex yet understandable and therefore not disorientating. This is a building students can decipher, like a second language. So drawing on the metaphor of the classical city space, all the areas beyond the enclosed classrooms were conceived of as an urban plaza, open to all students within the community, who are free to explore between lessons, at lunchtime and at the end of the day, just as they might explore the city itself. The main teaching accommodation

is formed as a dual aspect block six storeys high in places and almost 100 metres in length. There is also a vertical gallery carved out between the two classroom blocks, with intermediate half floors on either side of the void. The conceptual sketch illustrates how students benefit from views across the void, with opposite floors at intermediate levels to each other. This also facilitates stepped connections between the two sides, encouraging a constant physical dialogue which evokes a sense of spatial complexity, again a characteristic of the city. The connections across the void are bridged over in lots of places. This bridging accommodation is formed into stepped galleries where students can sit. It is a building which trusts the students with its openness. The desire to avoid compartments with fire doors everywhere has a cost,

however; the central void cannot be used as a primary fire escape. Instead the designers have provided external galleries, which connect to outside fire escape stairs at three points. On the ground floor, the plan appears to bisect, forming an additional splayed wing, which runs parallel to the adjacent railway line. This wing contains the main vocational teaching areas, large workshop spaces for the development of trade skills such as car mechanics, plumbing and joinery. The pre-eminent position of these areas and the generous well-equipped workshop spaces balance the importance of vocational training with that of the more academic subjects, which take place in the conventional, closed classroom areas. Between the two wings is the assembly hall, a space for a multitude of different activities.

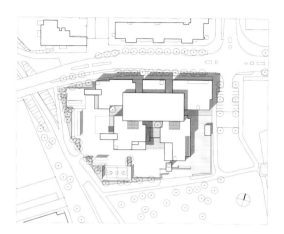

Site plan

Ground floor plan

1 Main entrance	**5** Arts class	**9** Technical crafts
2 Project classroom	**6** Music	**10** Administration
3 Home classroom	**7** Sportshall	**11** Central space, canteen
4 Library	**8** Home economics	

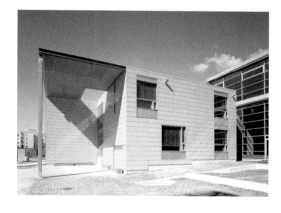

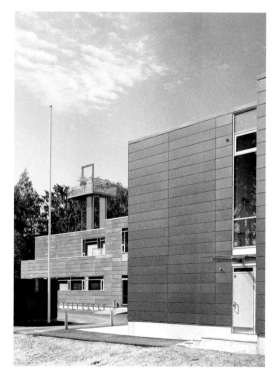

The lower school classrooms are in the yellow clad block | The observatory tower, a decorative feature which emphasises transparency | Main entrance orientated to the south with contrasting grey and brown cladding panels with the glazed atrium at the centre | Atrium with galleries | View inside the atrium looking down towards the main staircase

Aurinkolahti Comprehensive School

Vuosaari, Helsinki, Finland

Architect	Jeskanen-Repo-Teränne; Leena Yli-Lontinnen
Pupils	540 aged 9 -15 years
Building area	6,370 m²
Average classroom	40 m² (special classes 65 - 90 m²)
Parking spaces	10
Build cost	13.4 million EUR
Completion	2002
Year group system	Age-related 3 form entry

Complex office type structure with different departments identified by distinctive architectural treatment

The design incorporates departmental teaching areas arranged as clearly articulated colour coded mini-buildings or 'cells' in their own right. Each department is formed and enclosed by its own walls yet, at the same time, remains part of a coherent whole. The school classrooms and social study cell is clad in bright yellow painted steel panels, a gym block is picked out in brownish red panels, the science/technical workshop department is in grey cladding panels. A grand triple-height glazed canopy identifies the entrance or threshold to each of the three departments. This provides a further ordering device within this highly legible architectural composition.

Between the five blocks there is a three-storey high fully glazed central 'atrium' area, which not only acts

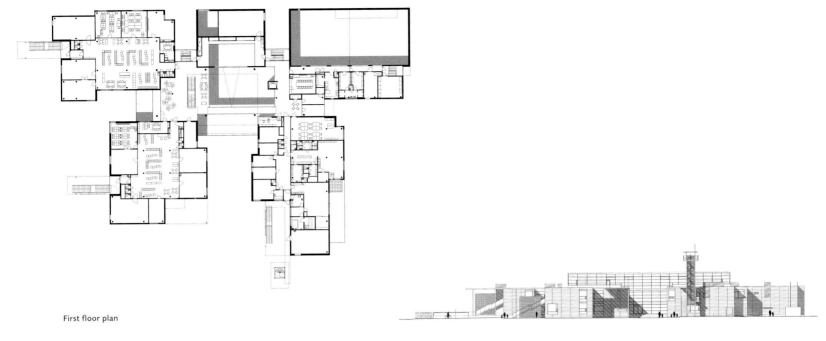

First floor plan

South elevation

as the main circulation route between departments, but also becomes a reference point for the social life of the school as a whole. It is a place where students meet by chance on the staircases and ramps running around and between each level and the various specialist teaching areas; the galleries and balconies which surround the atrium are used as break-out zones with computer and power access for study and smaller social groups outside the classrooms; the school's main canteen and dining area spreads out across the ground floor of the atrium to provide a vibrant social heart for the community, serviced by an adjacent kitchen. As staff and students rise up through the floors, they can look down and across to maintain visual contact with all parts of the institution.

The teaching departments consist in the main of traditional cellular classrooms, however, there is a strong emphasis on open-plan learning spaces, with three large homebase areas at the heart of each of the academic teaching blocks. These areas provide a variety of workspaces, together with storage areas for pupils, washrooms and a teacher's office; they give students a more intimate homebase area for each age range, and also open up the possibility for team teaching in a variety of forms. Each part of the building is clearly articulated yet slots effortlessly into the whole. Entire departments can be quickly identified through highly glazed components, which wrap the main central core areas, providing excellent visibility. This sense of transparency enables students to be visible, and at the same

time it promotes a sense of awareness of the user's own position within the building, whether it is on the ground floor or in the open galleries at the top of the building. It gives a sense of belonging to individual departments and the excitement of an adult environment where the next lesson is enhanced by the experience of built form; students can almost always see which part of the development they will be heading for next. The sense of order, which comes through this controlled use of colour and materiality, makes this an exemplar of the new architecture for schools.

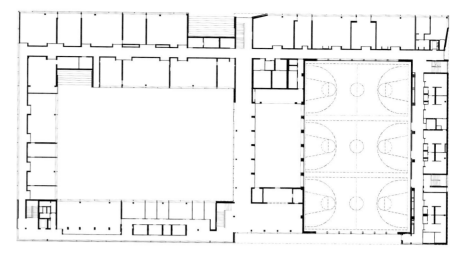

Ground floor plan

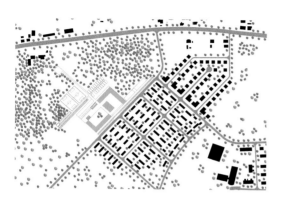

Site plan

The rooftop play deck is a generous gesture | Rear façade with contoured land stepping down to provide a natural amphitheatre for sports competitions | Typical corridor with coloured glassed lower panel and mesh paneling covering the large horizontal glazing panels above | Periscope showing mirror images of roof top | Typical classroom

Marie Curie Gymnasium

Dallgow-Döberitz, Berlin, Germany

Architect	Grüntuch Ernst Architekten, Berlin
Pupils	420 aged 11-18 years
Building area	5,184 m²
Average classroom	65 m²
Parking spaces	approx. 60
Build cost	14.7 million EUR
Completion	2006
Year group system	Age-related 3 form entry, 6 grades

Rigorous architectural cool in a suburban setting

This was a scheme won in competition by the young architectural practice, Grüntuch Ernst. The brief was for a specialist science academy for high achieving students. Located on the edge of a new suburban community, the idea was that the school would attract people to live in this town in former East Germany which is easily accessible from the centre of Berlin as an efficient suburban railway takes only 17 minutes from the Zoo Station. The feel of the building does not seem particularly at home in its suburban setting, where manicured lawns and picket fences jostle for attention with neatly parked rows of Mercedes family saloons. This is suburbia with a capital S, very much on the lines of middle America suburban models. The pitched roof single-family housing has a higgledy-piggledy disorder, which is intended

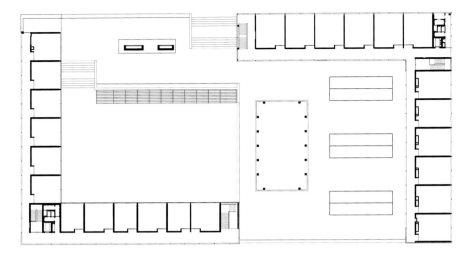

First floor plan

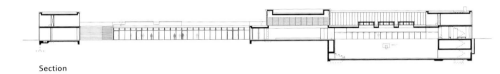

Section

to be homely. The precise high tech architecture of the new school is more like a science research centre than a school. It almost feels marooned out here, at odds with its twee rustic surroundings. According to the architects, the school fits into its surroundings by marking a clear edge to the housing development and the Brandenburg countryside beyond. It is a sort of inhabited wall, which is intended to limit the spread of suburban architectural mediocrity. The building is in the form of two main L shaped wings of classroom accommodation which are connected and linked at first floor level by a children's play deck (the roof of the first floor) leading down onto the sports ground to the rear. These two organising elements grasp and enclose an open play court on one side of the block and a large community hall and sports

hall on the other. The sports hall was deliberately buried within the deepest part of the building to reduce its triple-height bulk. From its sleek exterior, it is difficult to imagine that this building houses such a large volume of accommodation. The external façades, indeed the entire architectural treatment, emphasises the horizontal plain, with cladding panels in varying shades of shiny green aluminum. They are set within a precisely articulated module, which controls the window and wall panel proportions throughout. On the south-facing main façade windows, the entire face of glass is etched in tiny words from Marie Curie's Nobel prize speech. The glass is also intended to control solar penetration and keep students cool. Indeed the interior of the building can only be described as cool. We visited on one of the hottest days

of summer, and the environment was very comfortable. Naturally ventilated throughout, the building utilises a system of night-time cooling, shaded opening louvres, through ventilation and solar control glazing supporting a very successful passive environmental system. However, it is also cool in another way, almost austere in its interior architecture, full of colourless light, reflecting from white or grey floor, ceiling and wall surfaces. Certainly the building bears little resemblance to the secondary schools I knew as a child, rather this reminds me of a high quality corporate headquarters, slightly mechanistic, yet emphasising quality and expense at every turn. It is definitely one for the future, a vision of how education might feel in 50 years time.

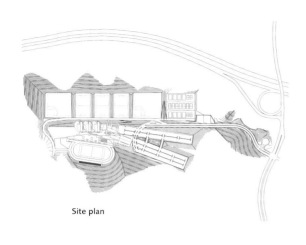

Site plan

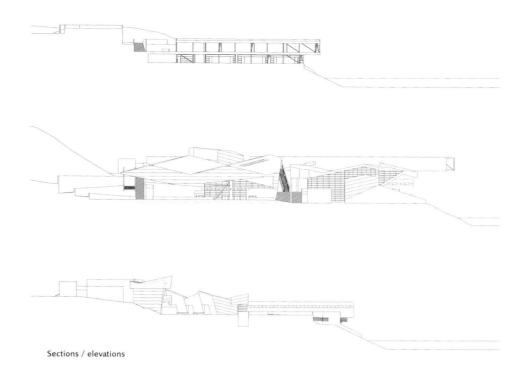

Sections / elevations

View of central social street with jagged metallic cladding precisely detailed in sharp relief to the mountains behind | Overall view of complex against the backdrop of the mountain range | Typical classroom | Performance space

Diamond Ranch High School

Pomona, California, USA

Architect	Morphosis; Thomas Blurock, Santa Monica
Pupils	1600 aged 11-16 years
Building area	15,000 m²
Average classroom	60 m²
Parking spaces	770
Build cost	n/a
Completion	2000
Year group system	Age-related groups in 50 classrooms

'Signature' architectural statement to elevate the image of schooling within the community and further afield

The jagged and inherently unstable forms of the Los Angeles foothills inform the language of the buildings as the architecture takes its organisational cues from the natural topography. Two rows of fragmented interlocking built form are set together tightly on either side of a long central 'canyon', or street, which cuts through the face of the hillside, as might a geological fault line. The street becomes the main social space sitting between the departmental areas and classrooms. As a counterpoint to the suburban nature of its surroundings, the street encloses and constricts this space to mimic the urban experience of a European town centre. The plan is organised around this street in the form of three schools within a single school plan, with two large classroom blocks and a sports and social building. The site, which runs parallel

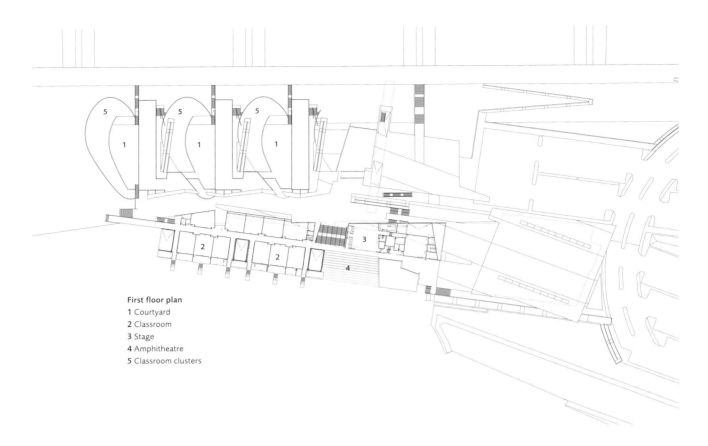

First floor plan
1 Courtyard
2 Classroom
3 Stage
4 Amphitheatre
5 Classroom clusters

with the suburban street below, is a steep slope. To develop this complex match between the topography and the brief, with its extensive architectural programme, provided a significant challenge. In a sense the architect optimises the relationship between the rocky landscape and the new building, so that the building takes the form of a highly jagged sculptural layer defined by a thin metallic continuously undulating roof. The terrain folds around the main buildings and is carved out to form a solid/void rhythm across the site, a strategy which creates outside courts or social meeting spaces between the blocks, giving light and air to the dense accommodation schedule; these courtyards provide relief from the tightness of the built form. The teaching spaces are organised in three 250 student classroom clusters (which was

a programmatic requirement). The lower block has two storeys of accommodation, the upper block has three storeys. However, these teaching blocks are articulated as solid slabs of building, which is in sharp contrast to the lighter, more fragmented shapes that define the central street. The blocks lean over the social street creating a surreal landscape which is protective and enclosing yet slightly threatening at the same time. The sports and social building contains a gymnasium with changing rooms and a cafeteria, which acts as the social heart of the complex. There is a monumental stairway which bisects the linear blocks. It functions doubly as a main pedestrian route from the entrance off the lower level street and up to the roof terrace and football field above; the stairway dissolves into an outdoor amphitheatre at its

highest point which is embedded in the hillside. There is an administration block, effectively a smaller fourth element completing the overall composition. It is at the main knuckle point of the north-south and east-west geometries providing a secure entrance threshold to the self-contained confines of the interior.

It is almost impossible to view this building in its totality, a series of fragmented architectural events interweaving with the landscape to create rich spatial tension. It is very unusual to find such a stirring sense of space within a school building, and time will tell whether this has a positive effect on the quality of learning. It is a building which emphasises architecture over and above almost anything else.

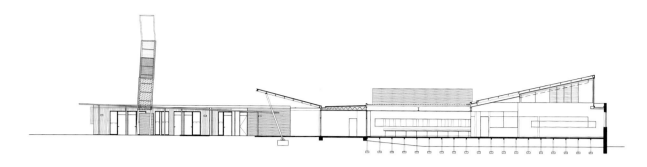

Section/elevation with tilting tower

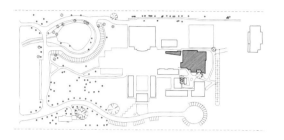

Site plan with new buildings shown in grey

Rear elevation with library block; every elevation has a different feel responding to the orientation and view | The building at night showing the tower and entrance canopy with the music wing on the left | Mondrianesque decoration illuminates the junior library entrance | Skylight feature in the senior library: natural light is reflected into the space to create a sense of drama

Ivanhoe Grammar School

Mernda, Victoria, Australia

Architect	Bates Smart, Melbourne
Pupils	600 aged 6-16 years
Building area	1,200 m²
Average classroom	71.8 m² (integrated learning)
Parking spaces	60
Build cost	1.8 million AUS
Completion	2001
Year group system	Traditional 2 form entry classbase system

New resources and enterprise centre for primary and secondary students located on an existing campus

This new student resource centre is composed of two buildings and a tower. The main building, recognisable by its large, sloping entrance canopy, contains libraries for the senior and junior schools together with rooms for creative arts performance, multi-media learning, study rooms, staff rooms and kitchen facilities. Adjacent is the much smaller music block comprising sound proof rehearsal rooms. The third element is a 14 metre high tower, a gleaming feature which is lit up at night, a transparent beacon which helps to compose the whole into a unified work. It is like a church in this respect, its startling presence on this disparate campus transforming the old-fashioned idea of library into a modernist edifice full of light and energy. The building was originally conceived conventionally as a series of separate functional

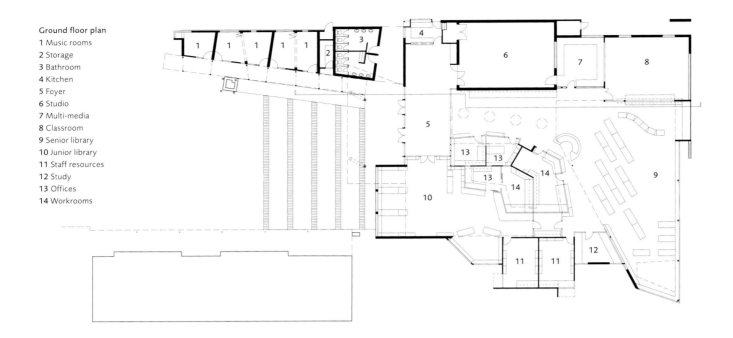

Ground floor plan
1 Music rooms
2 Storage
3 Bathroom
4 Kitchen
5 Foyer
6 Studio
7 Multi-media
8 Classroom
9 Senior library
10 Junior library
11 Staff resources
12 Study
13 Offices
14 Workrooms

spaces, a suite of rooms each with its own defined use; however, as discussions with the client developed, it became clear that creating flexible multi-use spaces would be to the students' advantage. The entrance foyer was expanded to become a space for hanging out. It in turn flows naturally into the senior library, predominantly open-plan yet serviced with a range of more enclosed study and classroom areas. It is, however, the range and diversity of windows and roof lights with sloping highly differentiated ceiling planes which create the sense of drama within the new building. Flexible technology is not just about computer aided learning, an individual working on his or her own, contained by four walls and the screen anyplace. Rather, as students have access to learning anywhere, so that in theory the classroom be-

comes less important, it becomes critical to ensure that social interaction between students is maintained and encouraged. Thus the new building will act as a classroom for 600 people at any one time. This concept of the building as a flexible mega-classroom will allow for learning in a less confined way than the conventional classroom permits. The space enables students to be quiet and isolated if they need to be; they can find hidden low corners, a window booth which orientates out rather than in. Alternatively, if they feel social as they work on a task, there are big open areas full of light which encourage a sense of interaction. It empowers the students to feel grown up, as it treats them with respect through the freedom of the plan and the strength of the architectural experiences it provides.

The new building with its tower and beautifully lit interiors conveys a sense of environmental sophistication to a previously mundane campus of portable classrooms and unremarkable institutional buildings. Strategically placed at the centre of the school's campus, it provides a heart and focus to both the school and the wider community (the centre is open for public use in evenings and at weekends). Each space has been designed on its own terms for the maximum emotional potential, exploiting views and orientation. The building is illuminated at nighttime, with each part of the composition highlighted with colour to provide legibility and order. The use of the strong vertical element is symbolic, a statement of the importance and pleasure of learning.

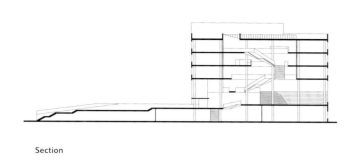

Section

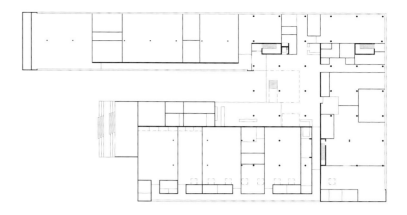

Ground floor plan

Entrance staircase | Lateral façade with technical classrooms in the 'base level' | View of central void | Grand staircase | Study area outside the classroom

Secondary Inter-mediate Vocational School

Hoorn, The Netherlands

Architect	Herman Hertzberger, Amsterdam
Pupils	600 aged 11-16 years
Building area	10,300 m²
Average classroom	65 m²
Parking spaces	6
Build cost	12.5 million EUR
Completion	2004
Year group system	Traditional 2 form entry classbase system

Compact multi-storey form to optimise site spread and keep construction costs low

The most compact solution was required here partly because of the limited site area, but in particular to keep the costs down, both build costs and running costs. Therefore the architects chose to stack the building on six storeys with classrooms around the outside, all served by a central void, with lifts, staircases and generous balcony/gallery areas at each level. As the most common form of school building is a single-storey volume spread across a green field setting, this is very unusual. Here is a more sustainable form with minimal external wall surface area to provide much lower running costs. However, the form provides a more immediate benefit in terms of common circulation areas, which are concentrated around the central 'core'. The most obvious benefit are the generous staircase areas, which

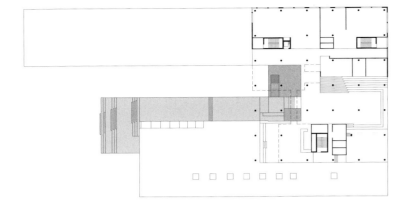

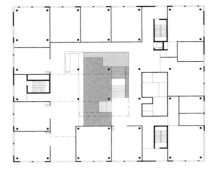

First floor plan   Second floor plan

act as spaces where students can meet and chat whilst changing lessons. There is a real sense of theatre about this movement corridor, with little bullying possible since everyone is in view all the time.

This school for intermediate vocational education naturally contains a considerable area devoted to practical instruction rooms and workshops along with the more conventional classrooms for teaching academic subjects. It seemed obvious that these vocational spaces, which needed to be larger and host activities such as applied car mechanics, should be at ground floor. In effect, the brief has forced the architects to dedicate two levels, a so-called 'base' level and the raised ground floor level, to vocational training spaces. The ground floor level

doubles as the main entrance area which is accesed via a grand staircase that uses above the base level and leads all students into a large entrance hall, or the so-called 'central square'. Here everything and everyone comes together. There is a café and entrance (with rooftop terrace) and a music room/stage for performances to the entire school and community beyond. There is no separate assembly hall or auditorium; instead the void defines the central space, which has large stepped seating areas forming a distinctive internal landscape, a trademark feature of this architect. The staircase leading up to the intermediate floors are approximately 17 metres wide, and quite clearly they are much more than stairs. The second floor contains staff rooms, multi-media spaces including a conventional library, art and crafts areas

and the central reception point. Each of the upper floors has a working space around the void before you get to the classrooms. Comprising an area approximately 7.5 x 25 metres (190 square metres), it is a secondary area for activities outside the classroom.

The architectural dexterity of the form is particularly evident in the central circulation void. It is no simple vertical hole; rather it appears to twist as each layer of accommodation adopts its specific layout. The open stairways are located in different positions as they lead up through each floor. Circulation becomes a real promenade, with constantly changing views as one ascends each level. At the top is an enormous roof light, which allows daylight to penetrate right down to the ground floor level.

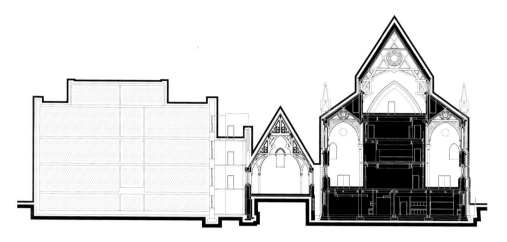

Cross section

The courtyard at night | School court with its glass atrium connecting the church to the old school | View of the new break-out space | The soaring volume of the original church

Packer Collegiate Institute

Brooklyn, New York, USA

Architect	H³ Hardy Collaboration Architecture, New York
Pupils	900 aged 3-18 years
Building area	6,317 m² renovation, 836 m² new construction
Average classroom	n/a
Parking spaces	0
Build cost	17 million USD
Completion	2003
Year group system	Age-related groups in pre-kindergarten to grade 12

Imaginative use of an old redundant church structure

Packer Collegiate Institute comprised of five loosely connected buildings, which had been added piece-meal over the course of a century from 1854 to 1969. In addition to these buildings, there was a church, St. Ann's, no longer in use, and a parish house all closely connected but not fully utilised for educational purposes. Prior to the new commission, Packer was using only the cramped main school building, due to the run-down and disconnected condition of the rest. The challenge for the architects therefore was to adapt and integrate all parts of this complex into a progressive 21st century academic programme exploiting all parts to benefit the expanding student body. Improvement work, which was on-going for over four years, has resulted in a complete re-organisation of the plan,

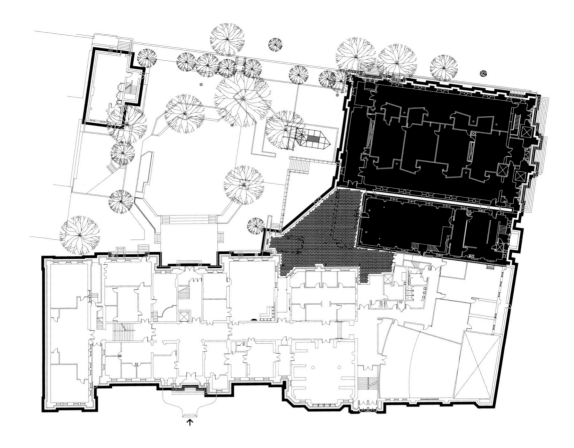

Ground floor plan

expanding accommodation into the Renwick Church, allowing for the lower, middle and upper schools to each have their own self-contained zones. The parish house has been re-configured as a shared dining room for the whole school.

The main challenge for the designers was converting and integrating the church interior into school accommodation. Space for more classrooms was a priority and the old church was too large for its traditional purpose. The key planning move was the insertion of 18 classrooms into the former church, serviced by two 'open' corridors positioned on either side of the nave. This provides two full-height aisles along both sides of the building. Corridors occur at each level alternating

between the north and south side of the church (see cross section). This creates a sense of spatial variety and dilutes the impact of noise from students changing lessons and socialising in the break-out areas.

Contemporary materials and modern lighting technology is used carefully to enhance the contrast between the exposed brick and gothic detailing of the original building, and the shiny futuristic new classroom pods with their lightweight bridges and high level access routes. It is this contrast between old and new which gives the project a rich and evocative spatial language. Lightweight, sensitive engineering solutions ensure that the original and the new structural elements work in harmony. The new steel and con-

crete structural system is set within a volume of load bearing masonry walls, cast iron columns and wooden floor joists which forms a single integrated composition. Mechanical equipment for ventilation was placed so that it does not disfigure the existing rooftop profiles, an issue of great concern to the community, who were consulted widely during the development of the scheme.

Equally the future of the original stained glass, which was felt to be inappropriate to the new secular function, was carefully considered. Some of the windows are of high quality with a vivid range of colours, others are more modest and some are only lightly patterned. 70% of the high quality glass was removed

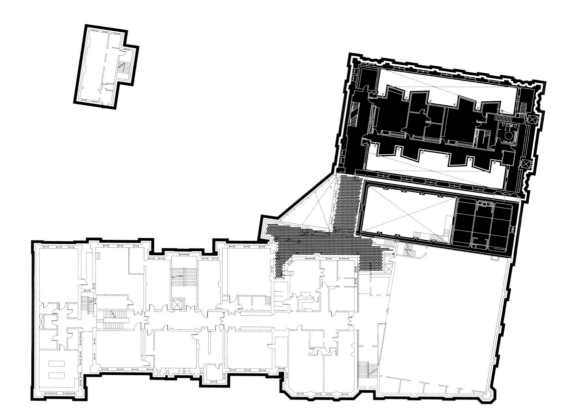

First floor plan

The main refectory in the old chapel | Student break-out area |
Restored stained glass window in the former church | Gallery with
tracery window

and taken by various museums including the Metropolitan Museum of Art, The Brooklyn Museum of Art and St. Joseph's Stained Glass Museum; all are institutions which can care for this artistic legacy. Where stained glass was removed, new insulated glass windows were installed to fit the original tracery profiles. An overlay of simulated lead frames gives the appearance of individual glass elements set in stone frames. The remaining stained glass was restored and reinstalled in the building's primary façade on the east street elevation. This creates a poetic symmetry between the past and the future.

By balancing the old with the new, the architects have retained the character of the original Victorian church,

with its gothic tracery and hanging chandeliers, and successfully inserted a new state of the art four-storey classroom structure, which is no mean feat. Faced with ghost mirrors and lit with warm fluorescent feature lighting, the design allows students to experience the original soaring church interior whilst moving between lessons or enjoying their social time, whilst benefiting from an up to the minute, technology rich learning environment. It is interesting to reflect on how well the internalised world of the classrooms function for study. Perhaps the lack of direct contact to the outside urban landscape beyond the school is in this situation an unforeseen benefit of the unusual design strategy.

Each part of the refurbished building has its own character so that the whole is an integration of dissimilar parts. The new structural system within the walls of the former church is an open and free flowing accomodation compared to the rest of the school which is more conventional and cellular with a central corridor and views onto the surrounding streets from outward looking teaching spaces. The new and the existing form an L shaped plan which wraps around a landscaped courtyard. The parish house, now the only free standing form, has been refurbished. A new circulation plan to cater for the 18 classrooms placed in the church joins up to existing corridors and pathways beneath a new glass atrium. This two and a half-storey volume forms a visual and physical connection to all

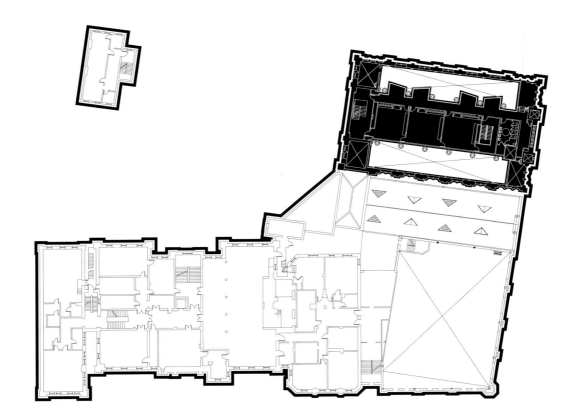

Second floor plan

levels of the school, and at night presents the illuminated façades of the church and Packer buildings at the back to the main school courtyard.

The architects believe that for buildings to survive they must be used, and however sad we may feel about St. Ann's fall into disuse as a place of worship, its transformation has brought new life and vitality to its venerable structure. The church's contribution to the wider community is clear as it retains its presence both to the surrounding streets and most importantly to the school's courtyard, a vibrant new urban space within the community with the school's main entrance (which is around the corner from the original church entrance). The fusion of old and new has been a sen-

sitive and respectful marriage, very much a result of the close working relationship between the designers and the client community to create a new building which fuses the old into its modern functions. In itself this is a fitting symbol of the school's ethos and philosophy, an environment for the future which respects and celebrates its past.

Authors

Dorothea Baumann

Dorothea Baumann received her piano diploma at the Musikakademie Zürich in 1969, she studied musicology, physics and German literature at the University of Zürich, obtained her Ph.D. in 1977 and finished her habilitation with a study on 'Music, Architectural Acoustics and Performance Practice' in 2000 (publication in preparation). Since 1974 she has been a lecturer for musicology at the University of Zürich, and from 1979-1993 she also taught at the University of Berne, Switzerland. In 1987 she was visiting professor at the City University of New York CUNY, Graduate Center, and in 1998 at the University of Innsbruck, Austria. She has lectured and published widely on interdisciplinary topics related to historical and systematical musicology. Her main research fields are architectural acoustics, musical acoustics, psychology of music and performing practice of music.

Mohamed Boubekri

Mohamed Boubekri is an associate professor at the University of Illinois at Urbana-Champaign (UIUC). He first studied architecture in Algeria where he received his diploma at the Université des Sciences et Technologie d'Oran in 1983. He then moved to the United States and obtained a Master of Architecture from the University of Colorado at Denver in 1985 and later a Ph.D. from Texas A&M University in 1990.

After teaching at the Center for Building Studies, Concordia University in Montréal, Canada, he joined the School of Architecture at UIUC where he became an associate professor in 1999. An important focus of Boubekri's muti-faceted research is on building daylighting and its effects on human health. Dr. Boubekri has lectured and published widely on the subject.

Mark Dudek

Mark Dudek runs a London-based design practice and is a consultant for education buildings, both in the UK and elsewhere. He has been involved in the design of numerous educational environments for some 25 years. Amongst his projects were four Children's Centres in the London Borough of Hillingdon, the Classroom of the Future at Yewlands Secondary School in Sheffield, an Ecolab at Stanley Infant and Nursery School in London and the ecological garden area Discovering Kids Playgroup in Magherafelt, Co. Derry in Northern Ireland (with Clare Devlin) as well as two prototype schools for Khorog, Tajikistan.

Mark Dudek's publications include *Architecture of Schools*, Architectural Press, 2001, and *Kindergarten Architecture*, Spon, 2000. He has spoken at numerous conferences in the UK, Ireland, Scandinavia and the USA and advises the UK Government's design association CABE. He is a Fellow of the Royal Society of Arts and a Research Fellow at the School of Architecture, University of Sheffield.

Susan Herrington

Susan Herrington is a landscape architect and an associate professor in the School of Architecture and Landscape Architecture at the University of British Columbia. She received her MLA from Harvard University and her BLA from the State University of New York. Her research concerns designed landscapes and child development. She has consulted in the design of play spaces for children in Canada and the United States for the past ten years.

Since 2003 Susan Herrington has led a five year long research project called 'Outside Criteria' that studies children's development in outdoor play spaces in the City of Vancouver. Herrington has conducted research in Germany and in Cambridge as a visiting researcher at Harvard University. She has won awards from the American Society of Landscape Architects, the National Endowment for the Arts and PLACES.

Susanne Hofmann

Susanne Hofmann, Berlin, studied architecture at the Technical University and the Academy of Fine Arts in Munich and the Architectural Association in London (diploma 1992). She worked for Alsop & Lyall Architects, Sauerbruch Hutton Architects and other architectural offices both in London and Berlin. Since 1996, Susanne Hofmann has been teaching at various universities in London, Melbourne, Auckland, Kairo, Hamburg and Berlin. Since 2009 she has been Professor for Participatory Design and Construction at Technical University Berlin. In 2003, she founded the Baupiloten in cooperation with the TU Berlin, an experimental new design course bridging education, practice and research, which became an independent practice in 2014. The Baupiloten specialise in participatory design and have worked on a number of schools, kindergartens and residential buildings. In 2012, Susanne Hofmann wrote her Ph.D. thesis on participatory design strategies and in 2014 she published her book *Partizipation macht Architektur*.

Peter Hübner

Peter Hübner first did an apprenticeship as an orthopaedic shoe-maker and then trained as a carpenter. From 1963-1968 he studied architecture at Stuttgart University. In the winter term he was a fellow at Deutsche Akademie Rom Villa Massimo and subsequently became professor for design and construction at Stuttgart University, retiring from this post in 2007. He is one of four partners in the architectural practice plus+ bauplanung in Neckartenzlingen near Stuttgart which he founded in 1980. The practice has some 100 buildings to its name, 25 of which are schools. Plus+ bauplanung has longstanding experience in the organisation of participation processes; some 50 buildings incorporated input from their users. The German architectural critic once referred to Peter Hübner as 'the master of messy houses.'

Pamela Loeffelman

Pamela Loeffelman is an architect and a principal at Perkins Eastman, a 700 person firm with offices in New York, Charlotte, Chicago, Arlington, Pittsburgh, San Francisco, Shanghai, Stamford and Toronto. Her focus is on the design of educational facilities, civic buildings and commercial developments.

In 2005, she was chair of AIA's Committee on Architecture for Education (CAE), and now she is a member of the AIA's Board Knowledge Committee. She is a North Atlantic regional council member of the Society of College and University Planners (SCUP). She was the co-chair of the AIA/SCUP 2006 Northeast Region Conference – 'Living in a Digital World: How Community Colleges Are Making the Connections'. Pamela Loeffelman is also an advisory board member for the National Clearinghouse for Educational Facilities (NCEF - www.edfacilities.org). The organisation provides information on planning, designing, funding, building, improving and maintaining safe, healthy, high performance schools.

Heather Marsden

Heather Marsden is a building services engineer and associate at the international engineering consultancy Buro Happold, which she joined in 2000. She is responsible for overall management of the buildings services strategy. Her career began in 1988, in the commercial and museum sectors and has gone on to cover education, healthcare, residential and retail developments as well as masterplanning for large projects.

In the late 1990s she gained experience in sustainable design which has been put to extensive use in Buro Happold, particularly on her work in the education sector. Most recently she has worked on the Bexley Business School and the Petchey Academy, a school specialising in medical sciences, both of which are in London.

Christina Niederstätter

Christina Niederstätter studied architecture in Innsbruck and Venice as well as music at the conservatory 'Claudio Monteverdi' in Bolzano and the conservatory in Cuneo/Turin, where her main instrument was flute. She taught music at several schools in South Tyrol.

In 1989, she received a grant and began to specialise in acoustics. She studied the relation between architecture and acoustics at the Technical University of Eindhoven, The Netherlands, and spatial acoustics at the University of Berne, Switzerland. Since 2003, Christina Niederstätter has been on the comittee for the development of 'Guidelines for the Construction of State Music Schools' of the province of Bolzano. In cooperation with Dorothea Baumann, University of Zürich, Switzerland, she was responsible for the design and the reconstruction of acoustically sensitive spaces. She has published and lectured widely on the topic of acoustics and architecture.

Selected Bibliography

History of Schools and Kindergartens

Architekt, special issue "Der dritte Lehrer" [The Third Teacher], no. 9/10, November 2004, p. 24-77.

Lloyd deMause (ed.), *The History of Childhood*, Northvale, New Jersey: Jason Aronson Inc., 1974.

"The First Model Schools", in: *Leningradskaya Panorama*, no. 9, September 1984, p. 32.

Susan Herrington, 'Garden Pedagogy: Romanticism to Reform,' in: *Landscape Journal*, vol. 20, no. 1, 2001, p. 30-47.

Nicholas Orme, *Medieval Children*, New Haven and London: Yale University Press, 2001.

Linda A. Pollock, *Forgotten Children – Parent–Child Relations from 1500 to 1900*, Cambridge: Cambridge University Press, 1983.

E. R. Robson, *School Architecture*, (with an introduction by Malcolm Seaborne), Leicester: Leicester University Press, 1972 (first published 1874).

Paul Rocheleau, *The One-Room Schoolhouse*, New York: Universe, 2003.

Andrew Saint, *Towards a Social Architecture – The Role of School Building in Post-War England*, New Haven and London: Yale University Press, 1987.

Richard Sennett, *The Fall of Public Man*, Cambridge: Cambridge University Press, 1974.

Design of Schools and Kindergartens

Giulio Ceppi and Michele Zini (eds.), *Children, Spaces, Relations – Metaproject for an Environment for Young Children*, Milan: Reggio Children/Domus Academy, 1998.

Childcare Directorate, Department of Justice, Equality and Law Reform, Ireland, *School Age Childcare in Ireland*, Dublin, 2005.

City of Zurich Building Authority (ed.), *School Buildings. The State of Affairs: The Swiss Contribution in an International Context*, Basel, Boston, Berlin: Birkhäuser – Publishers for Architecture, 2004.

Prue Chiles (ed.), Leo Care, Howard Evans, Anna Holder, Claire Kemp, *School Building: Key Issues for Contemporary Design*, Basel: Birkhäuser, 2015.

Michael J. Crosbie, *Class Architecture*, Melbourne: Images Publishing, 2001.

Detail, special issue, 'Konzept Schulbau,' no. 3, 2003.

Mark Dudek, *Kindergarten Architecture – Space for the Imagination*, London: E & FN SPON, 1996, second edition 2001.

Mark Dudek, *Building for Young Children*, London: The National Early Years Network (National Children's Bureau), 2001.

Mark Dudek, *Architecture of Schools – The New Learning Environments*, Oxford: Architectural Press, 2000, reprint 2002 and 2006.

Mark Dudek, *Children's Spaces*, Oxford: Architectural Press, 2005.

Thomas Müller and Romana Schneider, *Das Klassenzimmer. Schulmöbel im 20. Jahrhundert*, München, New York: Prestel, 1998.

Sharon Haar (ed.), *Schools for Cities – Urban Strategies*, New York: National Endowment for the Arts, 2002.

Didier Heintz, *Les temps de l'enfance et leurs espaces*, Paris: Association Navir, 1992.

Thomas Hille, *Modern Schools: A Century of Design for Education*, New York: Wiley, 2011.

Prakash Nair, Randall Fielding, *The Language of School Design: Design Patterns for 21st Century Schools*, Minneapolis: DesignShare, 3rd edition, 2013.

Anita Rui Olds, *Child Care Design Guide*, New York: McGraw Hill, 2001.

Bradford Perkins and Stephen Kliment, *Building Type Basics – Elementary and Secondary Schools*, New York: Wiley, 2001.

School Buildings and Design Unit, Department for Education and Skills (UK), *Classrooms of the Future – Innovative Designs for Schools*, London: The Stationery Office (TSO), 2003.

John and Frances Sorrell, *Joined up Design for Schools*, London and New York: Merrell, 2006.

'Oppimisrakennuksia' [Architecture for Learning], in: *Arkkitehti*, vol. 103, no. 1, 2006, p 24-67.

'Places of Learning,' in: *Canadian Architect*, special issue, vol. 51, no. 10, October 2006, p. 26-42, 53.

'Les Arcs, hier et maintenant,' in: *D'Architectures*, no. 153, March 2006, p. 19-20.

'Academies could do better,' in: *Building Design*, no. 1712, 31 March 2006, p. 3.

'Health and Education,' in: *Building Design*, special issue plus supplement, 26 May 2006, p. 3-34.

'Nyt I gammelt' [New in the Old], in: *Arkitektur DK*, vol. 50, no. 4, July 2006, p. 209-249.

Technical Requirements

David Adler (ed.), *Metric Handbook. Planning and Design Data*, (chapter 28, schools), Oxford: Architectural Press, second edition 1999.

Brian Billimore, Department for Education and Skills (UK), *The Outdoor Classroom*, (Building Bulletin 71), London: TSO, 1999.

Department of Health (UK), *The Children Act 1989. Guidance and Regulations Volume 2: Family Support, Day Care and Educational Provision for Young Children*, London: TSO, 1991.

Barbara E. Hendricks, *Designing for Play*, Burlington, VT: Ashgate Publishing, 2001.

Susan Herrington, *Schoolyard Park: 13 Acres International Design Competition*, Vancouver: Centre for Landscape Research, University of British Columbia, 2002.

'ICT must fulfil the aspirations of individual pupils,' in: *Architects' Journal*, vol. 223, no. 23, 15 June 2006, p. 49-50.

Marshall Long, *Architectural Acoustics*, Oxford: Elsevier Academic Press, 2006.

Mary C. Miller, *Color for Interior Architecture*, New York: Wiley, 1997.

Sue Roaf, *Ecohouse 2*, Oxford: Architectural Press, 2006.

School Buildings and Design Unit, Department for Education and Skills (UK), *Inclusive School Design* (Building Bulletin 94), London: TSO, 2003.

School Buildings and Design Unit, Department for Education and Skills (UK), *Acoustic Design of Schools – A Design Guide* (Building Bulletin 93), London: TSO, 2003.

School Buildings and Design Unit, Department for Education and Skills (UK), *Briefing Framework for Secondary School Projects* (Building Bulletin 98), London: TSO, 2004.

Lolly Tai, Mary Tailor Haque, Gina K. McLellan and Erin Jordan Knight, *Designing Outdoor Environments for Children*, New York: McGraw-Hill, 2006.

Education

Catherine Burke and Ian Grosvenor, *The School I'd Like – Children and Young People's Reflections on an Education for the 21st Century*, London and New York: Routledge, 2003.

Elinor Goldschmied and Sonia Jackson, *People Under Three*, London and New York: Routledge, 1999, second edition 2004.

Joseph Kelly (ed.), *School Building*, Manchester: Gabriel Communications Ltd, 2006.

Penelope Leach, *Children First – what we must do – and are not doing – for our children today*, London: Michael Joseph, 1994.

Andrew Pollard (ed.), *Children and their Primary Schools*, London and New York: Falmer Press, 1996.

Sharon Wright and Andrew Beard (eds.), *Century 21 Schools*, Birmingham: Imaginative Minds, 2006.

Eleanor Young, James Randall, Dani Hart (eds.), Department for Education and Skills, *Schools for the Future – Designs for Learning Communities* (Building Bulletin 95), London: TSO, 2002.

Index of Places

Page numbers in bold refer to illustrations

Amsterdam, The Netherlands
Montessori Primary School, De Eilanden 114-115
Montessori College Oost 227, 236-237

Auer, South Tyrol, Italy
Music School 29, 30, 33

Aurora, Ontario, Canada
St. Andrew's College 190-191

Berlin, Germany
Albert Einstein Oberschule 194-195
Erika Mann Grundschule 51-52
Heinz Galinski School **136-137**
Kindergarten Jerusalemer Straße 78-79
Kita Sinneswandel 56-59
Kita Taka-Tuka-Land 52-53
Kita Traumbaum 52
Marie Curie Gymnasium, Dallgow-Döberitz
227, **240-241**
Mary Poppins Primary School 111, **124-125**

Bilbao, Spain
Sondika Kindergarten, Sondika 68-69

Bordeaux, France
Lycée François Magendie **186-187**

Boston, Massachusetts, USA
The High and Normal School for Girls 14

Bolzano, Italy
Gasteiner Upper School 31, 33
Manzoni Elementary School 30, 33

Bury, Northwest England, UK
Hoyle Early Years Centre 74-75

Celbridge, Ireland
North Kildare Educate Together School
126-127

Chiba City, Japan
Utase Elementary School **47**

Chicago, Illinois, USA
Avery Coonley Playhouse 11, 12
Little Village Academy **120-121**
Perspectives Charter School 200-201

Clacton, Essex, UK
Bishops Park College 202-203

Copenhagen, Denmark
Nærum Amtsgymnasium 20, 192-193

Dresden, Germany
Sankt Benno Gymnasium 196-197

Dublin, Ireland
Ranelagh Multi-denominational School 122-123

Düsseldorf, Germany
Volksschule Düsseldorf 15

Eichstätt, Germany
Special Pedagogic Centre **108-109**

Fairfield, Connecticut, USA
Burr Elementary School 21, 111, **128-129**

Flims, Switzerland
Flims Comprehensive School 226-227

Fredrikstad, Norway
Kvernhuset Junior High School 180-181

Freudenberg, Zürich, Switzerland
Kantonschule Freudenberg 15

Gelsenkirchen, Germany
Protestant Comprehensive School 218-221

Gland, France
Collège des Tuillières 208-211

Grantham, UK
National Day Nurseries Association 76-77

Greenwich, Connecticut, USA
Greenwich Academy **188-189**
Glenville Elementary School **26**

Hamburg, Germany
Education Centre 'Tor zur Welt' 228-233

Helsinki, Finland
Aurinkolahti Comprehensive School, Vuosaari
238-239

Herbrechtingen, Germany
Pistorius School for Disabled Children 96-99

Hohen Neuendorf, Germany
Energy-plus Primary School **144-147**

Hong Kong, China
Jockey Club Primary School 152-153
Kingston International School 112-113

Hoorn, The Netherlands
Secondary Intermediate Vocational School
246-247

Hunstanton, Norfolk, UK
Secondary Modern School 15

Ingolstadt, Germany
Montessori School 172-173

Isle of Sheppey, Kent, UK
Sheerness Children's and Family Centre
80-81

Kearsley, Lancashire, UK
Prestolee School 10, 11

Köln, Germany
Internationale Friedensschule **48, 49**
Waldorf Schule Chorweiler 19

La Orotava, Tenerife, Spain
Instituto Rafael Arozarena 176-179

Ladakh, India
Druk White Lotus School 116-119

Liverpool, UK
Academy of St. Francis of Assisi 40-41

London, UK
Alma School 19
Archbishop Ramsey Technology College,
Southwark 18-19
Cherry Lane Children's Centre, Hillingdon **60-61**
Bexley Business Academy, Bexley 227, **234-235**
Exemplar School, Lambeth 184-185
Jo Richardson Community School, Dagenham
20, 222-223
Jubilee School, Brixton **148-151**
King Alfred School 19
Margaret McMillan Nursery School, Deptford 10
Phoenix High School, White City 13, **18**
Swiss Cottage SEN School, Camden 92-95
Tulse Comprehensive School 16

Lorch, Germany
Schulzentrum Auf dem Schäfersfeld 15, 21

Loup, Northern Ireland, UK
Nursery 17

Maihara, Japan
Bubbletecture Maihara Kindergarten 86-87

Markt Indersdorf, Germany
Gymnasium Markt Indersdorf 204-205

Medellin, Colombia
San Antonio de Prado Kindergarten 62-65

Minneapolis, Minnesota, USA
WMEP Interdistrict Downtown School 25

Mitcham, Surrey, UK
Lavender Children's Centre 66-67

Mollerussa, Lleida, Spain
Instituto La Serra 216-217

Morestel, France
Lycée Camille Corot 168-169

Neufahrn, Germany
Oskar Maria Graf Gymnasium 214-215

New York, New York, USA
Edward Everett Hale School, Brooklyn 24
Lucile S. Bulger Center for Community Life 26
Packer Collegiate Institute, Brooklyn 21, 248-251
South Bronx Charter School for The Arts, Hunts
Point 18, 156-157, 227

Nödinge, Sweden
Ale Upper Secondary School 166-167

Northwich, Cheshire, United Kingdom
Kingsmead Primary School 142-143

Norton, Sheffield, UK
Mossbrook Primary School **138-139**

Nummela, Finland
Kuoppanummi School Centre 174-175

Ohta City, Gunma, Japan
Gunma Kokusai Academy 170-171

Osterburken, Germany
All-day Secondary School 16-17

Paris, France
École Maternelle ZAC Moskowa 82-83

Pittsburgh, Pennsylvania, USA
Cyert Center for Early Education 22, 27
Helen S. Faison Academy 22

Pomona, California, USA
Diamond Ranch High School 163, 242-243

Potsdam, Germany
Montessori Secondary School 47

Rutland, Massachusetts, USA
Central Tree Middle School 20

San Felice, Reggio Emilia, Italy
San Felice Nursery and Preschool 12, 70-73

Santiago de Cali, Colombia
Industrial Public Secondary School 212-213

São Paolo, Brazil
Public School Jardim Ataliba Leonel 182-183

Schlanders, South Tyrol, Italy
Middle School 32

Seville, Spain
Instituto Villanueva del Rio y Minas 206-207

Shanghai, China
Concordia International School 26

Sheffield, UK
Joint Denominational School 134-135

Shenyang, China
Shenyang Xiaohajin International Kindergarten
84-85

St. Truiden, Belgium
BSBO De Bloesem School **90-91**

Sursee, Switzerland
Special School Sursee 100-101

Taxham, Salzburg, Austria
Taxham School Extension 140-141

Toblach, South Tyrol, Italy
Arts Centre and School of Music 29, 33

Tongjiang, Jianxi, China
Recycled Brick School 158-159

Überlingen, Germany
Janusz-Korczak School 46

Vernouillet, Eure-et-Loir, France
Collège Nicolas Robert 162-165

Vella, Graubünden, Switzerland
Multi-purpose Hall 32, 33

Victoria, Australia
Ivanhoe Grammar School, Mernda **244-245**

Wadenswil, Switzerland
Zürich International School 154-155

Westcliff on Sea, UK
Westcliff Primary School and After School Club
132-133

West Haven, Utah, USA
West Haven Elementary School 23

Wiesbaden, Germany
Campus Klarenthal 48

Winchester, UK
Osborne School 102-103

Wolfsburg, Germany
Heinrich-Nordhoff Comprehensive School 49

Woodbury, Minnesota, USA
Crosswinds Arts and Science Middle School
24, 25

Yuba City, California, USA
Feather River Academy 20, 104-107

Zichron Yaacov, Israel
Hachoresh School 130-131

Zürich, Switzerland
Lachenzelg School Extension 198-199
School complex Im Birch, Oerlikon 46
University of Zürich Musicology Institute 32, 33
Zürich International School 154-155

Index of Names

ADP, Beat Jordi, Caspar Angst 198
Aedas + Design Consultants 152
Akamatsu, Kazuko 170
Allford Hall Monaghan Morris 148
Allmann Sattler Wappner Architekten 204
Alsop Architects 184
AMP arquitectos 176
Andriolo, V. 31, 33
Architects Co-Partnership (ACP) 202
Architecture for Education – A4E 20, 104
Architecture PLB 20, 222
Architype 80
Arroyo, Eduardo 70
Arup Associates 116
Atkinson, William 18
Barney Ross Architects 120
Bassenge, Puhan-Schultz und Schreck 16
Bates Smart 244
Baukind 56
Baupiloten, Technical University of Berlin 50-53
Bearth, Valentin 32, 33
Behnisch, Behnisch & Partner 94, 196
Behnisch & Partner 15, 21, 172
Behnisch, Günther 15, 21, 172
Berthelier Fichet Tribouillet 162
Blurock, Thomas 242
BOF Architekten 228
Bolchover, Joshua 158
Borel, Frédéric Architectes 82
Brojet Lajus Pueyo 186
Bucci, Angelo 182
Buro Happold 40-41
Capua, Patricia 210
Cottrell and Vermeulen 132
Ctrl G Estudio de Arquitectura 62
Cuningham Group 24, 25
Dall & Lindhardtsen 21, 192
Deplazes, Andrea 32, 33
Desplat, Carme Pinós 216
Diezinger & Kramer Architekten 108
DSDHA 74, 134
Dudek, Mark 9, 17, 60, 76
Flöckner, Maria and Hermann Schnöll 140
Foster and Partners 227, 234
Froebel, Friedrich (Fröbel) 11f, 43, 55
Galli & Rudolf 154
Goldstein, Hein Architekten 214
Grafton Architects 126
Gropius, Walter 15
Grüntuch Ernst Architekten 240
H³ Hardy Collaboration Architecture 21, 248
Hampshire County Council Architects 102
Hecker, Zvi 136
Hérault Arnod Architectes 168
Hertzberger, Herman 114, 236, 246
Hillmann, Gustav 144
HMFH Architects 20
Hübner, Peter 19, 46-49, 218
IBUS Architects and Engineers 144
Jeskanen-Repo-Teränne 238
Kojima, Kazuhiro 170
Kudo, Kazumi 47

Kuwabara Payne McKenna Blumberg 190
Kwong & Associates 112
Lewis, Duncan 182
Lin, John 158
Lütkemeyer, Ingo 144
Malaguzzi, Loris 12
Mann, Graeme & Patricia Capua 208
Märkli, Peter 46
McAslan, John + Partners 66
Meskanen & Pursiainen 176
Mithun Architects 24
Morphosis 163, 242
Niederstätter, Christina 29-33
No.mad arquitectos 68
O'Donnell + Tuomey Architects 122
O'Neill, Edward Francis 10-11
Penoyre & Prasad 92
Perkins+Will 200
Perkins Eastman Architects 22, 26, 27
Perko Architects 174
PIR II Arkitektkontor 180
Plan B (Federico Mesa) 62
Plus+ Bauplanung 46-49, 218
Powsner, Shimon and Gideon 130
Puntoni, Alvaro 182
Robson, E. R. 13-14
Rockwell Architecture 24
Rural Urban Framework 158
Sabine, Wallace C. 30-31
Schader, Jacques 15
Schäfers, Carola 124
Scharoun, Hans 15
Scheitlin-Syfrig+Partner 100
Schmid, Hans-Martin 144
Schneider-Esleben, Peter 15
Schnitter, Beate 32
Schnöll, Hermann 140
Scholz, Stefan Architekten 194
Shenyang Huaxin Designers 84
Shuhei Endo Architect Institute 86
Simma, T. 32, 33
Smithson, Alison and Peter 14-15
SOM 'Education Lab' 128, 188
Speto 184
Staab Architekten 78
Steiner, Rudolf 55
Stiff, Michael 76
Suárez Corchete, Fernando 206
Takala, Asko 100
Terrados Cepeda, Javier 206
Trevillion, Andy 76
Uno, Susumu 170
VBM Architecten 90
VCBO Architecture 23
Wachter & Partner 29
Weisz + Yoes Studio 18, 156
Werknetz Architektur 226
White Design Associates 142
Wigglesworth Sarah, Architects 138
Wilson, Harold 14
Wingårdh Arkitektkontor 166
Wright, Frank Lloyd 11-13
Yli-Lonttinen, Leena 238
Zoeggeler, O. 33
ZPZ Partners 70
Zùñiga Gàez, Luis Fernando 212

Illustration Credits

The author and the publisher thank the following photographers, architects and organisations for the kind permission to reproduce the photographs in this book. Unless noted otherwise, all illustrations are courtesy of the authors or architects. Every effort has been made to trace the copyright holders of images. We apologise in advance for any unintentional omission and would be happy to insert the appropriate acknowledgement in any subsequent edition of the manual.

Cover Hannes Henz, Zürich

4 Jan Bitter, Berlin

8 from left to right
top row
Ria Stein (Babies)
Sieglinde von der Goltz (Classroom)
Leigh Simpson
Mesfin Ayalew
second row
Caroline Sohie
Wayne Soverns JR
Ria Stein
third row
Frau Pape
Herman van Doorn
bottom row
Herman van Doorn
Architecture for Education – A4E
Pamela Loeffelman

9 top Mark Dudek

12 bottom Miro Zagnoli

15 top Alison and Peter Smithson. From: William J.R. Curtis, *Modern Architecture since 1900*, London: Phaidon, 1996.

15 middle From: Heinrich Klotz (ed.), *Paul Schneider-Esleben, Entwürfe und Bauten 1949-1987*, Braunschweig/Wiesbaden: Friedrich Vieweg & Sohn, **1987**.

15 bottom From: Anna Meseure, Martin Tschanz, Wilfried Wang (eds.), *Architektur im 20. Jahrhundert – Schweiz*, exhibition catalogue, Frankfurt/Main, 1998.

16 top From: *Bauwelt*, no. 44, 1967, p. 1109.

17 Mark Dudek

18 top Mark Dudek

18 bottom Weisz + Yoes Studio

19 top © Museum of London

19 middle © Dennis Gilbert/VIEW

19 bottom Peter Hübner

20 middle HMFH Architects

22 top Jim Schafer Photography

22 bottom Denmarsh Photography

23 Paul Richer/Richer Images

24 middle Peter Mauss/Esto – Rockwell Architecture

24 bottom Art Grice Photography

25 top Peter Kerze

25 bottom Don Wong

27 Jim Schafer Photography

29 top and bottom right Ludwig Thalheimer/LUPE

29 bottom left Christina Niederstätter

30, 31 bottom right Ludwig Thalheimer/LUPE

32 top Christina Niederstätter

32 middle Bearth & Deplazes

32 bottom Ferrand Schnitter

36-39 Drawings: Mohamed Boubekri

40-41 Buro Happold/ Daniel Hopkinson

46 centre left Cornelia Suhan; centre right Peter Hübner; bottom istock/Ron Tech 2000

47 Peter Hübner

48 Cornelia Suhan

51-53 Jan Bitter, Berlin

56-59 Anne Deppe, Berlin

60-61 Ronald Chapman Photography

62-65 Sergio Gómez

66-67 © Peter Cook/VIEW

68-69 Eduardo Arroyo/ No.mad Arquitectos

70-73 Miro Zagnoli

74-75 Martine Hamilton Knight

76-77 Mark Dudek

78-79 Werner Huthmacher, Berlin

80-81 Leigh Simpson

82-83 © Frédéric Borel Architecte

84-85 Ma Tao

86-87 Yoshiharu Matsumura

90-91 Martin Lepej, VBM Architecten

92-94 Tim Crocker

96-98, 99 right Roland Halbe, Stuttgart

99 left Christian Kandzia

100-101 Christoph Eckert, Luzern

102-103 Hampshire County Architects

104-107 Architecture for Education - A4E

108-109 Stefan Müller-Naumann

112-113 Kerun Ip

114 Architectuurstudio Herman Hertzberger

115 left Kees Rutten

115 right Architectuurstudio Herman Hertzberger

116 left Caroline Sohie

116 right Roland Reinardy

117 left Roland Reinardy

117 right Caroline Sohie

118-119 Caroline Sohie

120-121 Steve Hall/Hedrich Blessing

122-123 © Dennis Gilbert/VIEW

124-125 Carola Schäfers Architekten

126-127 Grafton Architects

128-129 SOM 'Education Lab'

130 left Powsner Architects

130 right Albatros

131 Powsner Architects

132-133 Buro Happold/Adam Wilson

134-135 Morley von Sternberg

136-137 Michael Krüger, Berlin

138-139 Peter Lathey

140-141 Stefan Zenzmaier

142-143 White Design Associates Ltd

144 left Simon Cornils

144 right, 146 right Tomek Kwiatosz

145, 146 left and centre, 147 IBUS Architects and Engineers

148, 150 right Tim Soar

149 left and centre Allford Hall Monaghan Morris

149 right, 151 left Matt Chisnall

150 left, 151 centre and right Allford Hall Monaghan Morris

152-153 Aedas + Design Consultants

154 right Hannes Henz, Zürich

154 left, 155 Tom Bisig, Basel

156-157 Albert Vecerka/Esto

158-159 Rural Urban Framework

162-165 Philippe Ruault

166-167 Björn Breitholz

168-169 Georges Fessy

170, 171 left Hiroshi Ueda

171 right Kaname Yanagisawa

172-173 Christian Kandzia

174-175 Jussi Tiainen

176-179 AMP arquitectos

180, 181 left Jarl Morten Anderson

181 right PIR II/Duncan Lewis

182-183 Nelson Kon

184-185 Alsop Architects

186, 187 left Hervé Abbadie

187 right Philippe Ruault

188 left Florian Holzherr

188 right Aerial Photos of New Jersey

189 left Robert Polidori

189 right Florian Holzherr

190 Steven Evens

191 Eduard Heuber/Arch Photo Inc.

192-193 Jens Frederiksen

194-195 Reinhard Görner

196, 197 left Christian Kandzia

197 right Martin Schodder

198-199 Theodor Stalder/VISUS

200-201 James Steinkamp Photography

202 top left Alex Deverill

202 right Patrick Squire

203 bottom Alex Deverill

204-205 Stefan Müller-Naumann

206-207 Fernando Alda

208-211 Thomas Jantscher, Neuchâtel

212-213 Luis Fernando Zùñiga Gàez

214-215 Richie Müller, Christoph Knoch, Peter Frank

216-217 Duccio Malagamba

218-221 Peter Hübner, Plus+ Bauplanung

222-223 Architecture PLB, Bouygues, UK

226 Jos Schmid, Zürich

227 left Philipp Wieting, Zürich

227 right Ralf Feiner, Malans

228-233 Hagen Stier

234-235 Nigel Young

236 Duccio Malagamba

237 left Architectuurstudio Herman Hertzberger

237 middle Herman van Doorn

237 right Christian Richters

238 Jussi Tiainen

239 left Voitto Niemelä

239 right Mikko Auerniitty

240-241 Werner Huthmacher, Berlin

242-243 Timothy Hursley, Little Rock

244-245 Christopher Atkins

246-247 Herman van Doorn

248-250, 251 left Whitney Cox

251 right Bruce Buck

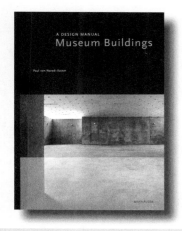
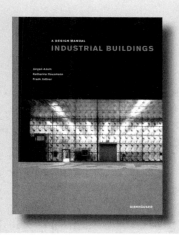

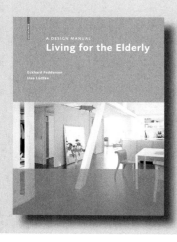